D1716516

On Screen and Off

ON SCREEN AND OFF

Cinema and the Making
of Nazi Hamburg

Anne Berg

PENN

UNIVERSITY OF PENNSYLVANIA PRESS

PHILADELPHIA

Published by
University of Pennsylvania Press
Philadelphia, Pennsylvania 19104-4112
www.upenn.edu/pennpress

Printed in the United States of America on acid-free paper
10 9 8 7 6 5 4 3 2 1

A catalogue record for this book is available
from the Library of Congress.
ISBN 978-0-8122-5380-1

für Lukas, Yannik, und Timo

CONTENTS

ABBREVIATIONS

BArch	Bundesarchiv (Federal Archive of Germany)
BDM	Bund Deutscher Mädel (League of German Girls)
BFI	British Film Institute
DA	Deutsches Tagebucharchiv (German Diary Archive)
DAF	Deutsche Arbeitsfront (German Labor Front)
DEFA	Deutsche Film-Aktiengesellschaft
Degeto	Deutsche Gesellschaft für Ton und Film
FIS	Foreign Information Service
FKB	Filmkreditbank (Film Credit Bank)
FZH	Forschungstelle für Zeitgeschichte
Gestapo	Geheime Staatspolizei (Secret Police)
HJ	Hitlerjugend (Hitler Youth)
KdF	Kraft durch Freude (Strength through Joy)
NS	National Socialist
NSDAP	Nationalsozialistische Deutsche Arbeiter Partei (National Socialist German Workers Party)
NSV	Nationalsozialistische Volkswohlfahrt (National Socialist People's Welfare)
RFK	Reichsfilmkammer (Reich Film Chamber)
RKK	Reichskulturkammer (Reich Culture Chamber)
RMVP	Reichsministerium für Volksaufklärung und Propaganda (Propaganda Ministry)
RWU	Reisen Wander und Urlaub (Office for Travel and Vacation)
SD	Sicherheitsdienst (Security Service)
SS	Schutzstaffel
StAHH	Staatsarchiv Hamburg (State Archive, Hamburg)
Ufa	Universum Film AG
Ufi	Ufa-Film-GmbH
ZAC	Zonal Advisory Council (Zonenbeirat)

Introduction

The Third Reich's designs for world power are beyond dispute. The making of Nazism was nonetheless a rather local affair. The *Volksgemeinschaft*—translating as "people's community" or (more accurately) "racial community"—was projected through national propaganda but performed and policed in cities, towns, and rural communities.[1] Some enactments of state power took the shape of seemingly innocuous gestures and interactions such as donations to party-run charities, the collecting of recyclables, personal greetings, and the exchange of gossip.[2] Others bore the imprint of a particular place, its idiosyncrasies and histories. In Hamburg, film was key. Deeply ingrained in urban life, the Nazi regime imagined film as a powerful tool to shape National Socialist subjects. In Hamburg, those very subjects chanced on film discourse as a seemingly apolitical opportunity to articulate their own ideas about what Nazism ought to look like.

Boasting a moviegoing public second in size to Berlin, Hamburg offered a dense web of theaters, avid cineastes, engaged journalists, and cultural pundits of many political persuasions. The site for a number of prestigious film projects during and after Nazi control, Hamburg sat at the intersection of the local practices and national policies that shaped the contours of the Reich. For Hamburg residents, film and film discourse were seemingly apolitical means for channeling local imagination and articulating ideas about how Nazism ought to work. They also provided a means for projecting the Hanse city's identity to the world, despite the many quibbles about what that identity was. Because Hamburg singularly embodied the contradictions between global aspirations and provincialism that characterized the regime, it serves as an excellent case study for understanding how Nazification worked.[3]

Hamburg's history as an independent port city and its self-conception as a cultural hub inflected the local flavor of Nazism that grew and changed throughout the 1930s and 1940s. As Germany's self-styled "gateway to the world," Hamburg rooted its parochialism in its claim to *Weltgeltung*—its aspiration for international stature.[4] Its sense of exceptionalism extended to

its embrace of National Socialism, even though its demonstrations of loyalty occasionally clashed with regime expectations.[5] Interestingly, political
polarizations and economic divisions served to bolster local pride, underscoring the claims of worldliness and openness that the city's mercantile elite
deemed instrumental to their reputation and affluence.[6] Hamburg was a center of the volkish nationalism, racial antisemitism, and imperialist *Weltpolitik*
handed down from the Weimar Republic.[7] At the same time, its vocal and
well-organized labor movement and its radicalized working class earned
Hamburg a reputation as a "red" city.

Hamburg's populace were not eager converts to National Socialism. Nazis
gained ground slowly, and in the elections of March 1933 the party underper-
formed even though conservatives and right-wingers were not rarities in the
city.[8] Once it became clear that Hitler's chancellorship would be more durable
than the preceding Weimar-era governments, Hamburg had to prove that it
had enough fanaticism to escape the scrutiny of Berlin. With ultra-right-wing
nationalism, patrician conservatism, bourgeois liberalism, and working-class
radicalism existing side by side, the city's commitment to National Socialism was far from self-evident. Equally problematic was Hamburg's unsavory
character. Inextricably linked to the city's economy, the amusement district of
St. Pauli was both an asset and a liability. A predominantly working-class district adjacent to the harbor, St. Pauli was home to an uneasy mix of shipping,
entertainment, prostitution, crime, poverty, and radical politics.[9] The district's
provocative and sexually permissive entertainment culture contrasted sharply
with the rustic, seafaring romanticism it inspired in movies, ensuring that
St. Pauli took center stage in the debates about national character in Hamburg.

Hamburg's self-avowed exceptionalism increased after it became the first
German target for aerial annihilation.[10] A test case for both the Allied strategic bombing campaigns and the Nazi organization of relief, Hamburg experienced spectacular destruction in the summer of 1943. In just ten days, around
one-third of its housing was destroyed and about thirty-five thousand people
died. Half the population fled as the city burned for days. With an administration helpless in the face of "the catastrophe," disillusionment, exhaustion,
Kriegsmüdigkeit (war weariness), and apathy characterized life in Hamburg
almost two years before Germans would experience these afflictions en
masse. In large part because wholesale destruction and political disenchantment arrived sooner than it did in Nuremberg, Cologne, and Dresden, the
feeling of being victimized not just by war but by the Nazi regime itself was
particularly acute in Hamburg.[11] This sense of victimhood congealed into

postwar myths that Hamburg had never been a Nazi city, that its lionized liberal traditions had survived in hiding, and that antisemitism and National Socialist fanaticism were less virulent and deadly here than elsewhere.[12]

Unlike Berlin, Hamburg wasn't the Reich's capital. Unlike Munich, it wasn't the city of the movement (*Stadt der Bewegung*). Unlike Nuremberg, it wasn't the city of the Reich's party rallies (*Stadt der Reichsparteitage*). Neither Adolf Hitler, who remained most at home in Munich, nor Leni Riefenstahl, who turned Nuremberg into the iconic Nazi city by sheer triumph of her artistic will, were ready to claim Hamburg as a canvas for the projection of unifying urban visions.[13] Instead, Hamburg boasted of its image as Germany's cosmopolitan center, making it an intriguing case study of Nazism gone local, one that has received little attention in English-language historiography.[14]

The comparison to Nuremberg is instructive. The southern German city also had a vibrant, radical working class that captured the regime's disciplinarian gaze. Moreover, Nuremberg's citizens had a clear sense of civic pride based on their history as a medieval center of German culture, art, and trade.[15] Riefenstahl's *Triumph of the Will* all but expunged these layered complexities that made Nuremberg similar to Hamburg, affixing a stigma that the Nuremberg Laws of 1935 further cemented. Decimated by air raids late in the war, Nuremberg did not have enough time to recontextualize its wartime victimization into postwar exoneration.[16] The tribunals that convicted regime conspirators of war crimes further cast Nuremberg as a locus of Nazi fanaticism rather than as a city of rich history and tradition. Hamburg, on the other hand, managed to escape the Nazi-laden fate that befell Nuremberg even though its authorities and cultural experts had attempted to echo Reich glories like *Triumph of the Will* as they mobilized film to boost their National Socialist credentials.

This book concerns the local usages of film in Hamburg from the ascension of the Nazi regime, through the city's destruction, and up to the early postwar years when the Hanse city began to rebuild its infrastructure and its self-image. Accordingly, this work is concerned only tangentially with the history of Nazi film production, the formalities of film aesthetics, and the mechanics of propaganda and censorship. Hamburg never attained international cinematic representation akin to Nuremberg. Neither did it become a film production center on the scale of Berlin. But the history of film in Hamburg demonstrates the use of film as a social technology, illustrating it as a cultural product, a referent for ideological debate, an instrument for policing, a tool for making claims on the state, and an infrastructure of political imagination and social control.[17] Film promised to capture Hamburg's history and to offer it up for general consumption while also aligning the city's local particularities with national imperatives. Moreover, film engendered a political space in which activists, welfare workers, cultural experts, and administrators could assert their views about current affairs, articulate criticism and praise, perform commitment to the regime, and police the boundaries of the *Volksgemeinschaft*. Finally, film was perhaps the most successful of the "people's products" because it extended the promise of economic prosperity and cultural preeminence even as living standards declined dramatically.

On Screen and Off brings a host of new actors and agents into view.[18] Thus far neither historians nor film scholars have considered the roles played by local administrators, cultural experts, cineastes, or welfare workers in defining the place of cinema in the Nazi state. This study shifts the focus away from national organs like Goebbels's Propaganda Ministry and sets its sights on a wide range of individuals who engaged with film and film discourse as part of their everyday lives. In the process, these actors imagined Hamburg, recast its history, and defined the roles of its citizens in explicitly National Socialist terms. In short, they transformed Hamburg into a Nazi city.

*   *   *

Although historians have carefully studied everyday life in various cities during the Nazi period, few scholars have seriously entertained the possibility that Nazism brought forth an urban order and form that was more than just a negation of existing structures and practices.[19] Fewer still seem to think that the Nazi city can contribute to our knowledge of cities in general or shed light on our understanding of the modern city.[20] Urban theorists who gesture toward Nazi ghettos and camps as the contemporary city's evil twin imply a fundamental break between modern cities and so-called totalitarian spaces, but they explain neither this rupture nor its presumed self-evidence.[21] The literature that examines the city in the Third Reich tends to privilege the built environment, the visions espoused by Nazi architects, and the perspectives afforded by urban planners.[22] Architects used design to represent the Reich's glory and repute. Planners stressed the organic nature of the city and its necessary integration into the larger racial planning for *Volk* and *Raum*. *On Screen and Off* demonstrates that the Nazi city was a product or more than models and plans. Abstract ideas about order, discipline, science, bureaucracy, hygiene, technology, and media certainly shaped the regime's interventions as it contended with urban conditions and mediated between the competing interests of decision makers at different levels of the Nazi hierarchy. But the city itself was also written into political pamphlets and tourist brochures. It was performed in rallies, marches, and public celebrations. It was experienced in mundane activities such as standing in line for groceries, exchanging news with a neighbor, and going to the movies. The city that I am concerned with is the one that was experienced, affirmed, and only occasionally contested in everyday life.[23]

Interdisciplinary in focus and methodology, *On Screen and Off* builds on existing scholarship that shows how the regime depended on the cooperation of actors at municipal, regional, and state levels to make Nazism work in the face of a promised prosperity that was slow in coming.[24] Following the early work that deepened our understanding of the antagonism between party and state,[25] the proliferation of competencies within the administration,[26] and the limits of social control,[27] historians began to investigate the processes by which the regime solicited consent and maintained legitimacy.[28] Subsequent studies focused more specifically on how ordinary Germans navigated the system and made it work for their own interests.[29] These works by younger scholars most directly inform the arguments in this book. In particular the studies on travel and tourism, sexuality and prostitution, soundscapes, and urban entertainment and consumption have prompted new and fascinating questions about politics in the Third Reich.[30] These analyses focus on local actors rather than the mechanics of policing and propaganda to demonstrate how everyday activities like consumption and traveling engendered an interplay between individuals, organizations, industry, cultural institutions, and the regime.

Moreover, these thematically informed studies highlight that political thought and practice are not neatly truncated by political caesurae. By drawing attention to the continuities between players and contexts, these interpretations render the Third Reich as less of an aberrant era than is often thought. As Victoria Harris poignantly concludes in her study of thirty years of prostitution in Germany, "national policy and local practice were two distinct entities: sometimes they intersected; at other points they contradicted each other."[31] Dagmar Herzog similarly demonstrates the embeddedness and after-effects of Nazi sexual politics in a longer transnational history.[32] *On Screen and Off* continues in this vein, demonstrating how ideas about film and the everyday practices of moviegoing forged continuities for ordinary people, their communities, and their political beliefs.

Following the lead of film scholars who have reshaped the field of Nazi cinema studies since the 1990s, this book approaches cinema as a complex set of participatory practices that provides multiple points of entry into everyday

politics for everyday citizens.[33] Viewing cinema as more than a means of
political indoctrination affords a broader window onto the ways in which the
Nazi state flowed in and out of the lives of ordinary people. After the Reich's
collapse, the observation that millions of Germans supported or at least failed
to object to the genocidal policies of the Nazi regime produced two kinds
of explanations, both of which took their vantage points from Nazism itself.
Because the regime presented itself as a product of the *Volk's* will and proclaimed the Führer to be its uncontested executor, scholars explained Nazism
as a manifestation of the intrinsic predispositions and internal tendencies of
the German people.[34] Other historians conversely took the Nazi drive for total
control as their starting point, focusing on the regime's masterminds, institutions, and ability to wield terror.[35] Along these lines, a "first wave" of film
historians and sociologists distanced themselves from Siegfried Kracauer's
seminal study, *From Caligari to Hitler*, first published in 1947. They rejected
Kracauer's reading that Nazism was a refraction of Weimar's failures, but they
retained the premise that film and propaganda offered compelling insights
into the relationship between the state and society in Nazi Germany.[36] By the
1990s the focus had shifted. Film scholars with an eye on ideology, aesthetics, and the workings of text interpreted film as a plastic, cultural product
whose nonnarrative elements, textures, excesses, and inconsistencies were as
telling (if not more so) than the story's "message."[37] Arguments belaboring
the dichotomy between propaganda and entertainment receded, allowing the
notion of "the popular" to emerge as the dominant theme.[38]

   On Screen and Off places Nazi film in the context of historical and transnational continuities, underscoring the fact that National Socialism didn't
operate in a cultural vacuum or serve as its own continuous referent.[39] The
attempts to "normalize" rather than exoticize the history of Nazi cinema
have inspired me to question the usefulness of a broad, national frame and to
examine the local resonances of, and contentions over, film. My aim here is
to uncover how film and film discourse served as a pathway through which
ordinary experiences related to national priorities. Consider the story of
Uwe Storjohann, who was an avid Hamburg cineaste and a teenager at the
start of the war. Uwe's father disapproved of the November 1938 pogrom,
exclaiming, "this could not have been in line with the Führer's will." The son's
recollections of his parents' political commentary sit uncomfortably next to
his reminiscences of singing the soundtrack of the latest blockbuster. From
a park bench, Uwe and his friend Hilde escaped into a world of stories and
stars, glamour and fame, "whose five continents were named Ufa, Terra,

Tobis, Metro-Goldwyn Mayer and Wien Film." They were fully aware that the world around them was about to burn.[40] Storjohann's recollections illustrate how discomfort with political developments and an infatuation with movie glamour didn't founder in dissonance. Rather, they show how continuities in everyday life—going to the movies or chatting about one's favorite actor—grounded normalcy in the midst of rupture.

*   *   *

In addition to telling the stories of individuals like Uwe Storjohann, *On Screen and Off* takes a fresh look at archival material to show how local administrators, welfare workers, cineastes, and self-styled cultural experts used film and film discourse to develop their political voices. Accordingly, institutions such as the Reich Film Chamber, Goebbels's Propaganda Ministry, industry spokespersons, and film directors play less prominent roles. This book examines films that were neither iconic nor foundational for Nazi cinema but that nonetheless inspired intense debate among Hamburg's avant-garde. Interdisciplinary, diverse, and somewhat unconventional, *On Screen and Off* draws on sources from local, state, and federal archives, including records from police precincts, youth organizations, tourism offices, and social welfare programs. It consults a broad range of local and national publications, including daily newspapers, periodicals, and trade journals. The personal observations recorded in diaries, letters, memoirs, oral histories, and interviews anchor this book in a particular place—Hamburg.

Cultural geographers have argued that space does not exist outside of representation, nor can space be rendered by representation alone. Here, my thinking has been influenced by Henri Lefebvre's concept of "social space" and Tim Cresswell's definition of "place—a meaningful location."[41] Nazi Hamburg was made by its inhabitants, inscribed onto the urban grid, written into representations, discussed in print, performed in the streets, and projected in theaters. Such *placemaking* had to contend with the regime's rigid prescriptions and proscriptions. It was further shaped by dramatic transformations in everyday life as the war effort started, progressed, and collapsed.[42] Nonetheless, as this book demonstrates, the making of Nazi Hamburg was a collective project, one that required and welcomed the participation of local citizens who legitimized the transformation of Hamburg into a Nazi city.

Chapter 1 of this book sets the stage for this placemaking, detailing how film shaped and disrupted Hamburg's entertainment landscape. The city's dense cinemascape gave the local regime an infrastructure for disseminating messages, whether entertaining, propagandistic, or both. The aryanization of the film production industries and exhibition venues was an integral component of the regime's effort to revamp film as high culture—the *Volksfilm*. Film became the favored means for aligning the infamous St. Pauli district to the Nazi rhetoric about wholesome and volk-bound pleasure. Yet the movies featuring St. Pauli kept alive a visceral connection to the district's salacious elements. Cinema stayed true to its original description as "living photography," bringing images to life but also bringing them to bear *on* life. Film in Hamburg thereby evaded the didactic clutches of political authority even as it helped ground that authority in urban space.

Chapter 2 approaches film as an infrastructure of political imagination, chronicling Hamburg's search for cinematic representation and the efforts to resolve the tensions that tarnished the city's image in the eyes of Berlin. Focusing on three Hamburg-specific films, this chapter analyzes the difficulty of capturing the pretzeled nature of a city that was both parochial and cosmopolitan, populist and elitist. Finding a representation that was both authentically Hamburg and acceptably Nazi took trial and error, not because these identities stood in contradiction, but because there was no consensus about what either of them entailed. The animated local discussions at the time reveal less about Nazi Hamburg than the process of its construction. Ironically, the film that best captured the emerging consensus reached audiences only after Germany's unconditional surrender.

Nazism was conjured through lofty claims of cultural ascendency, through pompous marches and obsessive flag waving. It was performed through the cleansing of inner-city districts and the production of documentaries and feature films. The representations that rendered the regime's contours visible were put to the test during wartime, when bombs threatened to blow to bits the collective performances of loyalty and sacrifice. Once war destroyed the fabric of everyday life and took scarcity and state terror to new extremes, cinema continued to nurture German ambitions of cultural preeminence and to promise better times to come. With repairs to infrastructure sluggish, the flickering images in makeshift movie theaters connected audiences across space as well as time, keeping alive the regime's promises for a prosperous future beyond the rubble.

This particular allure of cinema was never more evident than in the aftermath of Operation Gomorrah in July 1943.[43] As Chapter 3 illustrates, going to the movies in wartime was an enactment of normalcy, of resilience. It was a way of coping with uncertainty and loss, an escape from the drudgery of war. Even with the city in ruins, the project of reimagining Hamburg in National Socialist terms forged ahead. Cinema remained crucial to this effort, but here the story takes an unexpected turn. In the context of war, the Nazi goal of elevating film to the realm of high culture clashed with persistent fears about film's socially corrosive nature, its sexualizing effects. With the start of the war, concerns about how the movies would affect future generations produced an alternative discourse, and local administrators began to view cinema as a destabilizing force. Welfare workers insisted that movies corrupted the minds of youth and women, undermined the social order, and lured people away from their duties. Chapter 3 details how film "regressed" in the eyes of authorities, becoming a dangerous pastime that demanded vigilance and discipline from those who guarded the social order.

Chapter 4 demonstrates how the experience of aerial annihilation shaped the outlook and self-understanding of officials and private citizens in Hamburg. The razing of the city in the summer of 1943 anchored a transition from power to impotence that remained the dominant experience for the rest of the war. Almost overnight, the city of questionable allegiance to Berlin was transformed into a symbol of national resilience by dint of its victimization. After the city surrendered to the British forces, this sense of victimhood continued but to opposite ends. The city saw itself as a victim of a war the Nazis started and of an occupation that was forced on them, reinforcing the myth that Hamburg had never fully nazified.

The Hitler portraits were removed, the German greeting forbidden. Rubble was cleared away and the propaganda films were taken out of circulation. With Nazism outwardly dismantled and publicly disavowed, the British forces and their German partners came to view film as a means to transmit a new set of cultural values. But occupiers and the occupied had different views about what those values should be. Because the British considered most films made during the Third Reich to be apolitical, Nazism stealthily returned to the theaters in the form of reprises, feeding a nostalgia for "good" times and "good" deeds. Inadvertently perhaps, this suggested that authentic German culture had survived the Nazi interlude unscathed. Critics of the occupation began to mobilize an ahistorical ideal of *Kultur* to reinsert seemingly innocent German voices into a cultural landscape dominated by British, American, French, and Soviet productions. Film discourse and filmmaking became a tool to reclaim German heritage while burying Nazism in the visual motif of rubble. Chapter 4 zeros in on a prominent example of the short-lived genre of the rubble film, Helmut Käutner's *In jenen Tagen*, which took on the entire history of the Nazi regime. With a nod to the democratic sensibilities impressed on it by its censors, the Hamburg press went wild and laid a new-found sense of civic pride at the feet of the occupiers. By reclaiming the city's "cultural heritage" through a cinematic sleight of hand, Hamburg redeemed itself without acknowledging the crime.

CHAPTER 1

Living Photography:
Film and the City

It was in St. Pauli, that most controversial of districts, that the cinematic history of Hamburg began.[1] A cherished myth locates the city's oldest cinema in a
dive on Spielbudenplatz, where Eberhard Knopf supplemented his offerings of
booze and beer with "living photography." Apparently, Knopf understood how
to exploit this new technology. He placed the screen midway down the length
of the room and charged half the normal price of admission to customers who
didn't mind sitting behind the canvas and watching images that were flipped
as if in a mirror.[2] But Eberhard Knopf was neither a visionary nor the father of
film in Hamburg. He was a businessman, and it wasn't until a few years later,
in 1906, when Hamburg had at least five other movie theaters, that he officially registered Knopf Lichtspielhaus in an adjacent building. But his original
establishment occupies the center of the origin story of cinema in Hamburg
because of a commotion, an anonymous complaint, and a subsequent police
report that left the first public record of cinema in Hamburg in 1901.[3]

Although it may not accurately reflect the origins of film in Hamburg,
this myth of a savvy bar owner busted by the police because of unsavory
goings-on at his establishment encapsulates the complicated ways in which
the particularities of place, state power, and popular imagination charted the
trajectory of film in the urban landscape. This chapter traces the origins of
film exhibition in Hamburg, examining its transformation in the context of
the shifting political landscape as the Nazis assumed power. Focusing on the
development of the infrastructure of film exhibition, this chapter illustrates
the spatial connections between film and popular entertainment, showing
how the regime attempted to unmake those connections and recast film as
the embodiment of high culture. Theaters were aryanized, entertainment

Figure 1. Knopf Lichtspielhaus, 1930s. Staatsarchiv Hamburg.

districts whitewashed, and the "sanitized" *Volksfilm* advertised as the perfect
vehicle to bring the *Volksgemeinschaft* together. But for Hamburg's imagination, its self-conception, and even its reputation, the vulgar, salacious, and
racy character of St. Pauli remained key.

Film in Hamburg

At the turn of the twentieth century, traveling exhibitors sparked the curiosity
of urban dwellers with the first "movies"—short, nonnarrative, and sensation-
alistic—exhibited in markets, fairs, carnivals, and eventually concert halls.[4]
In 1896 Edison-Kinotoskop started showing short "films" at the Gänsemarkt
and soon farmed out its wares to the large beer halls in St. Pauli. Eberhard
Knopf happened to find his way into the story at a time of rising concern
about the droves of unaccompanied minors drawn to makeshift screens in
shady establishments. Describing the "Kientopp" as an epidemic that ripped
through the entertainment districts, Senator August Schröder spearheaded a
prohibition on the frivolous mix of living photography and alcohol in 1907.[5]
By this time, Knopf had already branched out with a cinematographic theater

in a neighboring building, allowing him to keep doing business with both booze and celluloid, just not under the same roof.[6] As moving images invaded the dense network of entertainment establishments over the next decade, cinema became a stable fixture of urban life in Hamburg.[7] It expanded Hamburg's entertainment economy in specifically spatial ways, heightening the connection between urban pleasures and the working classes, blurring the moral boundary that had originally separated St. Pauli from Hamburg proper.

Over the next two decades, Hamburg's cinemascape expanded rapidly. Initially, the inner-city, working-class districts of St. Pauli and St. Georg led the race with seven and nine theaters, respectively. The building boom of the late 1920s changed the distribution of theaters across Hamburg, reflecting the city's demographic shifts. The movies followed their audiences, with theaters popping up in new working-class districts in Hamm, Hammerbrook, and Barmbek. By the end of the 1920s, cinema had become a daily feature of urban life.[8] Generally located on a major street, the first cinemas were close to the bars, taverns, and dance halls that guaranteed regular traffic.[9] Moreover, movie houses mimicked the bombastic design styles of theaters and opera houses. Because only large exhibitors could afford such expenses, big franchises came to dominate the exhibition landscape. By the end of the 1920s, most of the city's large theaters were run by the *Schauburgen* (literally, show castles) of the Henschel Corporation, the theaters of the Emelka Group, and Ufa, Germany's largest production company.

Competition between the major players attests to the popularity of film. Hugo Streit and Hermann Urich-Sass, two sons-in-law of the early cinema czar James Henschel, had been Ufa executives before they began building a theater empire that rivaled the Ufa venues. Soon after purchasing the original Schauburg Hauptbahnhof, the Henschel Corporation built numerous Schauburgen and turned suitable buildings into movie palaces.[10]

The competition between Ufa and the Schauburgen manifested itself most visibly in St. Pauli. At the Millerntor, once the official gateway to the closed-off burbs of Hamburg proper, each corporation built grand palaces.[11] In 1929, colossal theaters with more than one thousand seats were erected in the densely populated working-class districts of Hamm, Hammerbrook, and Barmbek.[12] The Henschel Corporation's new movie palaces in Uhlenhorst, Fuhlsbüttel, and Wandsbek added at least five thousand seats to Hamburg's cinemascape.[13] In turn, Ufa built the largest movie theater in Europe in downtown Hamburg. The Ufa-Palast, which could accommodate a patronage of 2,667, opened a few days before Christmas in 1929.[14]

Figure 2. Schauburg Barmbeck, 1935. Staatsarchiv Hamburg.

Following the specious prosperity after World War I, the monetary crisis that peaked in 1923, and the currency reform that followed, the film industry plunged into a systemic crisis, which only deepened with the collapse of the world economy in 1929.[15] A host of factors exacerbated the vulnerability of film business in this volatile economic situation. Taxes on amusements were substantial.[16] Production costs increased significantly with the transition to sound in the mid-1920s. Hollywood aggressively pushed its products into the European film market. The explosion of movie theaters across Germany from 3,700 theaters in 1920 to approximately 5,000 in 1930 was not matched by an uptick in patrons, making for fierce competition between exhibitors.[17] Controlled by the anti-Semitic nationalist Alfred Hugenberg since March 1927, Ufa had willingly served Nazi interests by pushing nationalist themes in features films, agitating against "Jewish" Hollywood films, and redirect-ing capital for the production of reactionary and antirepublican newsreels.[18] Hugenberg openly joined forces with Hitler, the NSDAP, and other rightist and pan-German forces in August 1931. The world economic crisis disposed the giants of the German film industry to seek protection under the state.[19]

By the time the Nazis came to power, every burgeoning working-class dis-trict was outfitted with a megatheater. Barmbek led the way with twelve movie theaters and more than seven thousand seats. In contrast, the ritzy district of

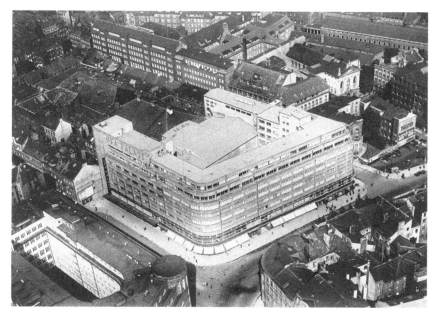

Figure 3. Ufa Palast, ca. 1930. Staatsarchiv Hamburg.

Rotherbaum and the middle-class Eppendorf remained underrepresented in the city's cinemascape. Smaller neighborhood theaters continued to play an important role in day-to-day moviegoing as the Weimar Republic gave way to the Third Reich, though Nazi policy furthered the trend set in motion during the Great Depression, strengthening the positions of franchised megatheaters. As market pressures and political aims aligned, vertically integrated film corporations such as Ufa and Tobis facilitated the regime's centralized control of film exhibition in the Reich.[20]

Joseph Goebbels ascribed a central function to cinema in the new state. He prophesized that film would triumph over established arts such as literature, music, and theater because of its potential to reach the urban masses and transform them into *Volk*. While the Nazi regime looked at Germany's urban centers with a mix of ideological reservation and economic enthusiasm, it was clear from the outset that urban growth was immeasurably important to the revolution of popular leisure and mass culture.[21] The movie theater occupied a particularly important place in the urban landscape, in both the actual fabric of the city and the Nazi zeal to reconfigure that fabric. Although

Nazification had a negligible impact on theater distribution (in fact, the regime placed a moratorium on the construction of theaters in 1934), it effectively implemented a hierarchical system of exhibition that redirected revenue from local institutions to state-controlled entities.[22]

The creation of the Film Credit Bank was as much a first step in establishing the policies of *Gleichschaltung* as it was a concession to the demands of film companies, cementing the relationship between the Reich and the film industry.[23] Advertised as an institution that would ameliorate conditions for medium-sized production companies, the bank primarily benefited the undercapitalized Tobis and the queen of German film production, Ufa. Goebbels, now certain of the industry's cooperation, began to turn film production, distribution, and exhibition into a state-mediated and increasingly state-controlled enterprise. The Reich's Film Chamber (*Reichsfilmkamer*, RFK), a model for cultural coordination in the Reich, was set up in preliminary form in July 1933. It was the first of seven operative chambers that made up the Reich's Culture Chamber (*Reichskulturkammer*, RKK), which was founded in September of the same year.[24] Membership in the RFK was mandatory for all individuals and industries engaged in film, yet membership was restricted to those who possessed "the necessary reliability."[25] Lacking precisely the (racial) reliability that the Nazis considered essential, Jews were systematically excluded from membership and therewith from the film sector.[26]

The apparatus put in place by Goebbels embodied and rendered visible the Nazi certainty about the connection between culture and politics. However, the backbone of the colossus was predicated on the compromise between industry, finance, and state interests. The effective nationalizations of Tobis, Ufa, Terra, and Bavaria began in 1937 and were completed in 1942 as the regime successively took control of the majority shares in these four major production companies. Private capital forged an effective alliance with the regime, industry converged with regulation, and military expansion guaranteed markets for more extravagant and expensive products.[27] The war ultimately delivered, if for a limited time, the long-awaited profits for a state-controlled and state-protected industry.[28]

The restructuring of film exhibition in Hamburg involved several steps that reflected the political and economic interests of both the Nazi state and the Reich's major production companies. The *Verreichlichung* (nationalization) of the film industry disempowered municipal regulatory agencies like the office for price regulation, giving franchised exhibitors a free hand when dealing with their independent competitors and the local administration. The four categories of Hamburg's cinemascape were topped by first-run theaters (*Erstauffführer*) that had the privilege of hosting any national premiere scheduled to take place in Hamburg. New films passed through one of these theaters before making their way down the rungs to movie houses that were categorized according to price and status.[29] Lower-ranking houses offered cheaper admission to films that had been in circulation longer. Accordingly, the situation for independent exhibitors in Hamburg steadily worsened.

In the 1930s movie theaters became a barometer of the reach of the state, a measure of modernization, and a standard for the cultural revolution.[30] When the Reich's Culture Chamber was founded on September 22, 1933, its subsidiary, the Reich's Film Chamber, oversaw a total of 4,265 movie theaters across Germany. With 4.2 million inhabitants and a total of 189,507 seats in 381 sound-equipped movie theaters, Berlin was the Reich's uncontested center of film production and exhibition, possessing a denser distribution of movie theaters than Europe's foremost cultural center, Paris. Hamburg was Germany's second most-important *Filmstadt*. In 1933 the city's seventy theaters were all wired for sound and had close to fifty thousand seats.[31] In most of these, the reels rolled almost continuously, and the average citizen saw a movie about ten times a year. Cinema attendance was highest in Berlin, Hamburg, and other large cities, trailing off significantly for smaller cities and towns. Audience statistics in rural areas were not captured by the Reich.[32]

In 1937, after the Greater Hamburg Law merged Hamburg with the Prussian cities of Harburg, Altona, and Wandsbek, the city possessed 104 movie theaters with a total of 66,605 seats. Close to 1.7 million people inhabited the city at that time and ticket sales were at an astonishing 21,772,138. The statistical average was thirteen viewings per person each year, but because the population total included the young, the old, the institutionalized, and those who preferred not to go to the movies, it can be assumed that the typical patron saw more than thirteen films a year.[33] Enthusiasts went to the movies weekly, sometimes even several times a week since the average admission price of less than one Reichsmark made moviegoing a more affordable pastime under Nazi rule than it had been in years prior. Programming generally consisted of a documentary (*Kulturfilm*), a newsreel, and a feature film, but it often included additional shorts or live performances. By 1937 growing audiences spelled the end of the economic uncertainty that had marked the film industry in the early 1930s.[34]

Aryanization

The history of Hamburg film exhibition cannot be separated from the aryanization of Jewish property, the exclusion of Jewish citizens from city life, and the ultimate deportation and murder of close to ten thousand Hamburger Jews.[35] In this section I focus on the combined effects of anti-Jewish and cultural coordination on the cinemascape of Hamburg, demonstrating how Hamburg's self-styled cosmopolitanism was rooted in greed, opportunism, and antisemitism.

The mass expulsion of Jews that commenced in the fall of 1941 was preceded by a stealthy expulsion of Jews from Hamburg's economy and society. This occurred with the silent acquiescence of the majority and within the context of pervasive opportunism. Middle-income groups and small to medium-sized businesses in particular benefited either directly from the aryanization or indirectly from the elimination of competition. For ordinary citizens, the regime's anti-Semitic policies offered public opportunities to denigrate Jewish neighbors, competitors, customers, and employees.[36] Interviewed decades after the war, Frau M insisted that 90 percent of all retail stores had been Jewish, "everywhere. In all of Hamburg. We all worked for the Jew. Had it up to here. Exploited to the max. After all, the Jews didn't get rich from nothing."[37]

The antisemitism that led to the eventual expulsion of Jews from Germany was readily accepted as an integral part of Nazi ideology. The *Hamburger Tageblatt* regularly printed anti-Semitic diatribes and took every occasion to distinguish itself with racist fervor. While most citizens neither objected to the silent redistribution of property nor protested the exclusion of Jews from local social and cultural networks, only a minority took pride in anti-Jewish violence. The open brutalization of Jews and the vandalization of Jewish property in the November pogroms met with near unanimous resentment in Hamburg as elsewhere in the Reich.[38] But when asked about the Night of Broken Glass, Frau M, a dockworker's daughter, insisted that in Eimsbüttel and St. Pauli "all the windows were unbroken" and that "only in Berlin" did much of consequence happen.[39]

The ways in which antisemitism underwrote the remaking of urban life were generally subtle. Aryanization of Jewish property and private enterprise was not consistently enforced before 1938 on a national level, yet local-level aryanization—the practices "from below"—long preceded the policies of Reich authorities.[40] Many Jews in Hamburg were assimilated members of venerable Hamburg families and part of the city's professional and business circles. The politics of aryanization thus provided the foil for middle- and lower-middle-class "Aryans" to imagine their antisemitism as a vehicle to express social "grievances" and advance their socioeconomic interests.[41]

The Reich's Film Chamber explicitly excluded Jews from membership, thereby denying them any employment related to film. Jewish film exhibitors had little choice but to sell or lease their theaters if they did not have "aryan" relatives who could act as fronts. When the film industry and individual exhibitors found themselves in economic turmoil between 1929 and 1933, a host of pressures were at work in the disposition of Jewish property. The indemnity trials conducted after the war naturally recorded conflicting viewpoints, yet it is clear that Jewish exhibitors increasingly yielded to pressure from the racist regime and their own neighbors who saw opportunities for personal gain. By 1938 all exhibition outlets were controlled by "aryan" citizens.[42]

Hamburg's smallest cinema franchise, owned by Manfred Hirschel, was aryanized during 1933. By 1934 its three theaters—Reichstheater, Theater at Nobistor, and the Waterloo—had new operators. The Waterloo Theater, one of Hamburg's first-run houses, retained its prominent position under the direction of Heinz B. Heisig after Hirschel sold the theater to him. Before the Nazi takeover, Hamburg's largest exhibition chain, the Schauburgen of the Henschel Corporation, had been seeking acquisition by Ufa because of its dire financial situation. The Henschel executives were Jewish, and Hermann Urich-Sass died only a few days before the Nazis seized power, leaving his share of the company to his heirs and his partner Hugo Streit. When the Reich Film Chamber made it unlawful for Jews to operate movie theaters in 1933, Streit leased the Henschel KG chain to Paul Rohmann, a former lawyer for the Henschel Corporation, and Gustav Schühmann, the leading executive of the Ufa subsidiary James Henschel GmbH (founded by the father-in-law of both Urich-Sass and Streit). By then, brownshirts had blocked access to the Schauburgen and Ufa no longer seemed interested in buying out its financially struggling competitor. The eventual sale of the Henschel KG theaters to Rohman and Schühmann in 1936 clearly reflected a changing political landscape. Both men had become members of the Nazi party.[43]

Next, Ufa saw an opportunity to dispense with their biggest local competitor. Schühmann's ties to Ufa made for a natural alliance between the Schauburg and Ufa. As of 1937, the state became the majority shareholder in all major film production companies.[44] The Ufa–Schauburg alliance thus entered into a direct relationship with the state. Others soon followed. The Emelka group and the Central Theater in Eimsbüttel likewise reached agreements by which they pooled their forces and shared their allotted slice of the national production budget, thus escaping the struggle for survival faced by other independent district theaters.[45]

The Reich assumed control over the cinemascape of the city without altering it much on the surface. Films were still printed on celluloid and shown in theaters to a receptive and eager public. Non-Jewish filmmakers, screenwriters, and actors who had learned their crafts during the "*Systemzeit*" (the System) of the Weimar era kept working. But Goebbels had succeeded in purging German culture of "degenerate" works and questionable artists. Nazi cinema had decisively broken with its predecessor.[46]

Whitewashing

Antisemitism not only afforded individuals an opportunity to enrich themselves and perform their commitment to the people's community, it also diverted attention from the lingering shadow that urban entertainment cast over film. The false dichotomy between base urban pleasure and culturally salubrious film ignored the spatial proximity between the two within the entertainment districts. As well, people were hardly drawn to the comfortable darkness of the cinema because of their national pride and racial consciousness. In the Third Reich, as it had been in the Weimar Republic, moviegoing was cheap, convenient, and entertaining. From the 1920s onward, the cinema became more popular and affordable for workers who joined middle-class patrons, allowing the largely separate strata of Hamburg's society to mix within the entertainment districts.[47]

Social divisions ran deep in Hamburg, well before the Nazi assumption of power. Behind a facade of bourgeois respectability dwelled an increasingly disgruntled mass of the unemployed and chronically poor. This was true not only in the inner-city districts like St. Pauli and St. Georg, but also in the newer working-class strongholds of Hamm, Hammerbrook, and Barmbek. St. Pauli, however, retained a unique character. Here, abject poverty coalesced with the mix of entertainment, amusement, exploitation, and vice that had been a stable feature of the district since the post-Napoleonic era. In 1833, St. Pauli, previously known as the Hamburger Berg, was formally incorporated into Hamburg and received its modern name from a church built in honor of the apostle Paul. Yet the gates that had long excluded St. Pauli socially and economically from the city continued to close at night and were passable only after a hefty payment that increased as the night progressed, functioning as a customs border that granted access to men in pursuit of sensual pleasures, shady bars, glittering vaudevilles, and later movie theaters. Even after the gates were permanently opened in 1860, the moral boundary they once marked remained. St. Pauli and the Reeperbahn in particular became the El Dorado of Hamburg's population.[48]

St. Pauli's reputation as an entertainment mecca continued to grow, attracting locals and foreigners alike. Over the course of the second half of the nineteenth century, fancy hotels, tasteful edifices, restaurants, and entertainment venues sprung up next to the dense, shabby quarters of deckhands and dockworkers. By the early 1900s St. Pauli had become a hotbed of radical politics, questionable business, flamboyant entertainment, and crime—both petty and organized. It also remained one of Hamburg's poorest districts.[49] Adjacent to the harbor, St. Pauli differed from newer working-class garrisons. Its streets were narrower and its houses seemed to bend under the weight of poverty and strife.[50] Prostitution, prevalent in all of the city's working-class quarters, had a more flamboyant quality in St. Pauli.[51] Vice had become a built-in component of urban entertainment and a supplementary service industry based around the harbor, the city's economic motor and relay station for people and goods.

St. Pauli didn't easily fit into the vision for race-conscious, salubrious, and volk-bound pleasures advertised by the official leisure organization, Strength through Joy (*Kraft durch Freude*, KdF).[52] Representatives from the Tourist Association (*Fremdenverkehrsverein*) and the local KdF office nonetheless tried to exploit St.Pauli's fame, forming the Consortium St. Pauli-Freiheit to address the "image problem" that beset the city's most infamous district. The Consortium, and by extension the Tourist Association and the city itself, were particularly concerned with reviving tourism to boost Hamburg's export-oriented economy.

In May 1935 a major national newspaper, *Deutsche Allgemeine Zeitung*, reported that St. Pauli rejected its reputation as "St. Slovenly." It described the efforts of the local tourist office to reassure tour guides that St. Pauli was not a sinister den of crime and iniquity. "The charm of this colorful district," the paper asserted, "were its folksy dancehalls, its homey alehouses and bars, its vaudevilles and its openness to meet visitors irrespective of status or purse strings." Accordingly, the Consortium announced that St. Pauli wished to be known as St. Slovenly no longer, welcoming guests instead to the "Anchor of Joy."[53]

As the economy of vice came under attack, the Consortium launched an aggressive press campaign in the name of moral and visual rehabilitation. The goal was to divest Hamburg's traditional playground of its questionable reputation and lure tourists into a city whose local economy had failed to respond to the regime's reordering of the national economy.[54] The Consortium sought to market *Hamburger Vergnügen* (Hamburg's delight) beyond the city's boundaries.[55]

In January 1938 district leader Johannes Häfker drafted a lengthy proposal for the beautification of St. Pauli that envisioned whitewashed facades, improved street lighting, a parking lot, a large open-air stage equipped with a loudspeaker system, and the removal of an unsightly public toilet. Häfker moreover dreamed of building an imposing portal at Millerntor that would physically function as a passageway to the hidden pleasures behind. In addition, the district leader called on the press to cease all negative reports of St. Pauli. He suggested that the state grant dance licenses to all establishments seeking them, decrease utility prices to make lighting more affordable, lift the curfew, lower the tax on public amusements, and eliminate the tax on alcoholic beverages.[56] In the end, Häfker argued that the entertainment district's reputation depended on the immaculate appearance of individual establishments and the conscientious and honorable conduct of their owners and patrons. Even though little changed in St. Pauli until the outbreak of the war, by the spring of 1939 German newspapers championed St. Pauli as Hamburg's Montmartre.[57]

The attempt to beautify St. Pauli and reinvent it as one of the Reich's major tourist attractions served more than one purpose. Certainly, boosting tourism was of economic interest because it would funnel revenue to small-scale entrepreneurs and family businesses at a time when many of St. Pauli's restaurants, bars, dance halls and entertainment establishments were incurring substantial losses.[58] The depression had wreaked havoc on local industry. When the office of price control contemplated lowering beer prices in 1932, Hamburg's innkeepers, supported by the NSDAP, threatened a beer strike.[59] After the Nazis assumed power, avoiding strikes while retaining the loyalty of workers and small business owners became imperative. Boosting traffic to the district was cheaper than bringing about real change. Moreover, it had the expedient side effect of papering over St. Pauli's limited loyalty to the new regime. Although the tourism office spent close to 90,000 Reichsmarks on advertisement materials in 1938, tourism statistics demonstrate only modest increases in overnight guests. Hamburg was hardly a vacation hotspot.

Visitors tended to pass through the city on business or stop briefly while en route to elsewhere.[60]

Despite the efforts by Hamburg officials, the Reich's leisure organization, and the Consortium St. Pauli, the district's dive bars, brothels, and shady establishments remained a visible part of the entertainment structure. The salubriousness that the press celebrated took the form of increased police presence. Inns and taverns often spent more of their revenue on police dues than they paid in income taxes. In 1936 Frau Johanna Peterson, a widow who owned and operated Ballhaus "Eldorado" in St. Pauli, sold 13,888 hectoliters (366,882.146 gallons) of beer. She paid 370 Reichsmarks in income taxes and 1,715 Reichsmarks to the police. The total revenue of "Eldorado" that year was just over 60,000 Reichsmarks, a decline of 20,000 Reichsmarks from the previous year.[61] Expensive press campaigns didn't transform these urban entertainment establishments; they continued to struggle for customers and St. Pauli remained a liability for city boosters.

In large part, the remaking of Hamburg after 1933 was confined to rhetoric portraying it as the healthy, clean, pulsating, modern epicenter of German culture. Designating Hamburg as the *Heimat der Kraft durch Freude* (hometown of Strength through Joy) hardly put money into people's pockets.[62] An acute housing crisis remained. The city's economy lay in ruins, showing no significant signs of recovery. Yet efforts to turn St. Pauli into an entertainment mecca and Hamburg proper into a *KdF-Stadt* merged seamlessly with the city's self-concept as Germany's "gateway to the world."[63] When Hamburg hosted the World Congress for Leisure and Recreation in 1936, men paraded down the lavishly decorated boulevards of the city of leisure dressed in neoclassical tunics, celebrating joy as the wellspring of *Schaffenskraft* (productivity). But that was about as far as joy and productivity manifested themselves. Such posturing did not effect lasting changes to urban structures or the self-conception of Hamburg's citizens. And it certainly didn't increase tourism.

Volksfilm

In St. Pauli and elsewhere in the city, drinking, dancing, and horsing around retained their air of debauchery and vice even when they took place in well-lit and heavily policed establishments. In contrast, the transformation of film into a *volksbildend* (educational) medium could be *shown* even as film exhibition remained rooted in the geography of urban entertainment. The

Propaganda Ministry signaled unmistakably the prominent role film was to play in German culture, inadvertently opening up a political space for local cineastes and city boosters, something I discuss in the following chapter.

To mobilize film as an instrument of the state, the regime attempted to extricate it from its associations with mass leisure and public amusement. The Propaganda Ministry and various trade publications recast film as a distinctive fusion of high art, political education, and *Volksvergnügen* (popular pastime). Goebbels insisted that film harbored the potential to dissolve the conflict between art and mass culture, reconciling them through a National Socialist solution of self-consciously political *Volksmassenkunst* (popular art).[64]

Official anxieties regarding film's detrimental effects on audiences dissipated within the first few years of Nazi rule, and the regime prided itself on rescuing the medium from those who hoped to "obliterate film as a form of art and denigrate it to a mere amusement."[65] In 1938 the *Film-Kurier* affirmed that "the cinema is not like a tavern; when you pay an admission fee, you're not buying a lottery ticket and there aren't any rowdy encores [*Zugabeunwesen*] like there are in the vaudeville shows."[66] Validating the "horror" with which parents "observed the influence of early cinema [*Kintopp*] on impressionable minds [*jugendliche Gemüter*]," the Hamburg press bragged that "today, thanks to a deliberate mopping-up operation, film stands at the center of cultural production alongside the stage and the book."[67]

The implicit reference to the progressive aryanization of the German *Filmwesen* (film sector) illustrates that all sexualizing, youth-corrupting, and morally compromising effects of film were attributed to the Marxist-Jewish conspiracy against German *Kultur*. In Hamburg, as I illustrate in Chapter 3, this perspective radically changed during the war, but throughout the 1930s, local authorities and journalists echoed the celebratory proclamations from Berlin. Only "after the internecine reckoning with and consequent liquidation of all unhealthy foreign influences," the *Hamburger Anzeiger* exclaimed, "did the film worker find a clean and secure platform whence he could undertake his constitutive labor."[68] The *Hamburger Fremdenblatt* added that only a clean, pure, and "Jew-free [*unverjudet*]" film that "does not hover over never-never land" but is true to life and "seizes themes with a healthy instinct that are dear to all our hearts" could be a reflection of the nation's soul.[69] In 1936, Hamburg's newspapers looked back with pride on the purge of the "undesirable elements" from the German film industry and enthusiastically exclaimed that "our German film is on the best path to become a cinema of the people [*Volksfilm*] in the most beautiful and truest sense of the term."[70]

The *Volksfilm* became the solution to cinema's potentially corrupting influences on the immature mind—Weimar cinema its opposite. Here the Nazi regime could build on the work of morality leagues and their campaigns against smut and trash, efforts by bourgeois reformers to censor sexually explicit or politically explosive films.[71] The *Volksfilm* forged a consensus between Hamburg and Berlin, short-lived as it proved to be, on the edifying powers of cinema. This made it possible for film to become the central vehicle for the constant insinuation of racism into the Reich's promises for cultural renewal and moral revival.[72] A July 1936 headline in the *Kölnische Zeitung* boasted that there were "no Jews in the German movies."[73] The *Film-Kurier* followed in April 1938 with comparisons of pre- and post-1933 conditions in the film industry, listing the complete elimination of Jews from German film production, distribution, and exhibition as the first and most important National Socialist accomplishment.[74]

With Nazi racism and censorship protecting adolescents from unsuitable films, the Reich deliberately enlisted film for youth education. Attempting to cast film as an art form accessible to a broad popular base, Councilor Peter Zimmermann of the Film Censorship Office in Berlin affirmed that film art "has nothing to do with wages or monthly salaries, with village schools or universities, with heavy labor or inwardly focused erudition." Rather, Zimmermann preached, "film wants *Volk*, film wants the entire *Volk*," and argued that it is precisely film's *Volksverbundenheit* (popular immediacy) that distinguishes it from and ennobles it in comparison to all other art forms.[75] Zimmermann and others argued for authenticity, folksy realism, and recognizably German settings. Nonetheless, they agreed that absolute verisimilitude (*Wirklichkeitsnähe*) should not be at the aesthetic center of German films. Ultimately, popular tastes would align with the changes signaled by films such as *Heimat* and *Du und ich*, which infused serious subjects with the glamour of stars like Zarah Leander and Brigitte Horney.[76]

The *Film-Kurier* assumed that cinema itself would "coax" rather than "convince" audiences to acknowledge its artistic qualities, even if it remained unclear what those qualities were.[77] The vagueness in the official discourse reflected Nazism's half-baked attempts to return to the roots of German *Kultur* while renouncing its Weimar precursors and aspiring to crush the hegemony of Hollywood.[78] As film historian Karsten Witte first pointed out and other scholars have subsequently corroborated, National Socialist film had little to call its own in terms of style or technological innovation.[79] Instead it seems that National Socialist film required a particular kind of *Haltung* (inner disposition). Audiences rather than aesthetics made up National Socialist film culture.

Despite the frequent affirmations of film's potential for societal renewal that were published in the daily and trade presses, the regime was not willing to cede control of a cultural revolution to an entity as politically ambiguous as the viewing public. Instead film policy attempted to use various institutions to transform the uncultured masses into model audiences for the National Socialist film, refining popular tastes while redefining moviegoing pleasure as a necessary element of national cohesion.[80]

The weekly *Jugendfilmstunden* provided a communal cultural experience for young people. Organized by Hitler Youth leaders in coordination with regional film offices (*Gaufilmstellen*), screenings were first carried out during a Hitler Youth initiative in the winter of 1934–35, drawing audiences of three hundred thousand boys and girls.[81] Two years later, the *Jugendfilmstunden* boasted an audience of over one million. In 1937–38 about three million young people went to weekly youth film sessions as the institution expanded to include virtually every established movie theater in the Reich.[82] Local theaters were required to screen films chosen from the regional film archives by district representatives of the Hitler Youth. These screenings were limited to certain days of the week and usually took place during the winter semester so they would not interfere with service in the Hitler Youth or the League of German Girls (BDM).[83]

The *Reichsleitung Film* (Reich Office of Film) placed great confidence in film as an educational tool. Youth film screenings were originally conceived of as entertainment for Hitler Youth and BDM groups, but educators and youth leaders increasingly realized that chosen films could be framed effectively in the context of a disciplined community of young minds. Observing "that films are experienced completely differently in the community of like-minded and similarly disposed comrades,"[84] educators now rejected earlier reservations that "film might negatively influence the development of adolescents and was therefore dangerous at least to young people."[85] Rather than the medium itself, the social settings in which films were received constituted the problem in the eyes of National Socialists. Hence, a new kind of film viewing experience was modeled after the great party rallies. Entire Hitler Youth units would march to a designated theater in lockstep to watch a "valuable" film after receiving an introduction to its political relevance by the youth leader (*Bannführer*). In the context of National Socialist discipline, film became an "enlightening and educational tool" that provided young people with "agile experience, role model[s] and a festive exhibit."[86] That the boys and girls used these outings to relax from their highly ritualized service in Hitler Youth and

BDM did not detract from the impressive public demonstration of their disciplined pleasure. The weekly film screenings for adolescents are the most dramatic examples of the Nazi attempt to transform cinematic experience.[87] These efforts to reinvent the cinema as a national *Jugendbildungsstätte* (youth education initiative) were meant to reach the "broad mass of adolescents passively interested in film" and subject them to the "far-reaching effects that would establish taste and will" as the result of a disciplined communal experience.[88]

Save for an occasional reminder in the *Film-Kurier* that youths were to be admitted only to approved films, National Socialist discussion of the effect of film on adolescents was unanimously affirmative. Film propagandists held out hope that this new generation would ultimately resolve the conflict between art and kitsch.[89] The youth film days held in Hamburg in October 1937 highlighted the commitment of German youth to the "film of tomorrow" and recognized the Hitler Youth movement as an active factor in shaping both film reception and film production. The younger generation were being groomed to create and consume a new kind of culture.[90] Once Hitler Youth service became mandatory, young people constituted a captive audience. But the regime hoped to reform and grow audiences beyond the rungs of the Nazi youth organizations.

The *Filmvolkstag* (People's Film Day) was meant to bring film novices into the theater, under the premise of familiarizing them with nationally spirited art. First organized on April 25, 1935, as part of the International Film Congress in Berlin, the event was a tremendous success, becoming a regular feature of the annual convention of the Reich Film Chamber and drawing increasingly larger audiences.[91] While the chamber intended the first *Filmvolkstag* to demonstrate German film culture to the entire world, the event itself exemplified the cooperation between Berlin film exhibitors and Reich cultural authorities in recruiting new filmgoing audiences.[92] Held on a Sunday (the most popular moviegoing day) in Reich movie theaters that agreed to suspend the programming they had already paid for, the *Filmvolkstag* was supposed to "bring film to the broadest classes of people and simultaneously function as a mass advertisement for the good film and the visit to film theaters in general."[93] For only one *Groschen*—one-fifth the price of the cheapest regular ticket—citizens could gain entry to any participating cinema and see an old-time favorite or the latest blockbuster.[94] Even though the *Filmvolkstag* drew large numbers into "life-threateningly overcrowded" theaters, it appears that the attendees were predominantly veteran audiences.[95] For participating theaters, the *Filmvolkstag* was a money loser that failed to secure throngs of new customers. It merely redistributed existing audiences to those theaters willing to collude with the state and extend the regime's reach into the social fabric of the city.

Following the removal of Jews from the film industry and the barrage of press coverage that attested to the sanitized rebirth of film, the *Filmvolkstag* and *Jugendfilmstunden* performed the kind of community that National Socialists envisioned crafting on a national scale. Yet overall, German films of the 1930s were neither more wholesome nor more suitable for young people than their Weimar-era predecessors. They did not attain the realism and verisimilitude (*bodenständige Wirklichkeitsnähe*) to which Nazi film ideologues aspired. It is doubtful that such films would have found receptive publics anyway. Audiences continued to go to the movies for pleasure rather than to exercise patriotic devotion. "We often went to the Ufa Palast in those days," remembered Frau M. "It was marvelous. There was even acrobatics [. . .] and around the back there was the great dancehall."[96] Neighborhood theaters that were less in the grip of the regime's ideology remained the mainstays for regular citizens who only occasionally treated themselves to more expensive outings at one of the city's extravagant movie palaces.[97] Ticket sellers continued to pretend that the hordes of adolescents seeking admission to *Hallo Janine*, a romantic musical with Hollywood-style glamour and glitz, were actually fresh-faced adults.[98] German film companies continued to work with the stars, directors, and subjects that proved popular. They were more interested in minting money than churning out obedient Nazis.

CHAPTER 2

On Screen:

The Search for Authenticity

As a medium through which cities are imagined and remade, film can be as powerful and totalizing as the designs of urban planners. In Hamburg, film resolved the tensions between the city's questionable commitment to Nazism and its desire to promote "Hanseatic traditions" as local *Eigenart*.[1] After rising to power in 1933, the Nazi regime disempowered local administrations and relegated cultural centers to mere tributaries.[2] The politics of *Gleichschaltung*, or coordination, stripped Hamburg of its historic status as an independent city-state and threatened to delegitimize the basis for its identity as Germany's "gateway to the world." As Hamburg administration was restructured in accordance with the leadership principle or *Führerprinzip*, the venues for local politics grew increasingly narrower.[3] The senate was reduced to a support staff for Governor Karl Kaufmann, the local economy was retooled for war, and cultural institutions were aligned with Joseph Goebbels's Propaganda Ministry.

In the realm of culture, the Reich not only insisted on loyalty but also depended on local participation, creativity, and initiative for the production, dissemination, and reception of National Socialist *Volkskultur*.[4] When it came to cultural politics, the fragmentation, splintering, and doubling of institutions and competencies within the Nazi state were replicated within administrative hierarchies and between different levels of local government.[5] The character of cultural politics reflected the push and pull of national and local agents who were coming to grips with a central tenet of Nazi ideology: the valency of *Volk*. In the name of the *Volk* and its own particular interests, the city of Hamburg reinvented its cultural legacy.

In film discourse, Hamburg's administration, cineastes, cultural experts, local audiences, and national production companies negotiated an ideological

compromise between local particularity, *Heimatverbundenheit*, and National
Socialist cultural cohesion with Berlin's Propaganda Ministry. In this chapter, I reconstruct this process by evaluating administrative correspondence
and giving contextual readings of three Hamburg films. The first picture,
known by the working title *Greater-Hamburg Film,* was a documentary that
was never produced.[6] Werner Hochbaum's *Ein Mädchen geht an Land,* which
translates as *Landward-Bound: The Journey of a Northern German Maid,* was
a first attempt at National Socialist film art. The prestigious *Große Freiheit
Nr. 7,* or *Great Freedom No. 7,* delivered, if in melodramatic fashion, a happy
ending to Hamburg's search for cinematic representation.[7]

At first sight, these films seem like odd choices. The first was never made,
the second proved to be a flop, and the third wasn't released until after the
war. Although none of these films had a lasting influence on German cinema,
they were important because they structured local discourses about Hamburg's identity, its relationship to the Reich, and its role in National Socialist
Germany. The vibrant local and Reich-level debates surrounding these films
illustrate how different institutions and agents deployed film as a tribute to
Hamburg's people and their history. These cinematic treatments were seen as
affirmations of the city's relevance to Hitler's "thousand-Year Reich." Yet, only
the impact of *Große Freiheit* endured. After the war, it represented the "sal-
vageable" remnants of German *Kultur,* waiting to be retrieved from beneath
the rubble of the Reich.

From this perspective, the Greater-Hamburg film is significant precisely
because it wasn't made. Even though Goebbels restricted funds for self-
aggrandizing cinematic projects, Governor Karl Kaufmann was not dissuaded
from his cinematic quest to memorialize Hamburg as an exemplary convert to
National Socialism. He solicited input from various city departments, and the
press repeatedly announced the impending release of a "Hamburg film." The
debates surrounding the Greater-Hamburg film offer insights into the attempts
by local political functionaries to perform their conversion to Nazism in front
of local and national audiences. The administration's attempt to rewrite Hamburg's history as a teleology culminating in the triumph of National Socialism
should be seen in the context of the striking social and economic predica-
ments facing the city's political elites. Aiming to construct the city's history
based on the promise of future prosperity, this film project diverted critics
even though the project was abandoned in the planning stages.

When it became apparent that the Greater-Hamburg film wouldn't go into
production, local papers shifted focus to *Ein Mädchen geht an Land* as the

promised cinematic tribute to Hamburg. Nationally advertised as a woman's film and welcomed locally as an artistic exploration of *Heimat*, this Ufa feature directed by Werner Hochbaum portrays the bereavement and subsequent struggle of a young woman in both the austere landscape of northern Germany and the "urban jungle" of modern Hamburg.[8] The film was celebrated as an example of Nazi avant-garde filmmaking that loudly promulgated ideals of National Socialist art.[9] But *Ein Mädchen* suffered from a certain artistic immaturity. Despite an impressive advertising campaign put together by Hamburg's Film Consortium and a local film club, *Ein Mädchen* met with ambiguous responses from local and national audiences. Its "authentic Germanness" stemmed from the Nazi tropes of verisimilitude (*Wirklichkeitsnähe*) and rootedness in the soil (*Bodenständigkeit*), holding little promise for a cinema that increasingly conceived of itself as the European alternative to Hollywood. Hochbaum's treatment resonated only with the cultural mission of the Hamburg Film Consortium and its most vocal advocate, Werner Kark, an editor for the Nazi newspaper *Hamburger Tageblatt*.

In contrast, the public embraced *Große Freiheit Nr. 7*, which was named after a famous street in Hamburg's entertainment district, one well known to this day. By the early 1940s, German filmmakers were consciously fusing visual excess, Hollywood-style glamour, and symbols of authentic Germanness into large-scale entertainment. Moreover, their confidence was fueled by military expansion that substantially increased access to audiences and catapulted Nazi cinema into the dominant position in Europe.[10] *Große Freiheit* successfully resolved the conflicts characteristic of National Socialist film art. It rendered visible the allure and repulsion of the controversial St. Pauli district, reviving the notoriety that earlier films had tried to suppress and placing it in the service of National Socialism. Because *Große Freiheit* was released after the collapse of the regime, it could be reclaimed as an example of the authentic Hamburg spirit that survived the war untarnished by Nazism. (The film's theme song still plays on local radio.) But if this historical melodrama captures the cinematic representation of Hamburg, the happy ending that epitomizes Nazi-era Hamburg film arrived after its moment of articulation had passed. *Große Freiheit Nr. 7* premiered under the auspices of the British military government.[11] This Nazified vision of Hamburg culture followed the irreversible collapse of the Reich in what philosopher Steve Neale calls *agnition*, a retraction of perspective. Neale argues that agnition has a particularly moving effect when it comes too late—after that which could have been is no longer possible.

Greater Hamburg

In January 1937 the Greater-Hamburg Law unified Hamburg with its neighboring Prussian cities of Wandsbek, Harburg, and Altona. During the June 7,
1937, municipal assembly, Gauleiter Karl Kaufmann entrusted Senator Wilhelm von Allwörden with ensuring that the necessary preparations were
taken for the production of a film that would illustrate the revolutionary
transformation of Hamburg following the Nazi Party's ascent to power.[12]
Over the course of the summer, Otto Hermann, the director of the municipal film archive, worked out a first draft of a manuscript for the Greater-
Hamburg film. Although municipal unification provided the rationale for a
feature-length documentary, it was little more than the impetus for setting
the bureaucratic wheels in motion.[13] Kaufmann's motivation for making a
tribute to Hamburg (and by implication to himself) ran deeper.

Kaufmann had been toying with the idea of a Hamburg film as early
as January 1936.[14] Production companies hoping to cover costs by means
other than box office returns vied for projects financed by the public sector.[15]
Kaufmann reviewed manuscripts from various independent studios, rejecting
most of the proposals. Instead of entrusting a studio with the responsibility
for producing a script, he enlisted the city's administration and its institutions
in the process of rethinking Hamburg in explicitly National Socialist terms.

The planning committee's vision was heavily influenced by the manuscripts filed away in Kaufmann's office. At the beginning of the Greater Hamburg docudrama, the camera would zoom in on hopeless faces, long lines at
labor offices, loitering citizens, and scenes of social disorder that documented
the moral decay and economic standstill of the Weimar "system." Labor
strikes and Communist agitation would then dissolve into orderly marches of
Storm Troopers and Hitler Youth. The hoisting of the National Socialist flag
at city hall and the celebration of the first Labor Day on May 1, 1933, would
signal the inauguration of a new era. Subsequent scenes would document
the improvement of working conditions and economic stabilization, focusing on infrastructure, living conditions, healthy workplaces, tourism, and the
economic bustle of Hamburg's harbor. Joyous smiles of gainfully employed
and well-educated workers would replace the frowns of desperation, which
the film would clearly link to what National Socialists derogatorily referred
to as the *Systemzeit*. Images of bikes, streetcars, railroads, planes, and ships
would show Hamburg connected to the larger world as if to reinforce the
city's cosmopolitanism. Shots of foreign cruise ships filled with delighted

tourists would signal the transformation of Hamburg's trade economy to one of industry and service.[16] Title cards filled with tourism statistics and images provided by the Congress of Leisure would link productivity with recreation and pleasure as the new economic model.[17]

The script asked the audience to visualize a range of economic achievements, starting with the turnover of goods in the harbor, while failing to note the dramatic change from *Kolonialwaren* to the industrial raw materials needed for war. Increased discipline and comradeship in schools, shown during lunch and, indeed, air-raid drills, was attributed to improvements by National Socialist welfare organizations. The leisure organization Strength Through Joy demonstrated that world-class leisure and international travel was available to the National Socialist everyman. The administration intended to come back full circle to the massive construction and improvements underway in Hamburg's harbor, thus preserving the image of Hamburg's economic motor and the center for the particular *Lebensgeist* (esprit de corps) and worldliness its citizens were clearly not ready to renounce.[18]

Kaufmann's interest in showcasing his own achievements in the name of the Führer was hardly unique.[19] Berlin prided itself on being represented in three short documentaries since 1933, and by the end of 1936 a documentary celebrating its seven-hundredth birthday was in production. Bremen, Munich, Frankfurt, Stuttgart, Düsseldorf, and Cologne were busy documenting their histories on celluloid, disseminating proof of their respective transformations throughout the Reich.[20] It comes as no surprise that Kaufmann, a zealous National Socialist and an even more ambitious politician, did not intend to lose this intercity competition by standing idly by.[21]

Since the 1920s, film had been used by cities and institutions interested in promoting tourism.[22] The attempts to mobilize film to make local histories, to capture the unique characteristics of urban areas, and to tell their stories cinematically was, if anything, *more* strongly developed in the Weimar Republic than under National Socialist rule. The best known example is Walter Ruttmann's *Berlin: Sinfonie der Großstadt* (1927). Even though scholars do not consider it a city film, it is an exceptional contribution to this genre, casting Berlin as the quintessential modern city.[23] It is the essential *urban* character, rather than the recognizable features of Berlin, that distinguishes this film as it takes the viewer through a day in the big city.[24]

Weimar-era treatments of Hamburg and its *Eigenart* (characteristics) include *Hamburg, die arbeitenden Hafenstadt* (1927), *Bilder aus Hamburg* (1929), *Hamburg, die schöne Stadt an der Alster* (1929), and *Hamburg, Welthandels- und*

Hafenstadt (1929). Films like these provide a framework for understanding the National Socialist ambitions to rewrite urban history. By the early 1930s, the city portrait had become a recognizable genre that provided a venue for local patriotism and pride, articulating a visual language for conceptualizing the nation within the contested republican frame.[25] As occasional variants of the obligatory *Kulturfilm* (cultural documentary), cinematic treatments of cities and picturesque German landscapes rarely exceeded the quality of advertisements.[26] Commissioned by a city's tourist office, these films insinuated that national and international travel was a stable feature of everyday life.[27] Unlike Ruttmann's *Berlin*, these latter films were usually short, aesthetically pleasing, and politically palatable visions of a prosperity yet to come.[28]

Hamburg's administration was not merely concerned with boosting tourism through a feature-length documentary. The city's greatest tourist attraction, the pulsating district of St. Pauli at the harbor's fringe, provided city administrators with more economic and representational problems than any advertisement could solve. St. Pauli's extreme poverty provided an uneasy contrast to the famous amusement mile, the Reeperbahn. Nazi economic policy, however, was not geared toward alleviating poverty or improving the quality of life for ordinary citizens. It was geared toward war. In September 1936, Hitler entrusted Hermann Goering with the implementation of what came to be known as the "Four-Year-Plan," which hitched the national economy to the Nazi imperial project by stipulating two interlinked goals. Within four years, both the German army and the German economy must be ready for war.[29] Infrastructural and construction projects of strategic significance took priority. Because neither the housing shortage nor chronic unemployment could be addressed within the frame of the Four-Year-Plan, tourism promised to bring economic relief by distributing revenue directly to the district's bars, restaurants, artists, performers, and service personnel. With economic policy failing to boost living standards, the consumer sector, or urban renewal, managing appearances and masking continuing economic disparities garnered political importance while the Reich boasted of full employment.

Nevertheless, the Greater-Hamburg film was clearly not capable of transforming St. Pauli into a reputable place. Up to this point, films had exploited rather than avoided the mix of pleasure, vice, sensationalism, and crime that characterized St. Pauli. The world-renowned anchor of *Hamburger Lebensfreude* was deliberately excluded from the plans for the Greater-Hamburg film to showcase the city's transformation into a National Socialist metropolis.[30]

The absence of St. Pauli cannot be explained by asserting that "the district with its bad reputation did not fit the image of a prim Nazi-Germany."[31] It was simply impossible to present St. Pauli visually according to the fiction that was invented by the Nazi press—a clean and vibrant cultural center that provided entertainment for every man's taste and wallet in an atmosphere of pirate-romanticism (*Räuberromantik*).[32]

Moreover, Hamburg's administration wanted to showcase its own political reliability rather than the lure of St. Pauli. As a substitute for real improvements in the quality of life, the film would offer images of smiling tourists availing themselves of Nazi leisure opportunities, carefully circumventing the problem of conflating Hamburg with its infamous, poor, and politically unreliable district. As if to make up for the absence of St. Pauli's conviviality, other districts contributed to the film their alternative ideas and materials that would attest to Hamburg's earthbound grandeur and its boundless capacity for joy.[33]

With St. Pauli excised, the film presented the administration with a near perfect opportunity to address the immediate concerns regarding the legitimacy of the Nazi state.[34] Until well into 1938, Karl Kaufmann's determination to turn Hamburg into a model National Socialist city had to contend with the reality of a sluggish economy that kept Hamburg languishing in a state of economic emergency despite the overall national recovery.[35] When the Nazis took over in Hamburg, unemployment had reached an astronomical 30 percent, slowly declining only in the first few years of the new regime. At the same time the cost of living progressively increased while actual income gradually declined.[36] By the end of 1934, the city's economy showed modest signs of recovery, but it would be years until one could speak of economic revitalization, much less celebrate the promised economic boom. The statistical full employment of which some contemporary German citizens occasionally boast was not reached in Hamburg until March 1939.[37]

The Nazis' determination to turn the German economy toward armament and subsistence was not a good match for a city dependent on specialized international trade. As a result of the new economic policy, Hamburg lost its international position as Western Europe's dominant export and trading hub.[38] Hard hit by the depression, Hamburg saw its economy reduced to largely import related.[39] As the trade sector plunged into permanent crisis, the Greater-Hamburg Law of January 1937 merged the industrial cities of Altona, Wandsbek, and Harburg with Hamburg proper, transforming at least part of Hamburg into an industrial city that could be stimulated by state-induced armaments production. The great dockyards came to occupy a central role in the new economy. Goods such as chemicals, rubber, asbestos, electronics, and steel helped turn Hamburg into an industrial center while traditional trading and shipping industries declined.[40]

Hamburg's harbor, its "gateway to the world," was now the most important site for the movement of raw materials *into* the Reich. The privately owned small and medium-sized port-operating companies all but vanished following their centralization into a port-operating cooperative in May 1934. Formerly a hallmark of Hamburg's mercantile independence and vitality, the harbor was transfigured into a centrally administered complex of national (read military) significance with dwindling economic sway.[41] Moreover, trade of consumer and luxury goods, of *Kolonialwaren* such as coffee, tea, and spices, no longer figured prominently in either the economy or public discourse. Hamburg's international importance decreased as a result of Nazi economic strategy. The city's identity as Deutschland's *Tor zur Welt* faced a crisis of credibility.

The Greater-Hamburg film was supposed to remedy this crisis at least in part. Moreover, local party leadership was painfully aware of the connection between the demographics that characterized the poorest districts of the city and the potential for political tensions. The election results of August 19, 1934, reminded Hamburg's National Socialists that they needed to demonstrate that Hamburg had successfully completed its transformation into a National Socialist *Führerstadt*.[42] In these staged elections, Hamburg Nazis registered the worst results in the nation. In some districts up to one third of the population either voted against the consolidation of the offices of Reich's chancellor and president or invalidated their votes.[43] Accordingly, the city demanded and promised itself a cinematic facelift that would embellish its meager social and economic achievements, allowing Hamburg to feel like an active participant on a national stage devoted to self-celebration.

At the request of Governor Kaufmann, the representatives of Hamburg's administration came together in the Phoenix Chamber of City Hall on November 11, 1938, to discuss the proposal for the Greater-Hamburg film. The politicians insisted on making the harbor the dominant visual and narrative focus.[44] The staff of lord mayor Carl Vincent Krogmann exhorted the planning committee to place Hamburg's uniqueness at center stage. The city's particular achievements should take precedence, and under no circumstances was the film to offer yet another locally inflected celebration of the national movement.[45] The administration chose otherwise. Given Hamburg's belated economic recovery, it developed a narrative meant to rebuild the city's official image in ways that would validate the sacrifices made by the population, obscure the limited availability of consumer products, glorify the National Socialist transformation, and celebrate historical "traditions" and the Hanseatic way of life.

Joseph Goebbels had boasted about the importance of film in the "New Germany" and called for the transformation of the German film industry in the early 1930s. By promoting German film production, setting high artistic standards, and guiding the masses in matters of value and taste, the authorities in Berlin hoped to sell the National Socialist idea through the careful deployment of a new kind of German culture, thereby binding individuals to the *Volksgemeinschaft*. In August 1936, Goebbels deliberately curtailed the ability of cities and towns to use public moneys for individual film projects.[46] He maintained that many of these films turned out to be "disastrous failures" and could not be released for public viewing. He decreed that every such film project needed to seek his personal approval before production.[47] The minister was particularly interested in preventing *Lokaltümelei* (navel-gazing localism).[48] The regime thus sought to implement clear directives regarding what kinds of films could be produced and by whom.[49]

Fearing that cities would squander public funds on self-aggrandizing projects, Goebbels stipulated that city films produced with public finances had to demonstrate prospects for profitability before production. Debates over the importance and value of the *Kulturfilm* reveal an acknowledgment that city documentaries were unlikely to be box office hits.[50] It was even less likely that a film about Hamburg that deliberately refused to meet the sensationalist expectations raised by feature films such as *Ein Mädel von der Reeperbahn* (1930) or *Razzia in St. Pauli* (1932) would draw a large audience beyond the boundaries of the city.[51] Even as an advertisement for tourists, the cinematic opus of the city did not hold much promise.[52]

The functionaries and film enthusiasts in Hamburg who already recognized the extraordinary powers of film listened carefully to Goebbels. Yet these ardent National Socialists deliberately pursued local visions and interests that did not reflect the goals of the propaganda minister in the slightest. Kaufmann himself did not care about the imposition of national authority. The earliest discussions of the Greater-Hamburg film violated Goebbels's directive requiring his personal approval for public funding of a *Stadtfilm*. Kaufmann believed that his personal relationship with Goebbels, which dated back to the early years of the National Socialist struggle, would lead the minister to turn a blind eye to Hamburg's transgression.[53] Furthermore,

Kaufmann's system of personal patronage had expanded to such an extent that he could have financed the film from specialty funds amassed from commercial gambling, auctions of "subversive capital" (the spoils of aryanization, that is), and voluntary or compulsory donations. Even the specter of reimbursing public funds in the event of the film's failure did not move Kaufmann to abandon the project.[54]

The Hamburg administration had bought into Goebbels's definition of film as the National Socialist *Wunderwaffe* (magic weapon), and they decided to mobilize the local film elite to embrace this vision. Over the course of the 1930s, Hamburg's administrators grew to agree with the national rhetoric that redefined film as an educational implement of the state.[55] They discovered in film a tool with which to forge convergences of local and national identities. Even though film policy remained the sole prerogative of Joseph Goebbels and the Reich Film Chamber, within that frame the regional film apostles projected *their* mission to a national audience.[56] Thus, when the president of the Reich Film Chamber affirmed the function of film to grow into its role "as an intermediary of the *Volksgemeinschaft*,"[57] Kaufmann seemed ready to take him at face value and view film as an arena to publicize his political zeal and the transformation of his city.[58]

Between the *Machtergreifung* (seizure of power) and the German attack on Poland on September 1, 1939, local and national interpretations of the political and cultural impact of film were remarkably compatible. Film became an instrument to imagine and articulate the racial community and a venue for asserting local significance on a national stage. The imposition of tight control and supervision by the Reich Film Chamber and the Ministry of Propaganda notwithstanding, officials in Hamburg were almost able to forge a compromise between the aggrandizing aspirations of Goebbels's ministry and their own impulses to promote the city, write its history, and celebrate the achievements of local party functionaries.

Despite the near seamless convergence of local ambition with Goebbels's vision of film fostering *Volksgemeinschaft*, the Greater-Hamburg film failed to go into production. The project's urgency subsided once the reality the film was supposed to depict was no longer in danger of being publicly questioned. The goal of full employment and the imminence of war put to rest the urgency for self-representation. Making National Socialist achievements visible became less essential as war loomed on the horizon.

Kaufmann, too, seemed to have lost interest in the film project. Detailed suggestions continued to arrive from various administrative units such as the district of Bergedorf, the city of Wandsbek, *Landherrenschaft* (regional representatives), the Departments of Youth and Sport, the Building Control Department, and the Fire Department. Manuscripts from film companies continued to pass across Kaufmann's desk.[59] Most disappeared into file cabinets or ended up in the trashcan.[60] Kaufmann was increasingly occupied with his own political standing within the Nazi party as he sought to increase the city administration's financial independence from Berlin. Moreover, as his area of personal responsibility widened, Kaufmann continued to insist on dealing with the smallest administrative details himself.[61] Overwhelmed, he threatened to paralyze the administration with his leadership style. The last proposal that survived in the records dates to April 12, 1939. The film company Epoche informed Kaufmann about the short takes they were producing for Berlin and offered to do the same for Hamburg, thus archiving the city's transformation for future generations. The pencil marks on the document read, *Ablagern* (file away).[62]

The Nazi Avant-Garde: A Local Perspective

The desire to pay cinematic homage to the Depression-ravaged Hamburg extended beyond the tight circle of Karl Kaufmann's chosen administrators. While the ruling elites fixed their hopes on Hitler's grandiose plans to shape the harbor areas into a "gateway to the world," cineastes found avid support in the local press for a cinematic facelift for the city.[63] Even before the administration had abandoned the Greater-Hamburg film, the press offered Hamburg audiences an unlikely surrogate. In March 1938 the *Hamburger Tageblatt* welcomed Werner Hochbaum's *Ein Mädchen geht an Land* as the solution to the vibrant debate surrounding the Hamburg film.[64] In September 1938 the Nazi newspaper proclaimed that this Ufa feature was the answer for a large-scale, feature-length Hamburg film. "Hamburg—Your Film Has Arrived," chimed the headline of the article describing director Werner Hochbaum's idiosyncratic career and arguing for *Ein Mädchen* as an example of National Socialist avant-garde filmmaking.[65]

Hochbaum was hardly a model Nazi.[66] In the 1920s he had worked briefly as a journalist for the Social Democratic daily *Hamburger Echo*. His first successful film, *Brüder* [*Brothers*] (1929), was a leftist exploration of the dockworkers' strike at Hamburg's harbor during the winter of 1896–97. He had spent time in prison after attempting to reconstruct scenes from the 1918 Revolution for the Social Democratic *Wille und Werk*. Born the son of a professional soldier in Kiel in 1899, Hochbaum was committed to his *Heimat* and developed a fascination with the city and with St. Pauli in particular. After the Nazi seizure of power, Hochbaum was repeatedly arrested and questioned by the authorities for his Social Democratic sympathies. *Morgen beginnt das Leben* [*Life Begins Tomorrow*] (1933) was the first film he finished under the new regime. His most successful film, *Die Ewige Maske* [*The Eternal Mask*] (1934), brought him international attention and fame.[67] He was subsequently hired by Ufa to direct Marika Rökk's debut, *Leichte Kavallerie* [*Light Cavalry*] (1935).

Hochbaum returned to the Hamburg harbor milieu when a popular novel by Eva Leidmann, *Ein Mädchen geht an Land*, captured his interest. His goal as director was to "represent the landscape and atmosphere of the lowland-German [mentality] in a true and recognizable fashion."[68] *Ein Mädchen geht an Land* was a deliberate return to *Hamburg, das Erlebnis einer Welthafenstadt* and allowed Hochbaum to explore his fascination with the city and its harbor milieu while engaging with a subject cherished by Nazi ideologues. A simplistic morality tale, *Ein Mädchen* follows a skipper's daughter named Erna Quandt (played by Elizabeth Flickenschildt) who loses her fiancé during a storm at sea and decides to make a new life on land. Trapped in a world that lacks familiar, clear lines of authority, this plain but steadfast maiden transforms the lives of the people around her while the city threatens to thwart her destiny as a wife and mother.

The film's popular reception was complicated and ambiguous, as shown by the contemporary discourse among German film experts on the relationship between art and film in the Nazi state. The endorsement Hochbaum's film received in Hamburg before its release was highly unusual, and the picture's initial success must be seen in light of the concerted efforts to promote the film by local Ufa executives and the city's patrons of northern German art.[69] For weeks before the release, Hamburg's Film Consortium, a unique institution that brought together cineastes, members of the Reich's film chamber, and representatives of the local film elite, had plastered posters on advertisement pillars and projected announcements in movie houses across the city.[70] Speaking to a packed auditorium of more than eight hundred at Hansesche University, Hochbaum inadvertently provided an explanation for the attention and extensive coverage his film received before its opening in the prestigious Hamburg Lessing-Theater.[71] He affirmed his intention to "make legible the lowland-German man to the all-German space [*den niederdeutschen Menschen für den gesamtdeutschen Raum verständlich zu machen*]."[72] This film, the director told his audience, promised to give outsiders an opportunity to gain accurate knowledge "of the essence [*Wesen*] of our eternal homeland [*Heimat*]."[73] Following the film's release, local Ufa representatives invited the director, several actors from the film, local film patrons, and members of the daily and trade presses to the home of Hamburg's film club at the Blauer Peter.[74] They came together to celebrate Hamburg's uniqueness as "pioneers of the German film for the land of tomorrow."[75]

One of the guiding principles of film was to connect with the everyday lives of *Volksgenossen* and to engage authentic German subject matter to produce a pure (*unverkitscht*) film experience.[76] This resonated not only with local patrons of the arts but also with the Propaganda Ministry, which promoted cinematic treatments of serious, contemporary material. Initially Hamburg elites welcomed the film, less for the gripping story than for the promised devotion to *Heimat*. The first three screenings at the Lessing Theater on September 30, 1938, were crowded; the latter two were sold out.[77] Over the next several days, the film played to well-attended houses.[78] However, the success of *Ein Mädchen* was short and far from universal—even in Hamburg. The *Hamburger Tageblatt* praised the choice of "*hamburgische Stoff*" (Hamburg-related subject matter), the use of local talent instead of popular Ufa stars, and the film's atmospheric visuals rather than its plot. This defined Hochbaum's work in the public eye as an art film. Ultimately it proved less successful with broad audiences.[79]

The first notice of *Ein Mädchen* in *Hamburger Tageblatt* drew explicit connections between Hochbaum's film and Hamburg's general search for cinematic representation. It celebrated the female lead, praising the director's choice of a protagonist "who certainly did not possess the features of a star."[80] Elisabeth Flickenschildt, the daughter of a captain from Blankenese, was a beloved actress welcomed as one of Hamburg's own. This did not guarantee popular acclaim, however. Flickenschildt was typecast for the part, but Hochbaum's decision to place "for the first time, the ugly girl at the center of a film [*erstmalig das häßliche Mädchen in den Mittelpunkt des Films zu stellen*]" was bound to run counter to popular expectations and prompted the *Tageblatt* to revel in Hochbaum's courage to place artistic considerations above box office returns guaranteed by star-stocked features.[81] Even though critics applauded Flickenschildt's talent as an actress, the dowdy protagonist of *Ein Mädchen geht an Land* did not elicit enthusiastic responses from local or national audiences.[82] Stars like Zarah Leander in *Heimat* and Heinz Rühmann in *13 Stühle* exerted a greater audience pull than Elisabeth Flickenschildt in her first and last role as a female lead.

The Ufa trailer nonetheless advertised *Ein Mädchen* as a woman's film with a heroine both noble and plain. Like the prerelease report of the *Hamburger*

Figure 4. Advertisement for *Ein Mädchen geht an Land* in *Illustrierter Filmkurier*, 1938. Staatsarchiv Hamburg.

Tageblatt, the Ufa advertisements anticipated the limited audience for the film, preparing viewers for a protagonist "who must not be beautiful for her role, who must grow out of the image of city and harbor, whose moral and spiritual background rests in the stream, the ships, and the sea alone."[83] Nonetheless, female patrons may have struggled to accept "a protagonist who is far from the normative beauty of usual female appearances at the center our films" as the quintessential embodiment of Hamburg and the uniqueness of its people.[84] Hochbaum's film received an even less enthusiastic reception in the Reich.[85]

The absence of ebullient postrelease reviews in local newspapers further suggests that a wide audience for the film did not exist in Hamburg. Calling the reception "warm-hearted" the press used a politically palatable word choice to describe the city's reaction to the film. The local news outlets, which had been so important to the initial reception of the film, did not print any more positive endorsements. Werner Kark, the editor of the *Hamburger Tageblatt* who had previously written an unqualified recommendation for the film, described Eva Leidmann's novel as "very shallow" and remarked that such a story "could not have been the last, valid foundation for a real [*echten*] Hamburg-film."[86] *Ein Mädchen* was booted down the tiers of local cinemas quickly. It was never shown in many of the smaller neighborhood theaters, which opted to screen reprises instead.[87] On November 10, 1938, a month after opening, the film was listed in the classified ads for the last time.

At this point it is important to take a closer look at Hamburg's film elite. Over the course of the 1930s, Hamburg developed an extensive patronage system for film art that served and furthered local interests. In 1935 local exhibitors, film distributors, and film critics founded the Film Consortium (Arbeitsgemeinschaft Film) in cooperation with the Center for Adult Education (Volkhochschule) under the guidance of local cineast Werner Kark.[88] Proud of their pioneer status in the Reich, the members of Hamburg's Film Consortium felt emboldened to present themselves as authoritative spokespersons for the new German film. Their initiative to create a local institution for the promotion of film art was unique in the Reich, and the *Film-Kurier* regularly reported on the consortium's lecture series and other activities.

Consortia (*Arbeitsgemeinschaften*) were a stable feature of local and national politics, useful for maintaining the Nazi illusion of political participation. The regime benefited from collaboration and exchange in these circumscribed political spaces while retaining absolute control and decision-making authority.[89] In 1937 members of the Hamburg Film Consortium created a second organization called the Hamburg film club, a private association that focused on promoting regional and local art in all forms. Guided by Kark, the club conceived of itself as an institution committed to furthering the work of the consortium, serving in effect as a double. But in contrast to the consortium, which was associated with the regional propaganda office, the university, and the city's adult education center, the club uncoupled local interests from the national machine.

After the completion of the clubhouse in March 1938, the consortium increasingly promoted itself publicly through the film club's venues. The club organized weekly matinees that brought film connoisseurs together in Hamburg's last independently owned, first-run theater (*Uraufführungstheater*), the Waterloo Kino on Dammtorstrasse.[90] They screened valuable (*wertvolle*) documentaries and feature films, providing the basis for discussions between audiences and prominent individuals from the Reich's film elite.[91] The Waterloo Theater, which had made a virtue of necessity by specializing in foreign films (many imported from Hollywood well into 1940), promised to be a viable counterweight to the Ufa-dominated machine. In turn, the Waterloo benefited from the club's patronage—the Waterloo was thus able to sustain itself financially and demonstrate its support for the regime. The film club by no means harbored political tendencies that opposed the *Arbeitsgemeinschaft* or the local film-political authorities. Although the membership of the Film Consortium and the film club largely overlapped, the institutional split allowed for more variegated and localized events to take place in the clubrooms and thus retain an aura of private gatherings of like-minded art enthusiasts. As venues for cultivating local alliances and cementing hierarchies imposed by the restructuring of the film industry, the Film Consortium and the film club provided local experts and enthusiasts with the opportunity to celebrate their collective contribution to the National Socialist revolution. In these pseudopolitical organizations, local patriotism and pride were easily assimilated and reinforced by Nazi doctrine.

The members of the Film Consortium took Goebbels seriously when he proclaimed the "primacy of art."[92] They conceived of themselves as sponsors of a National Socialist avant-garde, stripping the term of the meaning and connotations it held under their Weimar precursors. They espoused quintessential Germanness, and as filmmaker Wolfgang Liebeneiner said in Hamburg, "to be German, is to be lucid [*Deutsch sein, heißt klar sein*]!"[93] On December 11, 1938, Dr. Johannes Eckardt, director of Degeto (Deutsche Gesellschaft für Ton und Film), explained the new National Socialist avant-garde vision of film to the patrons of the Hamburger Film Consortium. He insisted that the new avant-garde "mustn't ever lose its connection to the larger group." It should "push forward while looking back [*zurückschauend vorwärts treiben*]."[94] Eckardt insisted that a National Socialist avant-garde is revolutionary only "when it does not fade into and distort itself in a vacuum of abstract, formal constructions."[95] It must assimilate "the breath of the tilled earth" that the National Socialist revolution has liberated as a result of "ploughing up the life of an entire nation." The "buried forces that for centuries had been hidden" would finally be set free.[96]

Grounded in a rigid adherence to the concept of verisimilitude, Nazi avant-garde cinema nonetheless relied on the suggestive effects of film. Rather than merely depicting reality objectively, the Nazis wanted film to articulate its own claims of objectivity (*Wirklichkeitsanspruch*). Eckardt explained that the "illusionary effect of film can be so strong that it creates the impression not just of reflecting reality, but of being reality."[97] Film historian Sabine Hake has shown that Nazi cinema's thrust for *Wirklichkeitsnähe* was politically as well as aesthetically motivated. She argues that "a momentous shift from text-based to reception-based definitions of filmic realism" had the "elevation of the motion-picture audience to a model of the racial community, the *Volksgemeinschaft*" as its main goal.[98] Hake convincingly illustrates that "Being true to life meant making political tendentiousness an integral part of cinema."[99] However, there was no clear consensus on what that tendentiousness entailed. Initial experiments like *Ein Mädchen geht an Land* displayed elements characteristic of an earlier period and were criticized for their supposed expressionism.[100] Still we can follow the "code for illusionism," the visual production of mood and atmosphere that Hake identifies as central to the cinematic realism espoused by the Nazis.[101] National Socialist film attempted to articulate an authenticity that transcended the real. Although ideas of authenticity and verisimilitude were at first connected almost literally to an ideology of blood and soil (as appears to be the case in *Ein Mädchen*), these concepts were broadened with the maturation of Nazi film production to include more extravagant cinematic treatments such as *Große Freiheit Nr. 7*.

Because the great production companies had national and, increasingly, international audiences in mind, the interests of the nationalized film industry did not naturally connect with local patriotism. *Ein Mädchen* promised to present Hamburg's film enthusiasts with a near perfect product by placing the city at the center of the production without visually exploiting "that which has been painted countless times in song, film and word."[102] It also offered the "naturalism" that chief censor Heinrich Zimmermann had called for back in 1938, demanding that "the entertainment film must become incomparably more realistic [*lebensechter*]."[103] Locally, Hochbaum was celebrated as a leading figure of a new avant-garde that utilized lucid optical means to "show people in their relationship to objects and to the landscape, both of which are suddenly imbued with great spirit and strength [*Beseelung*]."[104]

Ultimately, the film's rigid adherence to an ideal of verisimilitude that reflected the Nazi call for *Bodenständigkeit* (rootedness in the soil) may have been the main reason for the initial enthusiasm of the Film Consortium. The ambiguity that characterized popular reception of *Ein Mädchen* was also the result of its commitment to this kind of "realism." The call for *Bodenständigkeit* reflected the contradictions inherent in the use of filmic techniques associated on the one hand with lofty art and on the other with folk-bound ordinariness. Hochbaum's commitment to these two fundamental concepts of Nazi film art did not produce a vision of Hamburg that nurtured the spirit of self-celebration that audiences expected of a grand Hamburg film. The film was simply too *bodenständig* and *wirklichkeitsnah*.

It is almost impossible to reconstruct how *Ein Mädchen* (or any other film for that matter) was received by regular audiences. Only film critics and

National Socialist authorities left written accounts. Both the daily and the specialty presses followed the regime's instructions, discussing films in a descriptive and generally affirmative language. Caustic remarks and accusations of failure were generally reserved for international films.[105] Reports from the security service give insight as to what viewers thought or said about a film, but these anecdotal references must be seen as snapshots that do not invite historical generalizations.[106] We may never know whether audiences in Hamburg *liked* and *enjoyed* Hochbaum's exploration of the city in his stylized tale about feminine virtue. However, a careful contextual reading of the place of visual pleasure in *Ein Mädchen* will allow us to make educated guesses about the emotive resonances and their relationships to the official purpose this film was meant to serve.

Because *Ein Mädchen* was supposed to capture the essence of the northern German *Heimat*, any analysis of the film should begin by situating it in the context of the emerging genre of *Heimatfilm*, which affirms rural communities as bulwarks against the encroachment of the outside world (generally urban) into the primordial idyll.[107] Within the genre there are variations on the conflict between tradition and modernity, the individual and the sublime.[108] As a contribution to *Heimatfilm*, Hochbaum's feature was extraordinary. Not only did he highlight his lowland German homeland, but he also located his exploration in the *Heimat's* quintessential other—the modern metropolis.[109]

On both a formal and a narrative level, *Ein Mädchen* fails to resolve the tensions between the bourgeois home, the harbor as the city's economic motor, St. Pauli as the city's pleasure colony, and a landscape defined by the endless comings and goings of tides. Offering neither wholeness nor a brighter version of everyday reality, *Ein Mädchen* conflates Hamburg with one of its poorest districts as Hochbaum searches for the city's essence in and around its harbor. As a counterweight to the conflicts of a modern city, *Ein Mädchen* locates the potential for reform in the protagonist Erna. Yet instead of resolving the opposition between city and nature, Erna remains irreconcilably part of nature and thus foreign to her urban surroundings. Rather than sleep in a room of her own, she chooses a cove in the kitchen that reminds her of her bunk on her father's ship. Her sailor's almanac, the anchor of her moral compass, is never far from reach. Erna is not welcome. She does not belong to Hochbaum's city.

The visual strategies associated with the emerging genre of the *Heimatfilm* were translated into a northern German context a few years later by Veit Harlan's *Opfergang* (1942–44). Unlike *Ein Mädchen*, Harlan's film integrates the protagonist, a child-woman named Adele (Kristina Söderbaum), into the landscape in a way that suggests an elemental form of belonging and identity. In a particularly compelling scene, Söderbaum rides a horse along the beach of the Elbe River unconfined by the essentialized boundaries separating water from land. Yet wholeness in *Opfergang* is bittersweet. Adele's *Fernweh* (longing for faraway places) is the flip side of her youthful and melancholic vitality. Her illness and subsequent death—the inevitable consequences of her drifting—unmake her eternal homelessness (*Heimatlosigkeit*), reclaim her body as part of the natural landscape, and assimilate the contradictions between land and sea.

In contrast, Hochbaum attempts to dissolve the boundary that separates city from sea. He visually merges the natural landscape with man-made iconography of docks, chimneys, and ships. Juxtaposing the tropes of industrial modernity with a natural landscape dominated by water, the film's narrative unmasks the panoramas of Hochbaum's *Stadtlandschaft* (urban landscape) as fundamentally flawed. Like the return of the repressed, St. Pauli emanates from the city's fabric as an organic threat to the unadorned humanity of the German north. The loading cranes, steeples, and ships' bows that point upward to the eternal sublime hardly achieve the humbling effect of the monumental mountain ranges found in the *Bergfilm* sub-genre.[110] Compared to the urban spectacle of the city, the colorful bustle of St. Pauli is shortchanged. Seen through Erna's eyes, the pretty girls, dancing couples, ritzy bars, and amusements appear inauthentic and fake. In the few street scenes in which it appears, St. Pauli is populated by geezers, drunks, and whores, none of whom seem to enjoy themselves. The film robs St. Pauli of its allure and renders it a mere emblem of Hamburg's legendary urbanism.

City life eventually bends the upright Erna. Immune to both the extravagant lifestyle of her Viennese employer and the vices of St. Pauli, Erna's moral compass is nonetheless dislodged, her integrity called into question. Her selfless friendship with the marriage swindler Jonny Hasenbein (Carl Kuhlmann) sullies her name. Erna attempts suicide—the only logical step following female (sexual) transgression.[111] The children of the widower Semmler, clad in white nightgowns to resemble angels of providence, rescue the disoriented Erna, who "must have lost the solid path." Her life saved, she surrenders to her destiny. At the end of the film, Erna sits outside Semmler's petty bourgeois home, cradling his youngest in her lap while the inarticulate bachelor fumbles for words. The child's preemptive exclamation of "Mutti" seals Erna's fate as a mother who will know neither love nor sensuality.[112] By conflating the city with its pleasure colony, Hochbaum argues that Hamburg has no place for virtue. Even though Erna stays on land, she returns to a

Figure 5. Still of Hamburg Harbor, from *Ein Mädchen geht an Land*, 1938.

petty bourgeois milieu on the city's fringe, one that functions as an interme-
diate space safe from both the compromising bustle of the metropolis and
the elements raging at sea. In the house of the portly, middle-aged widower
Semmler and his three Germanic children, Erna finds a home at the price of
forsaking *Heimat*.

Hochbaum attempted to *show* Hamburg rather than *tell* its story. Despite
the "finest, atmospheric paintings of light [*Lichtmalerei*]" praised by the *Illustrated Film Kurier*, Hochbaum's film paints a bleak picture that refuses to
follow the conventions of melodrama.[113] The film's conclusion is an affirmation of duty, not happiness. *Ein Mädchen* may have been "a first discussable
attempt in German filmmaking to fashion the face of the Hanseatic city and
its people in a large scale feature," but it was hardly an opportunity for self-
celebration and pride, much less a showcase of local glamour. Hochbaum does
not present St. Pauli for visual consumption. Instead, the director produces a
nonvoyeuristic morality tale that affirms duty to the *Volksgemeinschaft* while
cynically calling into question the pursuit of happiness. In contrast, *Schatten über St. Pauli* (Kirchhoff, 1938), an unoriginal mystery set in Hamburg's
harbor milieu, established its allure by instrumentalizing the atmosphere of

the entertainment district.[114] Where *Ein Mädchen* stylizes the elemental and natural characteristics of both the northern sea and the modern urban jungle, *Schatten über St. Pauli* presents an action-packed crime drama about a beautiful maiden who is kidnapped by an unscrupulous industrialist and rescued when her fiancé and his fellow harbor skippers capture the scoundrel and turn him over to the police. In Hochbaum's exploration, the cityscape accentuates the "otherness" of the wholesome Erna, thus making visible the ambiguity and anxiety of a land-bound character caught between the primordial force of the sea and urban, man-made modernity. What makes Hamburg Hamburg is never clear.

Credited as emerging from folk-bound *Bodenständigkeit* rather than the seed of individual genius, *Ein Mädchen* was duly celebrated as the realization of a National Socialist avant-garde. Though the film was reasonably successful, it failed to deliver the long-awaited Hamburg film.[115] The day after it left the prestigious inner-city screen, *Fracht von Baltimore* (Hinrich 1938) opened in the Schauburg St. Pauli. On October 14, Max Baumann asked whether Hans Hinrich's film was finally "the Hamburg film." He answered, "No certainly not! Hamburg remains mostly in the background and one begins to wonder whether it is at all possible to present this conflicted city of rich and poor, of harbor dive-bars and exquisite restaurants, of work and evermore work by day and night, this city on Germany's fringe to the wide world in a mere film."[116] The search for the ultimate Hamburg film would have to continue.

Hamburg: The Nazi City

It was Helmut Käutner's *Große Freiheit Nr. 7* that produced a viable and lasting tribute to Hamburg. Mobilizing the same conflict between land and sea that was essential to *Ein Mädchen geht an Land,* Käutner's film explores Hamburg's harbor milieu in the story of a former sailor who reinvents himself twice over. The drama's two overlapping love triangles place the moral strictures of small-town morality in an urban setting where hard work, male honor, and feminine virtue prevail in the face of depravity and carefree entertainment. The main character, former sailor Hannes Kröger (Hans Albers), is the lead attraction in the Hippodrom on Große Freiheit Street in St. Pauli's amusement quarters. To the sounds of his accordion he sings hymns to his only true love—the sea. Fate keeps him on land, where he rescues his late brother's sweetheart, the beautiful and independent Gisa (Ilse Werner), from her dead-end, small-town life.[117]

Weary of his lover Anita (Hilde Körber) and his life at her brothel, Hannes falls for *das anständige Mädchen* (the good girl) who contrasts starkly with the lascivious women on the Große Freiheit. However, Gisa has her eye on Willem (Hans Söhnker), a saucy dockhand. Despite painful misunderstandings and the escalating rivalry between the two men, Gisa convinces Willem of her virtue and they find love and happiness together. Hannes, encouraged by his friends, returns to his true love—the sea.

The film first reached German audiences in October 1945. Enthusiasts and scholars have since focused on the film's nonconformity.[118] Journalists generally cite the film's representation of gender and sexuality as incompatible with Nazi ideology when explaining Goebbels's decision to ban the film for German audiences.[119] Film scholar Karsten Witte juxtaposes Helmut Käutner with prototypical Nazi filmmaker Veit Harlan, arguing that *Große Freiheit Nr. 7*'s aesthetic reflected the impending defeat of the Reich. Witte suggests that Käutner realistically illustrates the disintegration of social relations, whereas Harlan mystifies vanquishment as a death wish.[120] While Witte confines the presumed nonconformity of the film to the realm of the aesthetic, critic Michael Töteberg, who admits that *Große Freiheit Nr. 7* was a "prestigious project," argues that the film highlighted the disintegration of morality and the destruction of bourgeois society.[121] But *Große Freiheit* was far from an example of subversive defeatism.[122] Instead, Käutner's colorful melodrama survives as the most convincing National Socialist tribute to the city of Hamburg and possibly remains the most successful cinematic tribute to the city in popular imagination.

Even though the film was released after the end of the war, I read *Große Freiheit Nr. 7* as both a fulfillment of the Nazi promise of a Hamburg film and a celebration of Hanseatic *Eigenart*. A compelling testament to Nazi cultural grandeur no longer concerned with performing its conversion to National Socialism, *Große Freiheit* nurtured a nostalgia for the promised but unattainable realities in Hamburg. It continues to anchor the memory of Nazi "good times" by the grace of its belated release.[123] Reviewing the complicated production history of *Große Freiheit* and contextualizing Goebbels's decision to ban the film for German audiences in March 1945, I understand Käutner's "declaration of love" in the context of other popular wartime productions. It was this tale that was able to bring local sensitivity and national ambitions together in a glamorous testament to both the city of Hamburg and National Socialist cinema.[124]

After Goebbels approved the screenplay, Werner Krien, who had photographed *Ein Mädchen geht an Land,* started shooting *Große Freiheit Nr. 7* in

March 1943 on the expensive stage sets of Ufa studios in Neubabelsberg and Tempelhof. After the destruction of the Berlin studios in the summer of 1943, production continued at the Barrandv studio in Prague.[125] Käutner returned to Hamburg to film the harbor and various scenes in a Blankeneser coffeehouse in September 1943, mere weeks after massive air strikes had flattened the city. In August 1944, the film was completed and subsequently approved by Goebbels for domestic and international release.[126] It should be noted that by 1944, the international venues for Nazi film were limited to German-occupied territories, areas under Axis control, and the few neutral European countries such as Switzerland and Sweden.[127] It was the immense shortage of raw materials rather than the oft-cited disapproval of Great Admiral Karl Dönitz that further protracted the release of *Große Freiheit*.[128] Supposedly Dönitz took offense at the antiheroic depiction of sailors in the film. The only verifiable objection came from Gauleiter Karl Kaufmann, but the nature of his displeasure is unknown.[129] As a personal patron of dockworkers, Kaufmann may have supported Gisa's choice of the dockhand and rejected the romantic tragedy of Hannes' rejection.[130] It is less probable that Kaufmann complained that the film was too ideologically unorthodox, as Töteberg implies.[131] Hamburg's citizens and administration alike wanted to see the film. Film Intendant Hans Hinkel explained that the film "has to premiere in Hamburg. If a prestigious theater isn't available as a result of the terror bombing, it will have to start in five or ten emergency theaters [*Nottheater*], so that the Hamburg population, which has been hit so hard by enemy terror, will be the first to see its film."[132]

Kaufmann's objections likely concerned the conditions in Hamburg in the aftermath of the bombing raids. He worried that the support of the war-weary population could be further undermined by images of neighborhoods and pleasures that had fallen victim to British bombs. Moreover, since the beginning of the war the administration had opposed what it considered unsuitable entertainments. Kaufmann, faced with complaints from within his own ranks about lechery in the Ufa film *Münchhausen* as I illustrate in the following chapter, likely considered *Große Freiheit* untimely.[133] Due to Kaufmann's intervention, Goebbels ordered additional cuts in the domestic version but nevertheless remained committed to the film.[134] Irrespective of the fact that Goebbels found the script for Veit Harlan's *Opfergang* "slightly exaggerated," it had been shot in color and was ready to go.[135] Thus, *Opfergang*, rather than *Große Freiheit*, premiered in Hamburg on December 8, 1944.

Goebbels remained committed to Käutner, whom he described as "the lead avant-gardist among our German film directors" after he previewed

Unter den Brücken, another Käutner film that did not reach German audiences until after the war.[136] While he derided Werner Hochbaum as a traitor, Goebbels's diary references to Käutner are consistently positive.[137] *Große Freiheit Nr. 7* premiered in Prague in December 1944, and copies of the edited version were supposedly ready for distribution in January 1945. Yet on March 19, the Film Office (*Film Intendanz*) reported that Goebbels had decided to shelve the film. Because of this decision, the film acquired a reputation for political resistance, despite the fact that scholars such as Peter Hagemann and Michael Töteberg have stressed that *Große Freiheit Nr. 7* was a pet project of the propaganda minister.

In addition to Goebbels's decision to shelve *Große Freiheit,* there were two more reasons for the film's political reputation. Although Hans Albers continued to be one of National Socialism's greatest stars (his Jewish life-partner emigrated to Great Britain without him), he was no fan of the regime and didn't hide his sentiments. The second reason lies in the film's aesthetics and Käutner's cinematography, which miraculously recreate the familiar feel of Hamburg's harbor district so late in the war. Closeups of ships and dockhands with deck cranes in the background cleverly substitute for sweeping takes of the ravaged harbor. The director skillfully manipulates color and lighting to capture a sense of wistfulness and *Fernweh* within the proletarian panoramas of chimneys and docks. Dimly lit, shallow-focus shots blur backgrounds to obscure the harbor's massive destruction. Shots of waves and water reflecting the golden light of the evening sun, coupled with cross-fades of street signs and carefree amusements, recreate the iconic flair of St. Pauli. This cinematography of short takes, aggressive closeups, and oddly composed panoramas creates a makeshift collage of all things "Hamburg."

It is hardly surprising that the film is famous given the conditions under which it was produced. The director and cinematographer resurrected the port city out of the rubble in an extraordinary manner.[138] To this day the film resonates as a reflection of the indestructible Hanseatic spirit, spawning assertions that the film was an affront to the National Socialist ideals of femininity and sexual modesty.[139] Such interpretations reflect surprise about the direct treatment of sexual subject matter under the auspices of Goebbels's ministry. But as Dagmar Herzog has convincingly revealed, National Socialism's hostility toward pleasure and sexuality is a widespread misapprehension.[140] Far from culturally subversive, *Große Freiheit* was but one of many wartime color film productions that exemplified the inflated sense of political purpose and cultural hubris found in National Socialist culture. Films such

Figure 6. Still of Landungsbrücken, from *Große Freiheit Nr. 7*, 1944.

as *Münchhausen, Es war eine rauschende Ballnacht, Opfergang, Frauen sind doch bessere Diplomaten*, and *Die Große Liebe* placed the Third Reich's most stunning female stars in the spotlight and emphasized their sexual allure.[141]

Only through the mobilization of gender conflicts was *Große Freiheit* able to provide such compelling and lasting testimony to the city of Hamburg. Töteberg is right to assert that Ufa propagated the Nazi ideology of family,[142] but the studio did so in more variable terms than plastering celluloid strips with "faithful husbands" who reigned supreme while "the seducer was always a scoundrel."[143] There are countless examples of films in which the husband is neither faithful nor admirable. In the immensely popular 1938 Rühmann film *Der Mustergatte* (produced by Imagoton, not Ufa), a faithful husband is depicted as comical, boring, and ultimately dissatisfying to his young wife.[144] As for scoundrel males, Nazi cinema offers vast numbers. Ferdinand Marian in *Romanze in Moll* (Käutner, 1942/43), Paul Klinger *in Die Goldene Stadt* (Harlan, 1941/42), Hans Söhnker in *Nanette* (Engel, 1939/40), and Karl Martel in *La Habanera* (Sierck, 1937) are not portrayed as despicable despite their intentions to seduce married women or virgin girls.[145] This trend pinnacles in Veit Harlan's color drama *Opfergang*, when the transgressions of Albrecht (Carl Raddatz) are validated after he falls ill and his long-suffering wife makes daily, sacrificial visits to his sick mistress (Kristina Söderbaum) to spare the other woman the pain of losing Albrecht's company.

Unlike *Die Große Liebe* (Hansen, 1941/42) and *Das Wunschkonzert* (Borsody, 1940), which "turned war into revue," Käutner's nostalgic exploration of Hanseatic masculinity, with its seafaring freedom and comfortable strictures of marriage, sidesteps the problem of war and reiterates instead the pertinent responsibility of German men and women to accept their place, take charge of their fates, and not surrender to their fears of inadequacy.[146] Hannes, advancing in years and aware that he is wasting his talent and time singing in a shady establishment owned by his lover, wakes from his slumber because of unreciprocated love. In the end he remains true to himself in spite of his broken heart, finding purpose and wholeness. He was never at home on land, and was less so in Anita's *Bums* (cathouse). He dreamed of attending tillerman school, and we see him at last smiling at the helm of a sailboat. Willem too abandons his brazen ways (along with his bachelorhood) rescues Gisa from a life of urban vice, restoring the innocence lost when she relocated to the big city. At the same time, her innocence served as the catalyst for Hannes's embrace of the logic that runs through the film. Hannes' voice singing "*meine Braut is die See / und nur ihr kann ich treu sein* [My bride is the sea / only to her can I be faithful]" echoes in the closing frame.

Instead of belaboring feminine virtue, Käutner reclaims St. Pauli—and a color-shot version of it, too—as a repository for the romantic notions of a potent and unrestrained masculinity. In his representation of St. Pauli, Käutner reaffirms the community of men in the face of an inevitable erosion of feminine virtue. (As I illustrate in the following chapter, Hamburg's administration condemned this loss with draconian resolve.) Where Hochbaum contrasts stylized virtue with guileless criminality, *Große Freiheit* dissolves the conflict between respectability and vice as functions of male self-reliance and integrity. The female body serves as a canvas.

In both *Ein Mädchen geht an Land* and *Große Freiheit Nr. 7*, pleasure spells the ruin of a girl, but Käutner's film affirms that men remain unaffected by lasciviousness. The film does not invite the viewer to question the respectability of Willem, who coincidentally walks into the Hippodrom at precisely the moment when Gisa, for the first and only time, watches Hannes perform. When Willem, who came to settle his differences with Hannes, stumbles over Gisa, he immediately assumes she is a girl of the streets. All men make this

Figure 7. Still of Hannes and Anita, from *Große Freiheit Nr. 7*, 1944.

mistake, Hannes later tells Gisa, despite the striking differences in Gisa's composure and attire that set her apart from St. Pauli girls.[147]

The film resurrected the barrier that formerly separated Hamburg proper from its pleasure colony. The moral boundary, however, is permeable to men of true Hanseatic character. Sailors and workers remain untainted by the bustle of St. Pauli, maintaining their connections with respectability on the other side. Hamburg's working men—good-humored, decent, and sexually forward—can freely move across the city's divide, policing and reinforcing the boundary that is essential to the whole. Women, in contrast, are confined to one side. The social world defines them, as Anita's character illustrates and Hannes's assertions affirm. The amusement district of St. Pauli is no place for female virtue.

Emphasizing the bond between men, *Große Freiheit* validates the identity of a city that is neither whole nor broken. The film reclaims Hamburg's most iconic and embattled district in all of its originality (and depravity) as a colorful playground for the city's men. *Große Freiheit* depicts pleasure as part of an urban way of life that coexists with hard work, love, and respectability.

Figure 8. Still of Gisa, from *Große Freiheit Nr. 7*, 1944.

It promises that these virtues will be present in a better future. The film portrays men from different backgrounds as complex and vulnerable, without the parochialism that characterizes Hochbaum's film. *Große Freiheit* offers heroism and glamour and a different kind of realism than *Ein Mädchen geht an Land*. It celebrates Hamburg's uniqueness in ways recognizable to its citizens, effectively negotiating urban identity within the larger National Socialist frame. Serving as a bridge between war and a better future, *Große Freiheit Nr. 7* did exactly what it was supposed to do. The postfascist nature of this future was neither anticipated by the filmmaker nor necessary for the film's success.

For Hamburg's audiences, the prestigious melodrama of *Große Freiheit Nr. 7* was a corrective to the subdued depiction of Hamburg in *Ein Mädchen geht Land*. Käutner's choice of stars like Hans Albers and Ilse Werner added glamour to bleak times. Unlike *Ein Mädchen*'s obsession with translating the austerity of the German north to an urban streetscape, *Große Freiheit* celebrates the city itself. It employed the tenets of Nazi film art in fundamentally different ways than Hochbaum was able (or willing) to do. No longer suggesting that *bodenständig* represents the plain, the austere, and the unadorned,

Käutner rewrites down-to-earthness as down-to-folkness. Thus *Bodenstän-digkeit* becomes a category of popular accessibility rather than a particular visual style. In turn, Käutner uses *Wirklichkeitsnähe* as the emotive quality produced by the suggestive effects of film. Even though *Große Freiheit* does not attempt to represent objective reality, it presents the livelihood of St. Pauli so compellingly that its authenticity is *felt* rather than *seen*. Part of a cinema that unapologetically offered sensationalist and popular fare, *Große Freiheit Nr. 7* was a tribute to local *Eigenart* as well as an assertion of *Weltgeltung*.

Even though the film was never explicitly linked to the administration's attempt to provide Hamburg with a celluloid history, *Große Freiheit Nr. 7* fulfills that mission like no other film before or after it. Hamburg's identity straddling land and sea was inscribed in the geography of the city. St. Pauli functioned as an embodiment of Hamburg's transience. It came to epitomize the popular descriptor of Hamburg as Germany's "gateway to the world." Instead of monumental images of National Socialist achievement envisaged in the Greater-Hamburg film, instead of a stylization of an evanescent *Heimat* as was the case with *Ein Mädchen geht an Land*, Käutner's *Große Freiheit Nr. 7* masks the city's National Socialism in a tribute to its most controversial district. Even if *Große Freiheit Nr. 7* does not turn Hamburg into Paris and St. Pauli into Montmartre, it reinvents and translates in exclusively Hanseatic terms the analogy first invoked by the St. Pauli–Freiheit Consortium.[148]

CHAPTER 3

Off Screen: *Führerstadt* and
the Limits of Social Control

The scene opens with an aerial view of an old city, artfully blending old with new, visualizing conquest. Shot from above, the airplane casts a shadow over bridges, medieval buildings, and orderly columns of Nazis marching below. The camera renders both plane and cavalcade as harbingers of a new age, not of destruction but of renewal.[1] Although rarely described as a city film, Leni Riefenstahl's *Triumph of the Will* (1935) captures better than any document of its time the Nazi regime's architectural vision for reconfiguring both *Volk* and *Raum*. Its depiction of Nuremberg set the visual benchmark for representing National Socialism—the movement and the spaces it conquered—in the eyes of the regime and for generations of onlookers since.

In retrospect, *Triumph of the Will* makes evident just how important visual representation was to the regime. Moreover, it attests to the longevity of cinematically produced space. Film built Nazi cities and choreographed the movements of their citizens. Nuremberg, one of the five *Führerstädte,* is a case in point. The monumental buildings designed by Albert Speer and hammered out of the ground after the regime's ascent to power are now decrepit and overgrown with weeds. But their images live on. Riefenstahl built an entire world as a series of *Lichtbilder*.[2] Not surprisingly, that world was put on trial in the city that had rendered it visible.[3]

Nuremberg's transformation into a Nazi ideal may have been the exception for German cities, but this was not for the lack of grandiose ideas. Hitler's plans for remaking Hamburg started in earnest in 1939, following the steps taken by locals to boost their city's image. With a focus on "trouble spots," local efforts at change consisted mainly of cosmetics and posturing. The same held true for city planning in the Reich at large. The construction of affordable housing was paramount for many German cities, but the regime accomplished remarkably little in this respect.[4] Instead, planning and construction focused on industrial projects and pomp. Urban and regional planners chased ideas, drew up blueprints, and crafted models for reinvigorated German cities up until the end of the war. But implementation lagged far behind. Plans matured unevenly, often in a reactionary fashion driven by Hitler's whims and the changing realities on the ground.

The parting words of the director of the Viennese academy of fine arts to the young Hitler—that his talents lay more in architecture than in painting—must have made an impression as lasting as the academy's rejection.[5] After being appointed chancellor in January 1933, Hitler lingered into the wee hours in a little room next to the reception hall in the Reich Chancellery, as engaged with the architectural redesign of the Reich as with the struggle of the white man against "the non-aryans, the colored, the Mongols." He wanted to start his grand overhaul with the Chancellery itself, "a mere *Zigarrenkiste*" (cigar box) unbefitting a man who had ascended from the Viennese gutters.[6]

Emboldened by Hitler's rhetoric about the fundamental connection between race and space, urban planners dropped their mission of maintenance and modernization to embrace "a remodeling of the entire living space of the German people."[7] War unleashed their imaginations. Eastward expansion inspired the modernization of old cities and towns. Carpet-bombed urban areas were blank slates for fanatical visions of postwar reconstruction. At the center of these visions stood the five *Führerstädte*—Berlin, Hamburg, Nuremberg, Munich, and Linz.[8] However, unlike the regime's *Rassenpolitik,* architecture and *Städtebau* remained primarily proclamatory. After an initial cut into working-class districts and slums in the name of urban renewal, the regime did precious little to alter German cities, exhausting itself instead with endless planning for a postwar future. With materials scarce, waging war took precedence over refashioning cities. Abstract ideas about order, health, and discipline shaped the regime's urban vision, molding social rather than physical space.

War was not received with enthusiasm in Hamburg or elsewhere in Germany, yet it came as no surprise.[9] Rationing had returned in 1935, as had the draft. Foreign policy maneuvers left little doubt about the Third Reich's expansionist aspirations. By the summer of 1939, Austria and the Sudetenland had been incorporated, the Czech part of Czechoslovakia turned into a protectorate, and the rump state of Slovakia reduced to a Nazi satellite. Industry churned out armaments, children practiced air raid drills, and labor service prepared young men and women for the sacrifices to come.[10] The language of struggle characterized the Nazi movement from its inception, and the regime began planning for war in earnest in 1936. By September 1939, all nonessential construction had been halted, with labor and building materials reallocated to strategic industries. But existing environments did not remain static. With the cities of the future struck on the drawing boards, destruction became the dominant mode of urban transformation.

This chapter examines the tensions between imagining a new urbanism and policing an actual city. Initially, mass unemployment, poverty, prostitution, crime, and working-class dissent inspired interventions from slum clearance to mass incarceration—housecleaning projects that dominated urban visions in the latter 1930s. However, the designs for postwar grandeur drafted by architects and planners failed to sync the idea of cities as "show castles" of state power with the urban realities of citizens. The more that lived experience and representation diverged, the more apparent the lack of social control became to the architects of change, shifting the focus of local administrators toward enforcing order in a war-ravaged city.

By raiding alley quarters, reprimanding pleasure-seeking mothers, arresting loitering adolescents, and ultimately deporting the Jewish population, Hamburg's administration increasingly managed city life and thus oversaw the production of a particular kind of social space—one that bore the clear imprint of Nazi race thinking. Race thinking also lay at the core of the intellectual engagement with the city, whether in Andreas Walther's analysis of the "data" produced by the first slum clearance project, the designs coming out of the office of Hamburg architect Konstanty Gutschow, or the Reich's planning consortia for the "total city."

Although the parameters according to which the city was imagined remained constant, the tools did not, and the role that film played in Hamburg shifted along with the changing realities on the ground. The destruction of physical space and the experiences of wartime disruption drove more people to the respite of the movie theaters, drawing the suspicious gaze of the city's custodians. Film "switched sides" during the war, ceasing to function as an ally of the urban imaginary of local bureaucrats. Instead, the dark comfort of the movie theater became a culprit for corroding morality and tempting young people to shirk their duties. As the film industry churned out one mega production after another, the cultural value of Goebbels's favorite industry grew suspect in the eyes of Hamburg's youth wardens, as if the palaces of distraction diverted citizens not just from the pain of war but also from the labor and devotion that a nation at war required.

Housecleaning

For urban planners throughout Germany, the balance between honoring the historic character of the city and maintaining social control was essential. In 1934, authorities in Frankfurt called for the extensive rehabilitation of the old parts of its inner city. Almost everywhere, reconstruction was limited to the labyrinthine inner alleyways where "asocial elements and prostitution had secretly spawned for decades."[11] In large part, the parameters of what constituted healthy living conditions were inferred locally rather than communicated by national directive.

By 1937 most universities had organized consortia to address urban and rural planning. These groups considered questions such as rural exodus, utilization of resources, urban concentration, traffic regulation, and biological hazards of industrialization.[12] Urban planners in Cologne observed that "the complicated state of affairs [Verfilzung] brought about by traffic and construction advance[d] progressively" since the beginning of the nineteenth century, leaving the inner cities unhealthy and overcrowded.[13] Similarly, the municipal building authorities in Kassel recommended that all back buildings, alleyways, and makeshift slum dwellings be torn down to preserve the face of the beautiful old part of town, open the city to light, and improve living conditions.[14] Since the turn of the century, debates among urban and social planners focused on the presumed connection between urban Verfilzung and the congenial mix of urban amusements, crime, and prostitution.[15]

After 1933, planners justified the destruction of inner cities with arguments about social hygiene, bourgeois morality, and residential housing reform.[16] With its racial underpinnings, Nazi ideology broadened the scope to focus on population control.[17] Hamburg was a case in point. In 1934, the administration decided to raze the last of the alley quarters (Gängeviertel) before the Reich passed legislation to that effect. The threat of working-class opposition was addressed under the mantle of racial hygiene, social homogeneity, and Volksgesundheit (national health). The displacement caused by the demolition of the densely populated residential quarters sandwiched between Wexstrasse and Kaiser-Wilhelm-Strasse was outwardly defended as a remedial response to overcrowding and unhealthy living. In reality, the obliteration of this "site of infection" delivered a decisive blow to Hamburg's well-organized working classes. The experiment thus functioned as an initial test case for implementing ideological cleansing and biological determinism.[18]

In 1936, the sociologist Andreas Walther published a treatise titled
New Ways to Decontaminate the City, which analyzed effects of displacement after the destruction of the *Gängeviertel*. Walther assumed and subsequently "proved" a direct biological connection between communism and
asocial criminality. Walther's analysis not only demonstrates the pervasiveness of racial explanations to social problems, it also indicates what could
and could not be said. Arguments based on materialist considerations and
invoking questions of class, social status, and political affiliations had become
impossible. The specter of communist thinking could have easily threatened
Hamburg's reputation in the eyes of Berlin. Accordingly, Walther shifted the
explanatory approach to social ills in ways consistent with the National Socialist worldview.[19] He explained people's behavior and habits from a racial rather
than a structural vantage point, arguing against the folly that "people could
be changed by transplanting them into a different environment."[20] Walther
acknowledged the importance of the environment but emphasized the limits
of education and better living conditions in transforming the *Wesen* [essence]
of people. Instead, he cast the problem in biological terms and argued that "in
the malignant regions [*gemeinschädigende Regionen*] of the big cities, hopeless cases accumulate and proliferate like a tumor on the national body."[21]

In this multiyear study, Walther and his colleagues, known as *Notarbeit 51
der Akamdemiker Hilfe*, sought to identify regions of the city for decontamina-
tion by cataloguing and mapping "asocial elements." Based on their interpretations of criminal and welfare statistics, they made detailed recommendations
regarding the treatment of dislocated individuals and families. Rather than
justifying the razing of Hamburg's *Gängeviertel*, they argued against dispers-
ing the "agents of contagion." The destruction of the *Gängeviertel* may have
been well-intentioned, but it exacerbated the problem. The inhabitants of the
Gängeviertel had been left to their own devices and resettled in "terrible areas
that were similar to those they left behind." (Systematic resettlement of the
dispersed population had never been envisioned.) Accordingly, the displaced
elements "contributed to the infection of healthy districts, so that nests of asocial people can be found in even architecturally superior new apartment buildings; yes even on the rural fringes of the city."[22] Walther's team thus refuted
Weimar-era claims that changes in milieu would foster social integration and
transform the trouble spots of big cities.[23]

Walther was informed by the longitudinal studies conducted by E. J. Lidbetter, who argued that debased individuals generally marry within their own
ranks, and hence "only several thousand clans in each generation account for

the mass of those who burden and pollute the general community."[24] Walther concluded that the concentration of "defective" individuals was a natural development and the only socially responsible solution would be to "eradicate the genotype of hopelessly defective individuals." His team thus argued for concentration, not dispersal, explaining that "National Socialism would act rather ineffectively, if it were to disperse these nests of malignant, morally inferior and biologically defective individuals."[25] It was precisely the predisposition of inferior individuals to flock together that facilitated social control, Walther argued.[26]

In 1936, Walther outlined the logic the regime implemented during the war, not just in Hamburg but also in occupied Poland. His work prefigured and scientifically justified the mass incarceration, ghettoization, expulsion, and extermination of undesirable populations under Nazi rule. Walther further provided support for the regime's ambivalence about cities by insisting that over the previous decades the influx from rural areas consisted primarily of "defective" individuals, increasing the danger of unrest, social disruption, and biological deterioration.[27] The pervasive rhetoric around blood and soil, the celebration of manual labor, and the idealization of the German peasant appear to support the idea that Nazi ideology espoused hostility toward cities. The more mystical among Nazi ideologues certainly idealized village life and rural simplicity. However, most did not envision a return to premodern roots, recognizing the importance of cities for industrial production and cultural refinement.[28] The evocative idyll of the "countryside" functioned more as a metaphor for the transposable notion of *Heimat* than as an ideological alternative to the city. Attempts to discipline urban space, enforce public order, curtail the movement of people, and increase surveillance had little to do with the mythical affirmation of village life or fantasies of rural communities. They had everything to do with supposedly immutable biological characteristics of certain people that gave them a talent for escaping the state's watchful eye.[29]

Cities presented Nazism with a "wicked problem."[30] The concentration of labor in Germany's urban centers rendered cities both promising and threatening. Workers were essential to Germany's economic revival, but the politicized working classes also presented a threat to Nazism, at least initially.[31] Urban dangers ranging from squalor and overcrowding to vice, prostitution, and political radicalism had occupied social reformers since before the turn of the century. They remained a constant reminder of the inconsistencies that characterized National Socialism more generally. Those inconsistencies could be "resolved" only through representation. Accordingly, urban design picked up where planners like Baron Haussmann, Ebenezer Howard, and Le Corbusier had left off, capturing on camera and affirming in print an artful marriage of architecture and propaganda.

Blueprints

Architectural designs for prestige projects and plans for urban reconstruction were all about optics—a reciprocal gaze between state and subject that would reproduce state power.[32] Some of the grandiose building projects were launched soon after the regime consolidated. In 1933, Albert Speer started construction on the Zeppelinfeld at the Party Rally Compounds in Nuremberg, aspirational structures recognized worldwide by way of Leni Riefenstahl's *Triumph of the Will* (1935). Other prestige projects followed suit. The Berlin Olympia Stadium was erected in 1934. The Air Ministry headquarters opened in Berlin in 1935. Between 1936 and 1939 the regime founded the industrial centers of Herman-Göring Werke in Salzgitter and the City of the Strength Through Joy Car (*Stadt des KdF-Wagens*), now known as Wolfsburg.[33]

Planning for the redesign of German cities commenced in earnest in 1937. Hitler anointed Speer as the inspector general for the redesign of the Reich's capital city.[34] Although Berlin commanded special attention, the transformation of other cities into display cases of state power was equally important. Hitler, who had designated Hamburg (along with Bremen) as the maritime capital of Germany, had visited Hamburg numerous times. Keeping in line with the slogan that cast Hamburg as Germany's "gateway to the world," he envisioned reorienting the city center toward the Elbe and the harbor, away from the *Rathaus* and the *Börse* (stock exchange) on the Alster, the bedrock of Hamburg's liberal traditions. Accordingly, plans for Hamburg showcased the regime's power, aspiring to the worldliness and cosmopolitanism of cities like New York and London. Seeing in Hamburg "something American," Hitler cautioned against imitating the architecture of Berlin and Munich.[35] He imagined skyscrapers and bridges comparable to the New York City skyline and San Francisco's Golden Gate Bridge.[36] Hamburg held out the promise of a glamorous future. An entertainment mecca with numerous parks and inner-city waterways, it fit perfectly into the Nazi conception of mass leisure and man-made nature—an inspiring site for urban planners.[37]

Between 1933 and 1939 Hamburg had little reason to celebrate itself. International trade declined and its national relevance dwindled as its economy

Figure 9. *Führerstadt* Hamburg, model Konstanty Gutschow, ca. 1942. Staatsarchiv Hamburg.

failed to respond to Nazi policies of self-sufficiency. But these realities would be negated by the grandiose plans for reconstruction. In discussions with Mayor Krogmann, Hitler identified three important elements. First was a *Gauhochhaus* (skyscraper) with an imposing open plaza for mass assemblies and marches. Second was the riverfront itself. Third was a massive bridge across the Elbe that would rival the Golden Gate Bridge. While the bridge designs were relegated to the jurisdiction of Fritz Todt, who oversaw the Reich's Ministry of Transportation, Konstanty Gutschow won the national competition for the *Neugestaltung* (redesign) of Hamburg itself.[38]

Gutschow understood architecture as a national responsibility, a duty to the *Volksgemeinschaft*. He further understood that architecture and urban design were about more than erecting buildings and rearranging traffic. The disciplines forged a new order, shaping community policy by setting its parameters in steel, concrete, and granite.[39] The fact that Gutschow's interests stretched from single-family homes, swimming pools, and city quarters to traffic flows, bridges, and state buildings illustrates how he understood what Henri Lefebvre would later theorize as the production of social space.[40] Gutschow's models for the towering *Gauhochhaus* and the redesign of the riverbank appealed to Hitler because of their sleek and efficient designs. But the Führer was not without criticism. The roof of the skyscraper looked to him as if it had been flattened with a hammer, something the failed artist turned statesman and wannabe architect predicted would be easy enough to rectify.[41]

By September 1939, Albert Speer, the Reich's general building inspector at the time, told Governor Kaufmann to put the preparation for reconstruction on hold until the cessation of wartime hostilities. Planning continued nonetheless because the Führer wanted to see more drafts and sketches.[42] In any case, Hitler and Kaufmann agreed that land clearance would have to be the first step. The war would take care of that.

While architects deferred massive representational construction in the interest of defense, urban planning continued "especially for the redesign of German cities."[43] Instead of slowing down the ambitions of planners, the war seemed to accelerate them. Plans for the *Führerstadt* of Hamburg were taken up again with renewed verve as the war progressed.[44] In August 1940, Kaufmann instructed Gutschow to devise a general building plan for Hamburg, explaining that Hamburg faced "unanticipated opportunities for development."[45] Gutschow was thus in charge of redesigning the social, economic, and aesthetic organization of much of Hamburg. Under the aegis of social hygiene and population control, Gutschow imagined an ideal cityscape that would build houses, strengthen the appearance of "downtown," and sanitize the inner-city districts.[46]

Gutschow was not the sole champion of a new urban order. War had been on the minds of the Reich's planners from the get-go. In 1934, plans for housing developments on the outskirts of cities and towns cited protection from aerial bombardment as an advantage along the lines of ventilation, light, and green spaces.[47] In June 1939, architect Martin Mächler warned that "the aggregated and sandwiched populations in German cities are nearly defenseless in wartime and can be protected from obliteration only by extraordinary expenditures."[48] Mächler and others advocated for total planning, and after the aerial bombardments commenced, city planners stressed the *Totalitätsgedanke* (totalizing conception) in urban design.[49]

Because the family constituted the smallest unit of the Nazi *Volksgemeinschaft*, it functioned as the nodal point for urban designers. As the smallest community, the family should be able to integrate into *Hausgemeinschaften* (house communities), which would aggregate into *Strassengemeinschaften* (street communities). The equivalent of party political blocks, the *Strassengemeinschaften* would combine to form subcenters comparable to the party structure of *Zelle* (cell). Individual subcenters would be connected by a ring street that functioned as a supply artery to shops and services. A collection of subcenters would make up a town center that held schools, Hitler Youth homes, kindergartens, medical services, and so forth. Between four and eight town centers would make up the city center, which would house the district party office, administrative buildings (city hall, post office, fire station, banks), and cultural institutions such as libraries, theaters, and, of course, movie palaces. Moreover, the city center, the equivalent to the party-political structure of *Kreis*, was to have a plaza with arterial roads collecting traffic from the subcenters. Plazas would feature a short and narrow shopping street that allowed pedestrian crowds to mix comfortably. All subcenters, town centers, and city centers were to be surrounded by grass borders that channeled pedestrian traffic and provided space for recreation.

As a design premise, the total city reflected the organization of both party and *Volksgemeinschaft,* providing inhabitants ready access to necessities under the aegis of total legibility.[50] The vulnerability of cities to air attacks had led planners like Martin Mächler and Gottfried Feder to advocate star-shaped or concentric designs of self-sufficient minicities interrupted by open spaces and connected by multiple traffic arteries, infrastructural redundancies that would make these enclaves more resilient during war.[51] Such designs were extensions of the working-class settlements conceived according to Garden City models.[52] These plans both prefigured and outlived the flattening of German cities and the thousands of *Bombenflüchtlinge* (bombing refugees) who fled Berlin, Hamburg, Nuremberg, Dresden, and Cologne for the countryside. Self-evidently, perhaps, the grandiose plans for total cities were never implemented, remaining instead a grotesque of Nazi hubris.

Policing Urban Space

While architects and planners quibbled over designs, municipal welfare administrations managed the wartime realities. Rationing, curfews, and oppressive regulation further complicated the questions of child and youth welfare, education, *Kriegsfürsorge* (war pensions), and poverty relief. After September 1, 1939, the memories of world war and revolution weighed heavily on the minds of local administrators, and the conditions that guaranteed governability were inextricably connected to the pressing national questions of victory and defeat. Since the 1920s, the Nazis had made a point of reminding their supporters and foes alike that the First World War had not been lost on the battlefield.[53] They cited the conspiratorial *Dolchstoß* ("stab in the back"), according to which Jews, communists, socialists, "women of lesser means," and more generally the German home front undermined national unity and sabotaged the Reich's war effort.[54] Exploiting this legend, they turned the focus back onto the enemies within the state, allowing them to scrutinize the actions of "aryan" women, the only potentially "subversive" group not specifically targeted by the regime's population policies.[55]

In years prior the Reich had moved decisively against the racial and political enemies within German borders, preemptively attacking potential saboteurs and building support for a repressive regime by enlisting citizens in everyday brutalities.[56] In Hamburg, administrators anticipated that discontent, unruliness, and *Zersetzung* (erosion) would primarily be gendered and generational. The moral and cultural decay that paralleled the weakening of the *Frontgeist* in the last war served as a primary frame of reference.[57] Based on the country's experiences from 1917 and 1918, administrators were determined to confront the early signs of disobedience and disorder before these threatened political stability in Hamburg and undermined the war effort.

Even before bombs rearranged the physical environment, war transformed the social parameters of urban life. Both the Reich and Hamburg's administration, unable to shape a new order in concrete and steel, marshalled images and narratives to shape realities while mobilizing a state apparatus to enforce discipline. Cinema came to the forefront of the city's wartime effort to control the flow of information and people. The weekly newsreel, nearly doubling in length in response to the war, drew large crowds, providing one of few tangible connections between *Heimat* and front.[58] Across the Reich, movie theaters added additional screenings (*Sonderveranstaltungen*) to satisfy demand for news and short documentaries.[59] Hamburg theater operators responded to the community's call for a smooth and consistent flow of information, with many theaters instituting an afternoon program so that patrons could get home before dark.[60] The wartime newsreel, even more than the Hitler youth film screenings (*Jugendfilmstunden*) and the national People's Film Day (*Filmvolkstag*), accomplished the Nazis' goals of drawing new audiences into movie theaters.[61] Cinema attendance rose continuously and allowed an ever-growing number of people to participate in the "great events of the German existential struggle [*Lebenskampf*]."[62]

Hamburg's weary social welfare workers cast this "struggle" in highly particular terms. Observing the behavior of citizens in the early months of the war, they worried about the negative effects of smut and trash in film in particular, revisiting arguments that morality leagues and bourgeois reformers had been making since the late nineteenth century.[63] The cinema that had thus far been an emblem of National Socialist culture, Hamburg cosmopolitanism, and technological modernity now energized the imaginations of disciplinarians. The local state fixed its gaze on women and children stripped of paternal authority, explaining urban ills such as promiscuity, pleasure seeking, child neglect, vagrancy, petty crime, and indecencies as products of war. What is more, the pursuits of pleasure that would have hitherto appeared as normal and healthy now raised eyebrows. Uwe Storjohann remembers agonizing over whether to ask a girl "who already wears silk stockings, high heels, a bra with a lot underneath" to go for ice cream or to the movies. Heartbroken when someone else asked her to dance, he was scared to press his luck for fear that she might turn him down. After all, he was not even old enough to wear long pants.[64] Young people hadn't begun to act differently, but war had changed the frame within which local welfare workers and administrators evaluated the status quo. Fourteen-year-old Uwe would have been cast as a victim of neglect, the girl of his affections regarded as a vector for venereal disease.

There had been no reason to explain increases of *Verwahrlosung* (debilitation), *Kinosucht* (addiction to cimena), and *Vergnügungssucht* (pleasure seeking) in the years following the seizure of power—such behaviors were by definition impossible in a successfully nazified city.[65] But memories of the previous war rendered the collapse of civilian authority a looming possibility in the eyes of local administrators. Hitler, as his most eminent biographer documented, reacted with outrage to reports about the "bad mood" of the population. Addressing members of the Reichstag on the day that the German army invaded Poland, Hitler ranted, "Don't anyone tell me that in his Gau or his district, or his constituency [*Gruppe*], or his cell the mood could at some point be bad. *You* are responsible for the mood."[66] Accordingly, it was up to local administrators, the field staff of the *Führsorge* in particular, to monitor the popular mood, provide relief, and enforce discipline.

The NSV (*Nationalsozialistische Volkswohlfahrt*) was the first of Hamburg's institutions to address war-related dangers to youth. In October 1939, the NSV suggested setting a curfew for adolescents, but Police Chief Hans Julius Kehrl rejected the proposition as both unnecessary and unfeasible.[67] The office for social welfare, however, increased its surveillance efforts at the request of Senator Oscar Martini. The reports of *Führsorgerinnen* and

Oberführsorgerinnen subsequently became essential tools for monitoring public morale and conduct.[68] During the fall of 1939 these reports indicated the administration's discontent with young women who quit their jobs after marrying active soldiers and becoming eligible for state support.[69]

After the invasion of Poland, stories of juvenile transgressions increased, with 160 police reports of adolescents loitering in Hamburg's red-light district. The frequent acts of public dancing were also lamented. To protect female minors from moral dissolution, the Hamburg police intensified their surveillance and relied more and more on Hitler Youth patrols for information.[70] This is how the police stumbled on Hamburg's most famous agitators of civil disobedience, the Swing Kids, who gathered to listen to English-language swing and jazz records.[71] In early March 1940, the Nazi regional political director Karl Kaufmann set out to investigate and counteract the "false or at least greatly exaggerated rampant allegation" of the rapid increase of dangers to young people in Hamburg as a result of the war. Gauleiter Kaufmann empowered Senator Martini to convene district leaders, the chief of police, local experts on juvenile delinquency, and social welfare workers to discuss the rumors of "already advanced threats to our youth [*Verwahrlosung*] due to the war."[72]

To coordinate the agencies involved in juvenile oversight, Senator Martini established the Consortium for the Protection of Youth in Wartime under the direction of Professor Rudolf Sieverts. This occurred just days after the police had broken up a large gathering of Swing Kids in the Curio Haus.[73] A few days later, the Reichsführer SS and chief of police Heinrich Himmler decreed the Police Ordinance for the Protection of Youth in Wartime, which was posted to all police departments across the Reich.[74] Until superseded by the Protection of Young Persons Act of 1943, the Police Ordinance provided the legal basis for curbing juvenile mobility and crime, allowing authorities to take action against "roaming adolescents" and "gathering of hooligans [*Halbstarke*] for the purpose of debating, flirting, and other kinds of horseplay."[75] Local administrators and welfare workers quickly realized that the Police Ordinance was unenforceable without tools such as short-term incarceration or weekend arrest. By September the necessary measures had been put in place. Reinhard Heydrich, chief of the Reich's Security Office (SD), extended the disciplinary authority of the Hitler Youth and allowed incarceration for infractions against mandatory service in the organization. The municipal police would enforce these rules on instruction of a special agent (*Sonderbeauftragten*) of the Reich's youth leadership.

Members of Hamburg's Consortium for the Protection of Youth were convinced that the decline of moral values and public obedience resulted not merely from wartime realities but from the increasing sexualization of life due to modern entertainment media.[76] They devoted special attention to the "deplorable" conditions in literature, theater, and film, organizing a workshop for the identification, collection, and abatement of *Schmutz und Schund* (smut and trash).[77] The workshop focused on the effects of erotic references in film and pulp fiction. Sieverts argued that it was hardly a coincidence that criminal and morally compromised adolescents "read pulp fiction and viewed films of appalling quality on a large scale." He further claimed that the cinema clearly lacked any positive influence on the spiritual proclivities (*Geisteshaltung*) of young people.[78] Insisting that the highly sexualized materials in film and pulp fiction had a negative effect, from both a biological and a moral perspective, he explained that "the life of youth in the big cities, especially during adolescence [*Reifezeit*], is often meaningless." Young people were predisposed, he suggested, to seek out leisure activities that had the most harmful moral and biological effects. As a result, "urban youth are subject to a general process of acceleration." Boys and girls were not only physically taller but they also entered puberty "on average two years earlier than before the World War."[79]

Figure 10. Children's show, Schauburg St. Georg, 1937. Staatsarchiv Hamburg.

Pediatricians were concerned that such developments were unhealthy and surmised that they resulted from "the boundlessness of stimuli that to an ever-increasing extent assails our youth." Street traffic, cinema, and print media were thought to be the most powerful sources of overstimulation.

Claiming that the annulment of the law against *Schmutz und Schund* in 1934 had hidden from public view the problem of filth and trash in literature and film, the workshop set out to examine insidious publications. Slamming some twenty magazines onto the table, Sieverts exhorted workshop participants to get busy in the hope that Governor Karl Kaufmann would, in his office as the Reich's defense commissioner, utilize "the instruments of power of the New State" to ban and confiscate objectionable material in Hamburg, setting an example for the Reich.[80] The "cinema problem" proved to be harder to solve.[81] Accordingly, the Consortium demanded that cinema owners be held accountable if adolescents were admitted to films that had not been approved as suitable for youth. This deflected the responsibility for adolescent transgressions to the purveyors of unsuitable fare—local cinema operators and national production companies who remained utterly unresponsive to the emergency.

Workshop participants noted that the cinema merited greater attention than theater or vaudeville revues because "adolescents are much more affected by film than stage plays" and attended movie screenings in much larger numbers.[82] They argued that the artistic value of film would be lost on the immature mind, a conclusion based solely on the "findings" of Alois Funke.[83] In 1933 Funke had interviewed boys and girls about their cinematic habits, finding that film moved adolescents in a way that compromised their sense of reality, that drew them into the action of the film, and that excited and aroused them unnaturally.[84] The Consortium failed to take into account that Funke's 1933 research was meant to support Nazi claims that Weimar culture and film were Judeo-Bolshevik plots to exploit the sexual sensibilities of immature individuals.

By concluding that almost all films in 1940 were "riddled with erotic scenes," the Consortium directly contradicted the national consensus among power brokers in the Reich that film was an ideological tool and called into question the benefit of Nazi institutions like the Hitler Youth's weekly film screenings. It insisted that "films which entail no love-scenes whatsoever, do not exist," which put the healthy sexual development of adolescents in *continuous* danger of being corrupted.[85] The Consortium explicitly castigated the Hamburg press for uncritically applauding every film, even those of the lowest quality. Its members leveled overt criticism at the party and the state for allowing the film industry to produce films of such cheap and corrosive eroticism.[86] The effects, Dr. Mulzer explained, were most noticeable in young women. Dr. Mulzer and prosecutor Otto Blunk explained that even films distinguished as "artistically valuable" by the Reich's censorship office had been found to "slowly prepare female adolescents for fornication."[87]

The Consortium's connection between moving images and illicit sex had a long history. Weimar-era social reformers stressed that material conditions drove women into prostitution. Because the 1933 proclamation of the classless society contradicted this logic, social workers adjusted their framework to fit the biopolitical imperatives of the new regime, explaining pervasive prostitution as a result of an inherited "condition" that physicians described as moral turpitude (*moralischer Schwachsinn*). Doctors and social workers placed under custodianship of the state "feebleminded" women whose hereditary conditions caused them to wander the streets seeking pleasure whatever the costs. When "necessary," the women who did not adopt a decent life faced sterilization, incarceration, or both.[88]

War again shifted the frame, making it difficult to explain undesirable behavior solely as a function of female biology. The Hamburg administrators, politicians, and social workers who were deeply concerned about the loosening of sexual mores saw the thousands of soldiers and military personnel stationed in barracks on the outskirts of the city as a threat to moral order. Young soldiers became the main culprits for the dramatic deterioration in propriety among Hamburg's female population. However, the police ordinance explicitly excluded soldiers from its strictures. As criticisms grew, *Fürsorgerinnen* and the Consortium lamented the lack of restraint by young soldiers and appealed to military superiors to reiterate the imperative of restraint, at least with regard to minors. But the Consortium stopped short of blaming military leadership for the problem, focusing its criticism on the dearth of authority figures to keep the sexuality of women and girls in check.

In 1940 the military leadership was still certain of wartime victory, and it considered sexual access to German women (or women of equal racial value) instrumental to German military viability.[89] In December 1939, Heinrich Himmler, who was obviously aware of the threat posed by soldiers congregating in German cities, had considered "whether the moral dangers to adolescent girls might be attenuated through the establishment of additional brothels in which lecherous elements could find satisfaction."[90] Focused on alternatives for the sexual release of German fighting men, Himmler neither addressed nor felt the need to take seriously the suspicion of local social workers that "lecherous elements" were congregating in front of the barracks as much as within. Annette Timm has convincingly argued that National Socialist ideology built on existing views that male sexual urges were uncontrollable. The Nazis "took this belief one step further, equating sexual gratification with masculine power."[91]

Already in 1934, the Reich differentiated between two types of prostitutes. Registered prostitutes resided on designated streets and subjected themselves to mandatory medical examinations. The second group comprised women who engaged in secret or occasional prostitution, unmarried women with STDs, or women who were simply promiscuous. As the regime matured, so did its instrumentalization of female sexuality. Himmler considered sexual outlets for German soldiers of outmost importance for preventing homosexuality and enhancing military prowess.[92] By early 1943, Hamburg had settled on a municipal definition of a prostitute in an effort to set administrative guidelines in the struggle against venereal disease. Thereafter a prostitute was a female who engaged in frequent sexual encounters with varying partners, who enticed partners publicly, and who provided for her own life as a result of the compensation she received. When these conditions were not met, a woman could still be classified as a prostitute by a chief medical professional after careful consideration of her appearance and demeanor.[93]

Hamburg's health officials, police, and welfare workers cooperated in the control of prostitution, but they viewed sexually permissive behavior and extramarital sex as a side effect of war. Welfare workers realized that most men did not fit Himmler's model of sexual automatons and that women's needs for sexual pleasure undermined the functionalization of male sexuality within the bureaucratic machinery of war.[94] Taking seriously the wartime stresses on everyday life, welfare workers grew increasingly worried about what they perceived to be the local population's escalating addiction to pleasure and sensation. *Führsorgerinnen* in all districts linked the moral fragility of soldiers' wives to the growing numbers of dissolute adolescents. *Fürsorgerinnen* in St. Pauli explained that "many women suffer from loneliness; they can't bear the absence of their husbands very well." No longer were complaints about women going out at night limited to "enfeebled women." Increasingly women "who thus far made a sound and orderly impression, leave their children home alone while pursuing their own pleasures."[95]

Although Nazi leaders insisted that sexual activity had the power to revitalize and rejuvenate the nation, thereby justifying both "sexual violence on the front and the provision of sexual gratification as a reward for military service," they failed to account for the need for reciprocal human contact whether through sexual intercourse or flirtation and courtship.[96] Viewing promiscuity as a form of asocial behavior, Hamburg's local youth protectors assumed that young girls from respectable backgrounds were not likely to be seduced by soldiers unless they had been exposed to inappropriate leisure activities, reading materials, or films. Remarkably, the Consortium for the Protection of Youth in Wartime refrained from disapproving of specific films, a likely concession to the Propaganda Ministry. However, the challenge leveled by their excessively vague reports was far ranging.[97] The language pervading the 1943 summary insisted that most films and almost all entertainment films were detrimental to the moral and mental well-being of the younger generation, harming in particular the sexual ethics of young women.[98] Instead of criticizing a specific cultural product, the Consortium exposed the transience of the entire cultural project, implying that it was a failure.

Through its vague but damning reports on moral decay, the Consortium issued a municipal response to the perceived disintegration of society. It also provided a vehicle for the ideological zeal of welfare workers and youth reformers who were not prepared to surrender social reform to the repressive apparatus of the Gestapo. Placing responsibility for the growing dangers to youths squarely on the authorities in Berlin, the local state agilely relegated blame for moral debilitation both upward and downward. While reaffirming the essential National Socialist bond between the Führer and the *Volksgenossen*, it assigned the failure to maintain social control to both the Reich and the *Volk*, conveniently escaping culpability itself.[99]

Projections of War

Throughout Hamburg, observers noticed the apathetic resignation of men and women who were "under such duress due to work and duties and their own experiences that the strength . . . for strong, lasting human emotions— be they joy or sorrow—no longer exist."[100] People were exhausted from bombing raids, from standing in line for insufficient provisions, from waiting for news from the front. Although neighborhoods rallied together during the first bombing raids in May and June 1941, social networks had started breaking down by the following summer. Disagreements and quibbles became the order of the day, further straining social relations.[101] The case of Marie-Louise and Friedrich Solmitz is instructive here, for it also brings back to mind the exterminationist practice of the regime in front of which Hamburg mustered its response to wartime disruptions.

The Solmitzes were a mixed-race couple, according to the Nuremberg Laws. Friedrich was a German Jew who was protected by marriage and his veteran status from deportation but his ability to partake in normal life had been dramatically curtailed way before bombs reordered life for his wife. Excluded from economic and cultural life since late 1938, he wasn't even allowed to visit movie theaters or other public *Lustbarkeiten* with his wife. Marie-Louise felt frustration at her own guilt and her husband's griping about her visits to the movies, lamenting that he expected her to give up everyday pleasures just because he was no longer allowed to partake in them. Frau Solmitz petitioned the authorities for an exception based on her husband's service in the Great War. Her request was denied.[102]

For decades after the war, the myth of Hamburg's liberal *Sonderweg* persisted. According to this fantasy, National Socialism was a superficial phenomenon that never penetrated below the surface in Germany's foremost liberal stronghold. The persecution of Jews supposedly happened much later and more humanely in Hamburg than elsewhere in the Reich.[103] Like all of Hamburg's Jews and mixed families, the Solmitzes experienced the strictures the regime imposed on them and their children in a pointed fashion and the extent of their neighbors' antisemitism remained as a constant presence. Frank Bajohr has demonstrated that anti-Jewish measures in Hamburg started as quickly and proceeded as ruthlessly as elsewhere in the Reich. He has furthermore revealed that aryanization of Jewish property and the deportation of Jews in Hamburg did not wait for directives from Berlin. City leaders exercised restraint in communal anti-Jewish actions only to avoid worsening the city's precarious economic situation. Gauleiter Kaufmann was careful not to alienate current or potential business partners to a port city that attracted international attention. But as Bajohr has shown, Kaufmann ruthlessly pushed anti-Jewish measures in situations where economic interests did not demand restraint.

Citing the ridiculous pretense that Jewish apartments needed to be vacated to accommodate "aryan" victims of war, Kaufmann personally initiated the deportation of Hamburg's Jews in the aftermath of a severe air raid attack in September 1941. Supported by Baldur von Schirach and Joseph Goebbels, he had hoped to ingratiate himself with Hitler by reporting his *Gau* to be "Jew free" ahead of schedule. The deportation was blocked by Hans Frank, governor general of German-occupied Poland, who was himself pushing Jews eastward and hence was unwilling to accommodate Jews from the

Reich. Instead of one massive deportation in early October 1941, the majority of Hamburg's remaining Jewish population was deported in four segments between the end of October and the beginning of December. Deportations resumed in July 1942, but unlike earlier transports to the Jewish ghettos in Poland, the later expulsions led directly to the death camps, with the exception of those individuals specifically designated for Theresienstadt. In 1933, there were 19,643 citizens of Jewish faith (*Glaubensjuden*) counted in Hamburg. By the end of the war, only 647 had survived. Thousands emigrated after the November 1938 pogroms. Of the close to 8,000 people classified as "racial Jews" (*Rassejuden*) who remained by the end of 1940, approximately 5,000 were deported between 1941 and 1945. Scholars estimate that close to 10,000 Jews in Hamburg were exterminated by the Nazi regime.[104]

War intensified and radicalized the regime's persecutory mechanisms against Jews and other so-called community aliens, in turn raising awareness of "suspicious" or "subversive" behaviors and putting welfare workers on high alert. The more the regime cracked down on "undesirables," the more convincing became the notion of an "enemy within." After the obliteration of Hamburg in the summer of 1943, "the Polish resistance began chalking up the slogan 'October' to warn that the November 1918 revolution would come a month earlier to Germany this time," as historian Nicholas Stargardt notes.[105] This crisis brought into the open the most intimate beliefs and most dismal fears of Hamburg's citizens. People matter-of-factly explained the annihilation of their city as *Vergeltung*—a requital for German treatment of the Jews.[106] Defeatist rumors, derogatory remarks, caustic jokes, and mockery of Nazi leaders laced private and not-so-private conversations. But "dissent never progressed beyond idle talk of regime change and a separate peace."[107] The revolution never came, not in October and not in November. Instead, war dragged on. The bombardment of German cities intensified and the general mood acquired a new baseline of apathy and hopelessness. Carrying out the most menial tasks required immense determination. Instead of completing valuable services to the *Volksgemeinschaft*, women and adolescents took temporary leaves of absence to attend the cinema. Filmgoing was construed by the authorities in Berlin as a form of psychological recuperation, but local observers recognized the behavior of citizens for what it was: not merely an escape from personal hardship, but a retreat from a *Volksgemeinschaft*, which in any case increasingly resembled a community of duty and sacrifice.

Life constricted for the majority of the population, but the movie reels kept rolling. The leading trade journal *Film-Kurier* boasted production statistics as evidence of Germany's determination to intensify cultural output during the war.[108] Cinema attendance rose consistently until 1944.[109] Only when raw material shortages slowed down film production and aerial bombardments destroyed vast numbers of theaters in Germany's urban centers did the Reich statistics register a decline in cinema attendance.[110] Despite talk of rationing visits to the cinema late in the war, moviegoing remained the most consistently available form of entertainment, at least in urban areas.[111]

At the same time that local administrators called the beneficial role of cinema into question, the Reich stepped up its movie production, boasting of film as a weapon of war. With a few notable exceptions, the most popular and most (in)famous Nazi films were produced during the war years.[112] On the one hand, films such as *Der ewige Jude* (1940), *Jud Süss* (1940), *Ich klage an* (1940), *Achtung! Feind hört mit!* (1940), and *Heimkehr* (1941) were used to further antisemitism and visually present an existential threat to the German people. *D III 88* (1939), *Feuertaufe* (1939/40), *Wunschkonzert* (1940), *Kampfgeschwader Lützow* (1940/41), and the war epic *Kolberg* (1945) glorified war and celebrated military conquest. On the other hand, many films spoke to the seriousness of the times by highlighting tragic fates,[113] belaboring heroic sacrifices,[114] and celebrating the nation.[115] It was during the war years that Nazi cinema perfected its self-definition as popular cinema.[116] The expensive wartime color films such as *Frauen sind doch bessere Diplomaten* (Jacoby, 1939/41), *Die Goldene Stadt* (Harlan, 1942), *Immensee* (Harlan, 1943), *Opfergang* (Harlan, 1942/44), *Die Frau meiner Träume* (Jacoby, 1944), *Große Freiheit Nr. 7* (Käutner, 1943/45), and *Kolberg* (Harlan, 1943/45) attest to the regime's endorsement of pleasure as a remedy to wartime deprivation. No single film illustrates this particular phenomenon better than Josef von Baky's 1943 fantasy *Münchhausen*.[117]

Münchhausen manifested most clearly the discrepancies between local criticism of the cinema and the Reich's endorsement of film as a weapon of war. It provided vivid examples of the kinds of images that fueled the criticisms leveled by the protectors of youth in Hamburg. In fact, it was the only film the Consortium openly criticized, citing it as an example of the danger even "great art" poses for the immature mind. At the same time, *Münchhausen* was touted by the regime as one of Nazi cinema's greatest achievements.[118] Produced for the twenty-fifth-anniversary celebration of Ufa, Germany's most prominent studio, the film cost more than 6.5 million Reichsmarks to make.[119] Filming for *Münchhausen* preceded both the massive aerial bombardments of German cities and the defeat of the 6th Army at Stalingrad. When it premiered in Berlin on March 5, 1943, only three days after British planes dropped nine hundred tons of bombs on the city, the film was seen as a prescient example of Goebbels's attempt to "transform the military debacle into a spiritual renewal" in response to military losses.[120] The war's exigencies had justified cranking up the pleasure dispenser even before Goebbels began entertaining the possibility of winning the war through willpower alone.[121]

These circumstances notwithstanding, *Münchhausen* was primarily a tribute to Nazi film production. It embodied the transformation of a financially ruined, depression-era industry into an international cultural force that challenged Hollywood dominance.[122] Scholars have made convincing arguments for *Münchhausen*'s exceptional position in Nazi cinema. Certain features of the film, in particular its self-reflexivity and reliance on fantasy, were unquestionably unique, though hardly at odds with Nazism.[123] This refurbished tale of a liar-baron's adventures—men sowing their wild oats and returning home to devote themselves to their patient wives—connects with wartime reality in different ways than scholars have previously considered. *Münchhausen* was more than just an action-packed distraction from the drudgery of war. It offered profound, gender-specific commentary and commendations. In contrast to films like *Eine Frau für drei Tage* (1943), which tackled the issue of a potentially unfaithful wife caught in the constricting grip of bourgeois morality, *Münchhausen* advocated the betterment of men through a mix of three potent ingredients: adventure, war, and sexually available women.[124]

The adventure of war that *Münchhausen* celebrated was difficult to reconcile with the lived reality. The film invoked an atmosphere of blitzkrieg victories, of heroes returning home to a jubilant and intact society. When the film was released in Berlin in March 1943, the tide of war had begun to turn. By the time *Münchhausen* reached Hamburg audiences on September 16, British and American bombers had already leveled the city in the most devastating series of raids yet experienced in Germany.[125] The city was struggling to restore basic utilities, clear major traffic arteries, provide drinking water, and resume garbage collection as the population began to adjust to life in overcrowded quarters, makeshift shelters, and bunkers. The film did nothing to ameliorate the protracted struggle between local administrators and a war-weary population.

Earlier that summer, the *Hamburger Zeitung* assessed the local situation by inverting the prevailing sentiments. Offering a eulogy to the city's "tenaciousness" and determination, the paper exclaimed that "nobody between Elbe and Alster wants to shirk from their new duties."[126] The paper predicted that soldiers of the home front would return to their posts and hold their positions at all costs. It reassured readers that armies of volunteers would ensure the continued well-being of the population. It lauded the selflessness and communal sacrifices of a population that was exuding *Herzenswärme* (heartfelt warmth). If the *Hamburg Zeitung* had accurately captured the situation, the escape offered by *Münchhausen* would have given its Hamburg patrons a few hours of simple respite. Yet as the welfare workers had observed since the beginning of the war, indulgence in entertainment and pleasure rarely recharged public conscientiousness.

While the Ministry of Propaganda and the Reich's Film Chamber deliberately pursued a policy of entertainment and diversion, local debates over moral abandon, cultural decay, and myriad dangers to the young revived anxieties about the irrationality of the masses. This shift in perspective illustrates the continuities that survived the Nazis' cultural revolution. Old ideas were reintroduced to defend against the corrosive effects of the regime's cultural artifacts. *Münchhausen*, perhaps more than any other film, celebrated conditions that gave local administrators sleepless nights. The film translated into a fantasy world the assumption that sexually available women are essential to the fighting power of German men. *Münchhausen* may have perfectly captured the sexual policies of the *Wehrmacht*, but in the context of the home front's dissolution, women were both victims of and hazards to the inevitable self-assertion of male prowess, as Hamburg's army of youth reformers observed daily.

Although *Münchhausen* invited the kind of escapism most often associated with film, scholars tend to construe this escape in terms of "therapeutic relief."[127] *Münchhausen* appears in a different light when considering the protracted wartime disruptions. Much to the chagrin of Hamburg's welfare workers, the comfortable darkness of the cinema proved to be an escape from the duties of labor, family, and housework. Goebbels might well have believed his own rhetoric when he explained that the problem of overcoming the current setbacks of the war was "primarily a psychological one."[128] But the material shortages and the resulting production bottlenecks that strained the "psychology" of the population soon affected the apparatus designated to provide the cure. By 1944 the film production industry was severely hampered despite the fact that it had been designated as strategic.

The behaviors noted by Hamburg's welfare workers suggest that state-mandated escapism did connect with everyday life, but in unproductive ways. Schools operated irregularly, and when they were in session, they didn't have the personnel to enforce attendance or monitor student progress.[129] Willful and unexcused absences became the order of the day, and young people deliberately withdrew from the disciplinary grip of authorities. For an increasing number of adolescents, the much-despised Hitler Youth service meetings became an excuse to get out of the house. Their parents were often too exhausted to check or even care whether they had attended a sponsored event or sneaked out to the movies with friends instead.[130]

Much like their elders, adolescents went to the movies out of boredom rather than to satisfy their artistic or educational curiosity.[131] A careful reading of diaries confirms this for juveniles and adults alike. For example, the fifty-seven-year-old Hugo B., who was stationed as a guard at various branches of the concentration camp Neuengamme from June 1944 to the end of the war, wrote diligently to his wife in Hamburg, detailing his mundane tasks and his multiple visits to the movies. He went to see the same movie several times—he later couldn't even remember its title—but all of his attempts to finish watching this rather unspectacular film were interrupted by alarms. Nonetheless, he kept going back.[132]

Perhaps Konstanty Gutschow understood the impossible contradictions of planning the reconstruction of the *Führerstadt* in a thoroughly razed city. In November 1943, Gutschow resigned as director of the office for strategic effort (Amt für kriegswichtigen Einsatz), a position he had held since May 1941.[133] He instead followed Albert Speer's call to join the Berlin task force for the reconstruction of destroyed cities. Plans for postwar reconstruction mirrored the efforts of a film industry that churned out megaproductions to document German cultural superiority, mobilizing citizens' dwindling reserves of willpower and determination in the face of total destruction. Urban designs projected National Socialism into the future while cities experienced its escalating demise. Drawings and sketches presumed the eventual removal of the rubble that engulfed citizens who eked out lives amid an architecture devastated by war. Similarly, filmmakers painted resilience and respite onto expensive celluloid canvases while social workers bemoaned the shirkers who evaded their duties in makeshift theaters. Film celebrated *Kulturschaffen*, but moviegoing served as evidence of cultural decline.

CHAPTER 4

Rubbled: Remnants of a Nazi City

Operation Gomorrah stopped the clocks in Hamburg.[1] In just ten days between July 25 and August 3, 1943, British and American bombers dropped approximately 8,500 tons of explosives and incendiaries on the city.[2] The first attack on the night of July 25 was directed against the inner city, severely damaging areas west of the Alster tributary, including Eimsbüttel, Harveste-hude, and Altona's city center. With tons of tinfoil blinding and ultimately incapacitating Hamburg's antiaircraft defense, two subsequent daytime attacks focused on the harbor and surrounding areas.[3] The worst destruction occurred on the evening of July 28 when the densely populated, working-class districts of Hamm, Hammerbrook, and Borgfelde, which were crowded with refugees from the first raids, were flattened in three hours. The exceedingly hot weather compounded the immense pressure and heat generated by the explosions to fuel a tornado-like firestorm of 800 degrees centigrade. Thou-sands died from explosions, fire, suffocation, or excessive heat. On the eve-ning of July 30, another fleet of British planes struck the largely depopulated city, setting off further conflagrations across vast swaths of razed neighbor-hoods.[4] On August 3, the British conducted a last and less successful strike.

Rumors spread through the Reich that one hundred thousand people had died in Hamburg, the charred corpses lying in the streets cited as evidence.[5] Thousands fled after the first attack, violating explicit orders by Gauleiter Kaufmann to remain calm and defend the city. The exodus continued over the next several days until Kaufmann sought to take charge of an unstoppable situation and organized the evacuation of roughly eight hundred thousand of the estimated nine hundred thousand refugees, shrinking the city's pop-ulation to a quarter of its prewar size. Many inhabitants returned by the end of the month, and by the end of November the population again exceeded one million.[6] Scholars estimate that about thirty-four thousand people died during and after the raids as soldiers, police, and rescue workers struggled to free people trapped in the rubble and to salvage household effects from burnt apartments and bombed-out buildings.[7] Author Hans Erich Nossack, who watched the city burn from his cottage in the country, remembers returning to check on his apartment and seeing entire districts closed off with walls built from rubble, removing from the public's gaze the clean-up efforts of forced laborers and concentration camp prisoners who waded through swarms of flies and rats that "ruled the city."[8]

Nonetheless, Nazism survived. The National Socialist People's Welfare, supported by the Wehrmacht, offered hot meals in soup kitchens. The city enlisted bakers, butchers, grocers, restaurants, and canteen kitchens to provide for the population.[9] More often, however, survivors had to fend for themselves, dragging coal and wood-burning stoves into yards or cooking on balconies.[10] In many districts, more than 75 percent of the housing stock was destroyed. Large parts of the city were left without gas, water, and electricity for months. Multiple families would band together and share tiny, often unsanitary quarters. Feeling unwelcome elsewhere and afraid to leave everything behind them, refugees began to return over the course of August and September. Those who had family or friends willing to take them in were lucky. The administration tried to accommodate people in emergency housing, but it lacked the human and material resources to construct enough shelters and huts. Many people lived in air-raid shelters, found a place among the ruins, or moved into dark cellars dampened by the inner-city waterways. Shops and administrative offices remained closed for weeks after the attacks, reopening sporadically. Schools, which had operated irregularly since war began, remained closed. Enough garbage accumulated in streets and doorways that the population began to use the ruins as garbage dumps. In some districts, regular garbage collection did not resume until September. Even then, the biweekly collection barely managed to keep up with household waste.[11]

Through more than 130 air strikes that started on May 18, 1940, Hamburg had learned to live with bombs, but Operation Gomorrah exceeded everyone's worst nightmares. Still known as "the catastrophe," it became emblematic for the war at large. Hamburg's ruins, along with those of Cologne, Nuremberg, and Dresden, stood in silent testimony to the cataclysm that shaped the nation's collective memory. Hans Erich Nossack's 1943 memoir *The End* is one of the few accounts that details in plain language the destruction visited upon German cities, even if it falls back on metaphor and allegory, indulging in "philosophical exaggeration and false notions of transcendence."[12] Nossack portrays a city struck by disaster, yet his somber tone is informed by what historian Peter Fritzsche termed "intimate knowledge" of the German crimes that don't explicitly enter his narrative.[13] He refers to the anxiety that characterized urban planning and wartime administration, remembering it as an internal dialogue of the collective, the *Volksgemeinschaft*. "We all entertained the idea of an apocalypse. The events of our time suggested it."[14] Apocalyptic thinking was the only frame of reference that could render intelligible the city's annihilation. Nossack speaks of punishment and paralysis.[15] He laments the loss of the past, of history.[16] Such framing contributed to the nascent but rapidly growing discourse that viewed Nazism as an epidemic infecting the German nation, ripping it out of history. Nossack philosophized, "There once was a creature that was not born of a mother. A fist struck it naked into the world, and a voice called: Fend for yourself! Then it opened its eyes and didn't know what to make of its surroundings. And it didn't dare to look back for behind it there was nothing but fire."[17]

Historian Nicholas Stargardt perfectly captures the transition of the regime from power to impotence in the aftermath of the Hamburg raids. It became clear to the people in Hamburg that the "Allied bombing was both vengeful and possibly even exterminatory in intent," prompting a hitherto unprecedented discussion of Nazi racial politics.[18] With the Nazi press repeatedly blaming Jews as the string pullers behind the air war, people began to connect reports about mass graves in the east to their experiences of aerial obliteration.[19]

To understand the pervasive language of *German* victimhood in the postwar years, it serves to trace the experiences between the destruction of Hamburg in the summer of 1943 and the unconditional surrender of Germany in May 1945. Nossack's dystopian musings anticipate the erasure of National Socialism as an identity that was widely coveted, routinely performed, and zealously represented. In the aftermath of the firebombing, Hamburg's self-understanding changed. The "Anchor of Joy" and "gateway to the world" morphed into a national symbol of resilience, finally achieving its status as an exemplary National Socialist city at the cost of its own destruction. Its citizens, though, came to see themselves as victims, first as targets of the Allies, then as casualties of Nazism. Again, film was central to this transformation. It bridged the gulf of war and salved the sense of normalcy and cultural continuity that remained, perhaps surprisingly, untarnished by Nazism's excesses.

In previous chapters I have shown how film was instrumental to and symptomatic of the search for an authentic Hamburg. As such, it shaped and focused local discourses about Hamburg's place in the Reich. I have also discussed the ways film discourse shifted in the context of war as welfare workers worried about the corrosive effects of tantalizing images. After the collapse of the regime, film became the prime medium to bury and hide the Nazi experience and instead focus on the city's destruction. This new genre, aptly dubbed "rubble film," thus renders visible the end of Nazism and the unmaking of Nazis as a function of the physical destruction of the city.[20]

Resilience and Sacrifice

In September 1940 the reports by Hamburg social workers praised the "courageous spirit of the National Socialist soldiers" and detailed how it transferred "onto the racial comrades at home, who all are fellow combatants and fellow victors in this momentous struggle."[21] The initial victories in the West had made a great impression on the population and nurtured the hope for a quick and painless war. But when reports about victories dwindled, "trivial vexations and gripes returned to the forefront" of public consciousness.[22] As the air war intensified, the atmosphere cooled from optimistic and confident to serious and tense.[23] With the third *Kriegsweihnachten* (war Christmas) approaching, social workers in Hamburg noted the population's growing discontent, apathy, and sluggishness.[24] Even as their reports stressed the indefatigable will to emerge victorious and recognized the willingness of the population to bear with dignity and calm the grave sacrifices demanded by war, the disenchantment of the *Volksgmeinschaft* could hardly be praised away.[25]

Authorities observed with concern that the will to sacrifice had limits, bemoaning that women "with just one or even no child" began to draw on public welfare for undergarments, infant clothing, healthcare costs, and heating supplies.[26] In the long lines in front of understocked shops, women experienced the war as a force eroding communal and neighborly bonds as it sharpened attention toward inequality, class difference, and social injustice.[27] Most of all, the constant bombing attacks that sent citizens scurrying to cellars and shelters began to take a toll on nerves and property.[28] After the first bombs were dropped on the city in May 1940, air raid warnings and trips to the bunker became part of wartime normality. By the third winter of the war, thousands of people in Hamburg had lost their homes. In 1940 social workers observed the willingness of women to help each other out, but a year later the rhetoric of *Volksgemeinschaft* focused on personal shortcomings, pointing fingers at those who didn't help neighbors, didn't show compassion, didn't restrain their consumption.[29]

In Hamburg, Operation Gomorrah escalated the hopelessness that had gripped the population en masse since the German defeat at Stalingrad in February 1943. Blazing fires made the rescue work immensely difficult, and even after the conflagrations were under control, clouds of smoke hung over the city for days. Distribution of provisions was initially chaotic. Scarce food rotted in the streets. Rescue workers were forbidden from scavenging the ruins as a means for replacing their household possessions, but food and drink were up for grabs. In a letter to his parents, Wehrmacht soldier Herwarth von Schade, who was part of a rescue squad in the aftermath of the attacks, chronicled an unusual feast. Eating was concrete evidence of being alive. Hence, von Schade described the two cuts of pork, each the size of a toilet lid, that were sizzled in bacon (*klosettdeckelgrosse, in Speck gebratene Koteletts*) and allotted to each man in his unit after a day's work in the smoldering rubble.[30]

The indulgence of soldiers notwithstanding, provisioning for the general population was breaking down, with potable water particularly difficult to obtain. The city released extra rations of liquor, coffee, and sweets in the first days after the "catastrophe," but this generous gesture was hardly able to restore a semblance of normality.[31] Uwe Storjohann remembers the truckloads of sausages, butter, chocolates, smoked fish, and canned meats that seemed to appear from nowhere and were distributed free of charge, without the usual food ration cards. People neither asked where these rare delicacies came from nor wondered why they had not been available before.[32]

Operation Gomorrah dramatically altered life in Hamburg. To understand the magnitude of its impact on a city of two million, it is worthwhile to compare it to the aerial destruction before July 1943.[33] From the beginning of the war until June 30, a total of 3,906 planes attacked Hamburg, dropping 164,768 bombs, killing 1,431, and leaving 24,204 people homeless. By the end of August the cumulative statistics from the beginning of the war published by the police department listed a total of 6,756 planes and 3,972,124 bombs, though numbers for fatalities and estimates for destruction were unavailable at that time.[34] Later reports estimated the bombings killed more than 30,000 people, wounded an additional 37,000, and destroyed 270,000 apartments. The official report from December 1943 listed 900,000 people as homeless or missing, illustrating the impossibility of establishing reliable information regarding the whereabouts of individual inhabitants.[35]

In the bourgeois district of Eppendorf, 75 percent of the buildings were destroyed, yet by September the population of that district had increased by five thousand to six thousand as bomb victims from worse-off parts of the city migrated there.[36] In Eppendorf as elsewhere in Hamburg, people obtained water from hydrants and pumping stations, doing laundry and washing what dishes they had left in the streets to minimize hauling water across the debris. After streets were rudimentarily cleared of rubble, the city organized wagons and pull carts to facilitate the transport of water to residential areas. Because only a handful of filter stations were available, most tap water had to be boiled, forcing people to exhaust their supplies of coal well before winter.[37]

Long before basic utilities were functioning, Hamburg's movie theaters resumed operation. On Monday, August 10, the *Hamburger Zeitung*[38] listed the movie theaters that would reopen.[39] The next day, the Ufa Palast held two screenings of *Das Ferienkind* at 4 and 6:30 P.M.[40] In the Harvesthuder Lichtspiele, *Gefährtin meines Sommers* played at 5 P.M. and again at 7:30 P.M. In contrast, the prestigious Lessing Theater on Gänsemarkt was open from 10 A.M. to 9 P.M. Its continuous program consisted of a cultural documentary and the two latest German newsreels, Nr. 673 and Nr. 674, just in case the citizens of Hamburg had not yet heard Goebbels's latest take on developments.

The *Hamburger Zeitung* promised that by the weekend most remaining theaters would resume operation.[41] The list of newspaper advertisements printed the next week revealed that only twenty-one of the one hundred movie theaters in Hamburg were operable. The rest had been destroyed.[42] As a result, the August program in Hamburg's first-run houses was gloomy and melancholic.[43] Ferdinand Marian and Marianne Hoppe returned to the Ufa screen in Helmut Käutner's *Romanze in Moll*. Tourjansky's *Nacht ohne Abschied* started at the Lessing Theater. In contrast, Knopf's Lichtspiele supplied lighter fare with *Der kleine Grenzverkehr*. The Lichtburg Iserbrook and the Bahrenfelder Lichtspiele offered up the inconspicuous hero of everyday life, the reliably droll Heinz Rühmann, as an unswerving bachelor in *Ich vertraue dir meine Frau an*, bringing some laughter to the outskirts of the city.[44]

A typical Rühmann comedy, *Ich vertraue dir meine Frau an* offers some eerie perspectives on the contradictions of cinema's supposedly therapeutic relief. This action-packed romantic comedy affirms the importance of seemingly trite *Volksprodukte* (people's products) to a sense of wholeness, even if mockingly so. Rühmann stars as Peter Trost, a small-scale entrepreneur in the firm *Jungesellentrost* (*Bachelor's Comfort*), which is dedicated to alleviating the burdens of bachelorhood and facilitating male self-reliance with products like the mechanical sandwich maker (*Mefrühstrei*, short for *mechanischer Frühstrücksbrotstreich- und Einwickelapparat*) and the automatic sock mender (*Selstrühsto* or *selbsttätiger Strümpfestopfer*). These devices add little to the domestic skills of the prototypical bachelor. Peter's socks still have holes and he goes hungry when the sandwich maker mashes its wrapping paper into his meal. Enter the latest invention, the *Meknonä*, short for *mechanischer Knopfannäher*, a mechanical button stitcher. When Peter presses the *Meknonä* to his heart to demonstrate the superfluousness of women, it perfectly sews a clunky black button to the lapel of his suit. As his secretary coquettishly giggles, Peter smugly smiles into the camera, announcing the new age of the single man.

The remainder of the film chronicles Peter's reformation from a stalwart if benign bachelor (when he looks at his secretary's low-cut, high-hemline dress, he expresses concern that she might catch cold) into a conventional man. When Peter's high school friend Robert (Werner Fuetterer) proves unable to resist his own secretary's charms, Robert's wife Ellinor (Lil Adina) vows to commit adultery if the secretary accompanies Robert on a business trip. Trying to forge a solution, Robert asks Peter to act as a wife sitter, thinking that his friend's commitment to bachelorhood makes him a safe stand-in. After numerous chases, an arrest, a near drowning, a host of mix-ups, and some delicate embroilments, Ellinor ends up sewing Peter's buttons and making him sandwiches.

Ridiculing the consumer society that the Nazis had advocated with such fervor only a few years earlier, *Ich vertraue dir meine Frau an* comes to the predictable conclusion that gadgets cannot replace a wife's companionship. Reminiscent of the "people's products," the *Meknonä* was a composite of German philistinism and American mass production.[45] Starting in August 1933 when Joseph Goebbels launched the first of the prestigious people's products, the *Volksempfänger*, or people's radio, the promise of an intrinsically German consumer society had become an essential aspect of the National Socialist vision for a prosperous future. The regime's propaganda turned the wartime lack of consumer products into a virtue of the self-reliant German, transforming the broken promise of prosperity into a critique of lazy American consumerism.[46] It's just that when *Ich vertraue dir meine Frau an* first ran in Hamburg, there was a lot to mend and not nearly enough fixings for the sandwiches.[47]

The timing of the film was unfortunate, the message off-target as people combed through the rubble for a trace of a loved one or a cherished possession. By 1943, the notion of an automatic housekeeper and wife replacement appeared painfully comic. Perhaps "it was a moment where humans are no longer slaves to their furnishings," as Nossack muses, but his recollections contradict this very assertion.[48] Whether he talked about his own possessions or those of the people he encountered, he realized that suddenly "everything was valuable, a towel, a nail brush, a cast iron lamp, whatever else."[49] Ordinary things—teacups and books and photographs and plush sofas—were freighted with the value of a lost existence.

Despite the massive destruction, the city's economy rebounded relatively quickly. The dead, however, did not return. No other than Konstanty Gut-schow, the architect who was supposed to design Hamburg's pompous new façade, "created an enormous cruciform grave—measuring 280 metres from north to south and 240 metres east to west—to hold 34,000 victims."[50] People were emotionally exhausted and the general mood remained dull and desper-ate.[51] Alarms continued and a numbness characterized the new routine that developed amid the ruins.[52] With rationing recommencing on August 16, the queues returned in front of food and provisions offices, further demoralizing a traumatized population that had to wait to obtain ration cards and allotment certificates.[53] Frustration, anger, and lack of understanding contributed to a fatalistic atmosphere. To coerce a fatigued population back to work, the city made the assignment of available housing contingent on demonstrable effort and willingness to work.[54]

By the spring of 1944, the mood in Hamburg was one of resignation and apathy. The cacophony of propaganda about lightning offensives and potent new weapons could no longer counteract the crippling effects of exhaustion, depression, and fear. Bombings continued and the retreat of the Wehrmacht in the east became a systemic feature of the war rather than a temporary set-back.[55] In Hamburg, social inequality deepened and became ever more visible as the war entered its final phase. In fact, individuals who worked longer hours ended up being worse off. The effects were biased according to gender and class. Middle-class women spent their days walking all over town, standing in line, and drawing on networks of friends in the ever more time-consuming procurement of food and daily necessities.[56] Working-class women had to do all that *after* their paid jobs. Around Christmas the mood lightened slightly as the Reich distributed an advance of sugar allocations. Cake and cookies, potatoes and cabbage, dumplings, applesauce, and even meat graced the tables of the fortunate. With doomsday around the corner, pork roast was as tasty as duck, the German equivalent of Thanksgiving turkey. Indulging in such friv-olous feasts was almost an act of defiance, considering the general mood and the rapidly devolving military situation.[57]

Figure 11. Makeshift playground and emergency movie theater, 1943. Staatsarchiv Hamburg.

Movies were the last items of personal consumption that had not been subjected to the rationing imposed on the *Volksgemeinschaft*.[58] As Goebbels reviewed the latest film proposals, he contemplated how he might further elevate the caliber of German cultural production.[59] Veit Harlan's script for the war epic *Kolberg* promised the right tone for a drama befitting the Reich's undoing. When Harlan started shooting in the fall of 1943, Hamburg was slowly adjusting to life amid the rubble.[60]

Kolberg was the Reich's last massive mobilization in the realm of film.[61] Goebbels clearly had no intention of sparing either cost or effort when it came to celluloid testimonies to the German fighting spirit. At the same time, the Reich Film Chamber tightened the screws by simplifying the price structure for movie tickets, effectively increasing the cost to consumers. The chamber's circular of August 20, 1944, required a reduction in the number of seating categories and the imposition of one standard price that reflected the previous average across seating categories and price gradations.[62] By November 1944 the office for price regulation in Hamburg reported the surprising fact that theater income had risen dramatically, noting as well that less-privileged patrons had been penalized.[63] Nobody seemed to complain. Even though the war had made film distribution more difficult and had drastically reduced the number of movie theaters, people continued to go to the pictures regularly.[64] Hamburg's prestigious first-run house, Lessing Theater, counted 69,825 patrons in August 1944, increasing to 88,350 in October as the weather grew colder.[65] Collectively the twelve Hamburg theaters run by the Deutsche Filmvertriebsgesellschaft counted 450,462 patrons in August and 491,029 in October, reflecting an average of approximately 14,500 and 15,800 daily ticket sales in those months.[66] Theaters were packed day and night regardless of the program. In districts where no functioning theaters remained, schools and community centers filled the void.[67]

By March 1945, Hamburg's cinemascape had rebounded to 36 functioning movie theaters.[68] By that time, only a minority of people held hope—with eyes wide shut—for a favorable outcome of Hitler's promised *Endkampf* (final struggle).[69] To many, a victorious adversary was preferable to the continuation

Figure 12. Antitank barricades, Reeperbahn, 1945. Courtesy Axel Springer Syndication.

of the "senseless murder of the population."[70] Despite fears of vengeance and retribution, many people wished the "Tommy" would come.[71] Yet the anticipated *Zersetzung*, or erosion of discipline, never materialized. Hitler and Goebbels praised Hamburg's tenacious resilience and its indefatigable will to sacrifice.[72] The tide had turned. Amid the rubble, Hamburg's Nazification was beyond question, never mind that the ideological zeal had turned into fatigue and hopelessness. The desperation and exhaustion of the population anticipated the radical change that followed the end of war.

Erasure

After Hitler committed suicide in his Berlin bunker on April 30, 1945, Governor Kaufmann was not prepared to transfer his loyalty to Grand Admiral Karl Dönitz. Instead, he handed Hamburg over to the British forces, just a day after Berlin surrendered to the Red Army. On May 3 at 8 A.M., transmitters blasted the news through the city: "Over the course of the day Hamburg will be occupied by English troops. Start of the invasion 13:00 hours."[73] As of 10 A.M. all offices in Hamburg remained closed. Public transportation ceased to operate at noon. The raising of red or white flags was expressly forbidden. The police, responsible for guaranteeing public order, were instructed to revert to the military greeting of "bringing the right hand to the headgear."[74] The occupation commenced without significant interruptions or incidents. British troops took up residence in the Hindenburg Barracks or made themselves at home in the Hotel Four Seasons overlooking the Alster. The long-awaited *Stunde Null*, or zero hour, had arrived. People were anxious but hopeful. Nazi Hamburg went into hiding.

After the surrender, the changes to everyday life were many and far reaching.[75] The continuities of need and want, traceable since the end of the First World War, would take much longer to unmake.[76] The *Reichsnährstand* (Reich's food provisioning office) began to issue ration cards according to British specifications, and people in Hamburg began to complain about British inefficiency, comparing the military administration unfavorably to the exaggerated orderliness of Nazism.[77] People ceased to blame the war for the continuing food shortages, lack of raw materials, and sluggish administrative changes, finding fault with the caprice and incompetence of their occupiers instead. In short, the state of exception continued, but in the light of war's end it no longer seemed justifiable. The oft-quoted popular phrase, "Enjoy the war! The peace will be dreadful," illustrates how Germans had anticipated retribution.[78] More importantly, it expressed the expectation that the end of war was going to bring about dramatic change.

Historians have long questioned the validity of interpreting the *Stunde Null* of May 8, 1945, as a blank slate representing radical beginnings. Certain ruptures were pivotal for the course of postwar German development, such as the defeat at Stalingrad,[79] establishment of the Bizone,[80] monetary reform,[81] and the establishment of dual German states.[82] Nonetheless, historians have emphasized continuities in structures and personnel beyond the presumed, all-defining rupture.[83] Hamburg surrendered, but many of the hardships that had characterized the last years of war continued under British occupation, betraying local hopes for the abrupt and fundamental improvement of everyday life. Faced with British reeducation, men and women in Hamburg focused instead on their own suffering and cast themselves as three-fold victims—betrayed by the Nazi regime, punished by the international air war, and occupied by forces indifferent to their continuing plight.

The British military government focused on the denazification of the civil administration and the removal of Nazi officials. At first, the dismantling of Nazi Hamburg was symbolic. On May 6 the British mandated the removal of all national and military emblems.[84] Skilled craftsmen were ordered to remove the swastikas from the belt buckles of police forces and the "German greeting" was forbidden in all public places. Images of leading National Socialists, as well as the military leaders from the two world wars, had to be removed from books and magazines. National Socialist content disappeared from bookshelves and shops. Nazis and Nazism became invisible.[85]

As a first step in reestablishing the administration and economy of Hamburg, the occupying forces demanded a list of dismissed civil servants, teachers, professors, union leaders, clerics, political leaders, anti-Nazi organizers, and Jews (including a declaration of their professions). From this pool they would pick civilian partners and employees.[86] On May 15, the military government installed Rudolf Petersen as the new mayor. Petersen promptly fired all civil servants who had joined the Nazi party before April 1, 1933. As a demonstration of his "authority," he nullified all blackout regulations, certainly a moot point but one he made nonetheless.[87]

The ultimate goal for all reorganized German institutions was "to gain a respected and equal place for a Germany freed from Nazism among other nations in honest and honorable cooperation with the occupying forces."[88] On July 24, even before the schools reopened in Hamburg,[89] the mayor achieved a symbolic victory by obtaining permission from the military government to fly the Hamburg flag at city hall.[90] The British made no secret of their conviction that the German nation and the German people were responsible for the war, the destruction of Europe, and the atrocities known today as the Holocaust. Germans quickly learned to transfer responsibility for these crimes to an obscure and alien force that had coerced them, misled them, and then disappeared—the Nazis.[91]

At the same time, there was a sense that the Nazis had taken better care of the population during the war than the occupiers could do in the aftermath. This sentiment persisted beyond the hunger years.[92] In 1943 the average adult food intake amounted to roughly 2,000 calories per day, dropping to 1,412 calories in 1945 and 1946.[93] However, it was cruelty rather than efficiency that had guaranteed rations for the German population during the war.[94] After the war, Germans no longer enjoyed monopolistic access to the European food supply. Farmland destruction and population migration had disrupted production, and farmers were reluctant to exchange what food they produced for any of the devalued European currencies.[95] Food ended up on the black market, a significant symptom of postwar afflictions.[96]

Citing an exaggerated threat of unrest and riots, the British decided to fill people's leisure time if not their stomachs, an excuse to prepare the ground for the "projection of Britain." On July 10, 1945, the military government permitted ten Hamburg movie theaters to open their doors to show films deemed suitable by the Political Intelligence Department's Film Section.[97] The first films to play in the British zone were German movies made between 1942 and 1944, both a conciliatory move and a solution of convenience to meet the pressing demand.[98] The newspapers pointed out that the programs to follow would feature a roster of German, English, and American films changing every Friday.[99] The strategy was to wean the public off German wartime classics with a transition to dubbed British films.[100] Fading out German reruns, the British authorities hoped, would be easier than weaning Germans off of Hollywood films. In the US zone, in contrast, the American occupiers banned German films and tried to squeeze cash out of second-run and second-rate Hollywood movies.[101]

German films were vastly preferred across occupation zones in part because Germans resented being treated like a vanquished people. The "projection of Britain" that attempted to inculcate British ways, British mores, and British democracy was no match for German *Kultur*. Casting themselves as "victims of a war that Hitler had started but everyone lost," Germans viewed themselves as heroic survivors of an inhumane war. Precisely because these "bombs were faceless," the people of Hamburg could talk of war as an evil force that had befallen innocent, ordinary people.[102] The *Volk* had been misled and betrayed by a leader who "lured it onto a mountain, showed it the riches of the earth, and promised to lay them at its feet, if only it were willing to bend its knees before the false God." As if awoken from a bad dream, the German people found themselves beggars rather than masters of the world and seemed to grieve for broken promises more than for their own dead—not to mention the countless victims of Nazism.[103] Like other voices across the Reich, the *Hamburger Freie Presse* cast the *Volk* as a crippled and helpless victim of the Nazi state and its genocidal policies.

Starving, defeated, disoriented, and disillusioned, people in Hamburg hesitantly gambled with democratic principles. Saturated with a *volk*-bound mysticism reminiscent of Nazispeak, the *Freie Presse* defined democracy as "the spiritual sourdough [*Sauerteig*] soaking through [*durchtränken*] the life of a nation from beginning to end" with emphasis primarily on obligation (*Verpflichtung*) and probation (*Bewährung*).[104] While the Hamburg press quickly caught on that democracy implied the consent of a free people, they saw the British occupiers as a greater obstacle to democratic reconstruction than their own residual Nazism.[105]

Rejecting *Kollektivschuld* (collective guilt), the press asked the Allies to imagine how "trampled and deflated the innermost German friends of democracy" felt when faced with the "most generous concessions the world [*das Ausland*] granted to Hitler, the dictator" only years after "denying even the smallest the concessions the democrats [*sic*] Stresemann and Brüning?" Insisting on the coresponsibility for the massive and inhumane crimes of Nazism, the press implied that rigorous enforcement of the *Diktat* of Versailles drove Germans under the yoke of Hitler.[106] The majority of people in Hamburg and elsewhere in Germany resented allegations of collective responsibility. Focusing on their own suffering, they failed to grasp the magnitude of the crimes committed against Jews, ethnic minorities, Eastern Europeans, political dissenters, and all the others whom the Nazis deemed undesirable. The Hamburg paper insisted that "one cannot instruct a hungry people in the ways of democracy" and ventured that "if the plight of Germany is not to be overcome, there will be a new tragedy." Observers in Hamburg mused that if the hunger and hardship after World War I produced Hitler, one can only imagine what hunger after Hitler might breed.[107]

It was through culture that political positions were most clearly staked out. Occupiers and occupied alike thought of film as an important vehicle to communicate and negotiate without making programmatic statements or attributing blame. Historian Heide Fehrenbach convincingly argues that "in the aftermath of a war whose weaponry was as much psychological as technological, cinematic representation, reorganization and control constituted a crucial cultural component of both the victors' postwar plans to denazify and democratize Germany *and* German elites' attempts to construct a new uniquely 'German' identity cleansed of fascist traces."[108] The military authorities rarely recognized that cultural discourse was a two-way street. Germans often rejected as alien the cultural artifacts, films, and narratives that the Allies had selected as a means for instructing them in the ways of democracy or socialism.

Removing Nazi officials, restaffing the police, replacing teachers, prosecuting criminals, disarming the population, supporting new political parties, and imposing military authority destroyed Nazi bureaucracy but not Nazi ideology. All occupying powers agreed that "security does not rely solely on fortifications, soldiers and armaments; far more important is a radical transformation of the mentality of the enemy."[109] In the summer of 1945, the population of Hamburg still resisted the identity of a vanquished people. Social workers pointed out the scrubbed floors and the simple tablecloths in living quarters that were cramped, structurally unsound, poorly lit, unventilated, and exceedingly damp, insisting that "for us, poverty and filth don't belong together!"[110] Stressing the extraordinary resourcefulness of women at mending everything and making a virtue of necessity, they contradicted the impression among foreigners that "we're not doing . . . badly," explaining that "since destitution doesn't catch the eye . . . [foreigners] do not know of the suffering that hides behind the apartment walls."[111] Pointing to the orderliness with which the population accepted "the continuous shortages of victuals, especially the cuts in fat allocations," welfare workers drew attention to the untenability of current circumstances and defended the population's bitterness toward the British military government.

After the harsh winter of 1946–47, trust in the British ability and willingness to ameliorate conditions and facilitate reconstruction (*Wiederaufbau*) waned.[112] By fall 1948, social workers in Hamburg mused that "It is hard to evaluate whether the magnitude of bearability had already been exceeded and the certain [*gewisse*] apathy with which everything is borne is already indicative of the abatement of physical and psychological strength."[113] Whereas resilience and hope for the future defined the first months of occupation, defeat characterized the popular mood by the summer of 1947. Spent, worn, exhausted, and sick, men and women looked years older than their actual ages.[114] There was little the occupying authorities could do to change the perception that under the Nazis suffering was at least well-organized and evenly distributed.[115]

Modeling Democracy

In a postwar life filled with hardship, Germans affirmed the cruelty and injustice of war. They were unwilling, however, to accept a fundamental difference between their suffering and the suffering caused by the Nazi regime's systematic extermination of entire populations, particularly European Jews.[116] Like the Americans, French, and Soviets, the British saw film as an instrument of denazification and political education because it could *illustrate* rather than *legislate* a different social model.[117] Film was central to both British and American occupation policy and deemed particularly useful in confronting the German public with the crimes committed by the Nazis.[118]

As early as June 1945, the British military government lifted the ban on groups larger than five people, allowing concerts, operas, and plays to recommence in German theaters.[119] Libraries reopened. Newspapers resumed printing and book publishing began to revive.[120] By July a limited civil postal service allowed Germans to send personal postcards.[121] Although the British military authorities recognized the need for entertainment, Americans insisted that "it is not the policy of the occupying authorities to entertain Germans but to educate and inform them of events in the outside world as an antidote to the long dosage of Nazi propaganda."[122] The United States screened the first atrocity film, *Death Camp,* in Erlangen from late June through July 1945. As with the later British-American coproduction *Todesmühlen* (*Death Mills,* 1946), the occupiers stressed the collective responsibility for Nazi crimes, confronting the population with footage taken during the liberation of the Nazi death camps in Eastern Europe, some of which was quite problematically reframed and staged.[123] In many instances, the military government mandated the viewing of reeducation films or visits to concentration camps for the entire population of a city or town, children and all.

Because the British, unlike their American counterparts, allowed reruns of wartime German productions, German films remained an integral part of theater programming for the duration of their military occupation.[124] British film studios could not profit off the worthless Reichsmark, so the first British films to be introduced were reruns, too. *Rembrandt,* a 1930s production, opened in the British Zone in September 1945. But even after newer British and American films became available, audiences continued to prefer German reprises over British and American fare.

Film distribution remained in the hands of the Film Section of the British military government until January 1947, with various offices staffed by German civilians. Commercial distributors were licensed in the British and American zones during the second half of 1947, and German outfits began to compete against the British Eagle Lion and the American Motion Picture Export Association.[125] The British insisted on keeping exhibition, distribution, and production separate to prevent another Ufa-style monopoly.[126] All of the Allies agreed on the need to dismantle the Nazi film apparatus, but the controversial revival of postwar German film production followed different rationales in each zone.[127]

The military governments broke up the state monopoly of major film companies, the German Ufi, expropriating the property and administering what remained through a public trust.[128] The revenues from reprises of old German films, though, continued to flow into the frozen accounts of the defunct Ufi subsidiaries.[129] Personnel and sites used for either production or exhibition were seized by the occupying power in each zone. The two most important film production centers, the Ufa studios in Berlin, Tempelhof and the Ufa studios in Geiselgasteig, Munich, were controlled by Soviet and US authorities, respectively. At first, they lay fallow.

The Soviets granted the first license to produce a postwar film to the newly founded DEFA (Deutsche Film-Aktiengesellschaft) on May 17, 1946, ending the so-called *Filmpause,* the period between May 1945 and May 1946 in which no German films were produced.[130] Only ten days later the British military government issued a license to Helmut Käutner's production company, Camera. During the *Filmpause,* actors, actresses, scriptwriters, cameramen, and directors kept a low profile, many of them moving from Berlin to Hamburg or Munich to await political developments.[131] Wolfgang Staudte completed the first postwar German film, *Die Mörder sind unter uns,* in Berlin, while Käutner began working on *In jenen Tagen* in Hamburg. Both films tried to come to grips with the past, Staudte focusing on Nazis, Käutner on German citizens. Neither addressed the pervasiveness of Nazi ideology and both let ordinary people off the hook.

In 1946 four films were produced by German film production companies.[132] The Americans, who had inherited the intact production sites at Geiselgasteig in Munich, licensed the Neue Deutsche Filmgesellschaft in November 1946. Even then they preferred to saturate the market with dubbed or subtitled Hollywood fare. By 1947, a total of fifty-six German and German-language films were being produced.[133]

Germans eagerly received these first postwar films, taking them as signs of cultural regeneration. Most Germans had no qualms watching foreign-made films, but they generally preferred their homemade variants, whether new releases or old-time favorites. The British assumed that Nazi-era film tropes would become outdated and Germans would embrace British filmmakers, but the German reruns proved to have a surprisingly long shelf-life simply because they offered *German* alternatives. Under the guidance of media czar J. Arthur Rank, British films made a forceful appearance on the international scene, successfully pushing into the US market.[134] But German audiences were not enthused. Local cineastes and nascent political authorities expressed a desire for a national film revival and a return to self-reliance in the cultural realm. Although criticism toward the military authorities was expressly forbidden, neither occupying government could require that audiences *liked* the films they saw.

Hamburg's movie audiences had regularly attended Hollywood films until they were banned by the regime in the fall of 1940, replaced by Czech, Hungarian, French, and Italian films that also proved popular. In light of this history of cultural cosmopolitanism, audience reactions to British films were surprising. In December 1946, Hamburg's social democratic Mayor Max Brauer informed the city's British authorities that the population often misunderstood British films. In an obsequious letter, he insisted that "the interest of Hamburg cinema audiences in British film is extraordinarily great and the desire and readiness to acquaint oneself through these films with the British conception of life is no doubt genuine."[135] Beneath this servile tone, the mayor bluntly told the occupiers that British films were an unsuitable and inferior substitute for even average-quality German fare. British products were accordingly rejected for "being too primitive."[136] The mayor primarily blamed the substandard reception of British films on poor dubbing or confusing subtitles that destroyed "the subtleties of the dialogue." In particular, Brauer referred to *Brief Encounter* (1945), which he considered to be a good film that was ruined in the process of synchronization. Rather than faulting British film per se, the mayor invoked a culture and language barrier that supposedly prevented British films from fostering an "understanding of the British way of living [*sic*]" with Hamburg audiences. *Brief Encounter* (Lean, 1945), *I'll Be Your Sweetheart* (Guest, 1945), and *The Wicked Lady* (Arliss, 1945) apparently made British ideas and customs appear ridiculous to Hamburg audiences (or at least to Mayor Brauer), causing "foolish explosions of derision and laughter."[137] What exactly the people in Hamburg found laughable about these films the mayor would not say. However, he felt compelled to suggest that the Information Control Unit prescreen British films before a panel of regular patrons of Hamburg's prestigious and art-conscious Waterloo Theater to avoid causing "bewilderment of public [sic]."[138] All of the films the mayor singled out enjoyed a positive international reception when shown in the United States and other European countries.[139] When Brauer imagined that German reactions to the internationally acclaimed *Henry V* (Oliver, 1944) would be more positive, he simply demonstrated his awareness that British selections for the German film market excluded some of the most successful works.[140]

The Hamburg press continued to lambast British films and to insist that achievements of a *German* nature be included in Arthur Rank's British film empire.[141] Film critics and journalists made it known that they were happy to exercise their democratic right to disapprove of the Rank films that the British believed to be superior. Erich Lüth, the director of Hamburg's public relations office, invited military authorities to measure the achievements of the new German film industry with a critical eye, but only after granting it the necessary freedom to grow.[142]

Just as Hamburg had cultivated its famed cosmopolitanism throughout the Nazi period, adjusting its hue according to wartime developments, the city now negotiated a new position vis-à-vis its past and the occupying powers, whether grappling with the political reorganization of Germany or contemplating what to do with 40 million cubic meters of rubble. When reporting on the sustained interest of the public in learning about Nazi crimes through atrocity films, the press attempted to meld the crimes into "the history of human cruelty" from the crusades and the religious wars, to the witch trials and persecutions of Christians, to the conquests of Genghis Khan and Napoleon.[143] While the press would not go so far as to equate Hamburg's military occupation with the political oppression wrought by the Nazi regime, popular expressions such as "*Gott gib uns ein fünftes Reich, das Vierte ist dem Dritten gleich*" (God give us a fifth empire, the fourth is just like the third) illustrate the widespread discontent with the limits imposed by Allied forces hoping to transform Germans into democrats.[144]

Hamburg's advocates for democracy stressed that democracy does not compare to a piece of furniture that can be restored and decoratively resituated after thirteen years of neglect. Nor is it "a coin one picks up of the street when one's own political change has run out." Democracy could not be borrowed like a "political decal from other nations and plastered over the bashed-up facade of one's own state."[145] While the British attempted to revive German civil administration and encouraged the formation of political parties, Hamburg only grudgingly submitted to British guidance. Admitting that the destruction of Nazism "may have opened up the possibility for democracy to grow out of our own law, out of our own life," the press insisted that, "it was neither the objective nor the business of the victors to deliver democracy; we have to forge it ourselves, have to dig it out from underneath the rubble, discover it anew and render it precious and binding for our state."[146]

German film could do just that, even if few felt ready to say what the home-grown version of democracy was supposed to entail. Instead, filmmakers began to dig through the debris—almost literally. The first postwar film produced in Hamburg was *In jenen Tagen* (Käutner, 1947). Its production illustrates how film developed a language for unmaking Nazism, rehabilitating the German people, and celebrating a democracy that cleared away the rubbled past. Contrary to *Ein Mädchen geht an Land* or *Große Freiheit Nr. 7*, *In jenen Tagen* was not lionized as a tribute to Hamburg or its history. Instead, it was embraced as a local intervention in the national discussions about how to reframe the past in order to retain it at all.

In jenen Tagen offers an episodic history of the Third Reich through seven cinematic vignettes told from the perspective of an old car. The story starts in 1933 and ends in the rubble-littered cityscape of Hamburg, a foil on which the recent history of the nation is projected. Ultimately the film serves as a rebuttal to the Allies' insistence on the German people's collective responsibility. Guilt and suffering, Käutner's story insists, are borne by a wider collective than the Allied accusations imply. Only lightly alluding to the racial and political order created by the Nazis, the film focuses on the fates of a few individuals, attempting to restore their shattered belief in German humanity. In response to the hopelessness and uncertainty of the future, the omnisciently narrating car tells tales about "ordinary Germans" who, like the vehicle itself, were scarred by the brutal unfolding of history. Functioning as both a tribute to the wrecked city and a self-assured nod toward the British military government, the film played an important role in reviving Hamburg's exceptionalism that was a pillar of earlier cosmopolitanism.

Rehabilitated as anti-Nazi but pro-German, Käutner began shooting *In jenen Tagen* in June 1946 using the rudimentary technical equipment that was available.[147] Save for two scenes, Käutner's postwar debut was shot entirely under Hamburg's open skies, the ruins of the ravaged city serving

Figure 13. Shooting *In jenen Tagen*, 1946. Staatsarchiv Hamburg.

as the set.[148] For seven months the director's expediency and creativity were put to the test. The sound equipment was ex-Wehrmacht property used to transmit military information. After the lightbulbs on the relic of a camera burst, car headlights provided lighting for many scenes. In June 1947 the film opened in Hamburg's recently refurbished Waterloo Theater.[149] Like the film's director, the theater had morphed from the home of the Nazi-friendly Hamburg Film Consortium into the most prestigious movie theater in the British occupation zone and the home of the *Wirtschaftsverband für Filmtheater e.V.* under the continuing direction of Heinz B. Heisig.[150] On June 13, the film's main protagonist welcomed audiences to the premiere.[151] Leisurely parked in the theater's foyer, the Opel Olympia presented Käutner's version of recent German history as a collage of snapshots that recited the history of the "thousand-year Reich."[152]

In jenen Tagen intervened in the discourse about German collective guilt by mobilizing victimhood and suffering as universal human experiences in a landscape devoid of perpetrators.[153] The dilapidated automobile functioned as an unusual framing device that located objective authority in an inanimate

Figure 14. Waterloo
Theater, 1970. Sta-
atsarchiv Hamburg.

object. Rendering the "objective, unbiased, or heartless" car an expert witness
on German humanity (*deutsche Menschlichkeit*), Käutner deliberately sidesteps the polarity between the vanquished and the victors. Because an object
lacks a viewpoint, mobilizing it in a film as a narrative device functions as a
wide-angle lens onto the past, replacing perspective with a totalizing view.

Perhaps more significantly, using a car as the narrator embodies the Nazis'
promise of a better life that follows unrelenting sacrifice. The people's car,
or Volkswagen, had been the pinnacle of the consumer society promised by
the Nazi regime.[154] In its first sweeping takes, *In jenen Tagen* reveals the perspective of the Allies, a compassionless gaze that wanders across the rubble-
littered landscape of Hamburg, hardly noticing within the violated landscape
the hungry children, the veterans, and the bent backs of toiling women. But

Figure 15. Still of the omniscient car, from *In jenen Tagen,* 1947.

the car's storytelling reforms the camera, reeducating and softening its gaze to the suffering performed before it.

In the film's opening scene, two young men gut the car in the midst of this *Sauleben* (a hoggish life), symbolically deconstructing the Nazi promise for better times to come. The people's car is mined for parts in an inherited world characterized by absence. Willi (Gert Schaefer) summarizes the situation: "No smokes, no booze, no food, no coal, no real job, no apartment, no money, no news from Susanne, no future, no illusions, no . . . no . . . no . . ." The more educated Karl (Erich Schellow) brings the conversation to a philosophical level: "No humans [*Menschen*]." When his friend doesn't seem to understand, Karl explains, "There are no humans anymore, just like there hadn't been any in all those damn years." But Karl remains silent when pressed to explain, "what actually is a human?" Here the car's solemn introspection reproaches the men for their remissness and moves to answer the question.

Claiming to show *Menschen,* the car first presents the audience with victims. Dying German soldiers, uprooted refugees, disillusioned émigrés, a disenfranchised Jew, bereft wives, betrayed husbands, and hungry mothers are

shown to be victims of brutal circumstances, of war, of corrupting and corrupted times. At the end of the film, the car directly addresses the viewer:
"I haven't seen much of those days, no great events, no heroes, just a few fates
[*Schicksale*], and of those only excerpts. But I have seen a few humans [*Menschen*], that is whom you asked about, Herr Willi. The times were stronger than
they. But their humanity [*Menschlichkeit*] was stronger than the times. They
have existed, those humans [*Menschen*], and they will always exist." Invoking the format of the documentary by having an "objective" narrator mobilize
"evidence" for an argument articulated only in the frame, the film formulates
a response to British and American reeducation films by portraying Germans
as victims. The *Menschen* we encounter in this film are bound by suffering,
hardship, and impossible choices. The ideological battle for the reintegration
of Germans into the community of nations was a battle over the qualities of
victimhood. Juxtaposing the fate of a rank-and-file Wehrmacht soldier with
the suicide of the German-Jewish couple in the face of escalating anti-Jewish
violence, *In jenen Tagen* essentially denies the structural difference between
their respective suffering.[155]

Throughout the film, perpetrators remain faceless and unnamed. The
individual episodes are stitched together by the enlightened car to present
a totalizing collage in which the brown-shirted mob and the Nazi police are
presented in parity with allied bombs and tanks, the barbarous Russian landscape, and universal tragedies of hunger and cold. Stripped of Nazi symbols,
the tale mobilizes *Einzelschicksale* (individual stories) to counteract vilifica-
tion of an entire people and offers a starting point from which to re-imagine
a better future, a reformed people, and a new city.

Reruns and *Wiederaufbau*

As the case of Hamburg illustrates, postwar discussions about film took on
explicitly national overtones. In fact, film became a medium through which to
articulate hopes and claims for *national* cohesion and equality among nations
(*nationale Gleichberechtigung*). Patrons in Hamburg demanded to see films that
spoke *their* language and reflected *their* cultural sensibilities.[156] These cultural
sensibilities were intimately connected with a German suffering that was imagined and cast as a collective response to the allegation of *Kollektiveschuld*.[157]

In addition to the first postwar German films, the return of National
Socialist films to postwar screens within the British zone implied that German

culture could be rehabilitated even if Germans lacked the mechanisms to contest the political power of the occupying authorities. Political traditions had been thoroughly discredited, but the revival of German cultural production through films, books, and performances provided a space for safely challenging the superiority of the victors while demonstrating an understanding of the intellectual exchanges that democracy fosters.

The reruns of so-called escapist entertainment films and the continued employment of prominent actors and actresses, scriptwriters, directors, and support personnel in postwar film production reasserted the separation of art and politics that presumably allowed German artists to survive as inner emigrants in a regime that left no doubt about the functional subservience of culture to politics. Hans Albers, for example, the star of *Große Freiheit Nr. 7*, appeared in the first American-made postwar film.[158] In contrast, Veit Harlan, though acquitted of the charges of crimes against humanity, was widely seen as a filmmaker who with films such as *Jud Süss* had knowingly placed his "art" in the service of murderous ideas.[159] Like many artists who had contributed to overtly propagandistic fare, Harlan was singled out as a Nazi while the majority of cultural experts and artists connected to the wartime film industry escaped relatively unscathed by the thirteen-year parade of blood-soiled grandeur.

In Hamburg as elsewhere, individuals seemed prepared to cast themselves and their efforts as part of a national agenda of *Wiederaufbau* (reconstruction). Audiences rejected British films not for lack of understanding or because of essential incompatibility of British films with "German sensibilities."[160] In fact, Hamburg's film viewing public had been so well-versed in English-language films that the Waterloo Theater could profitably screen Hollywood releases with their original soundtracks up to 1940. Rather, Hamburg's cosmopolitan film public rejected Hollywood movies and Rank films because they could. Just like their counterparts in other cities, audiences snubbed movies made by the occupying powers, claiming their "democratic rights" to disapprove and speak out publicly for the value of German art and culture.[161]

Epilogue:
Filmstadt Hamburg

The end of war inspired new legends.[1] Nazism never took root in Hamburg. Antisemitism had been tangential and humane. Liberalism survived in hiding. Fanatics were hard to find. Kaufmann was a "good" Gauleiter who "saved" Hamburg from the apocalyptic *Endkampf* decreed by Hitler.[2] Rather than marking a radical break with the past, the *kampflose Übergabe* (surrender without a fight) on May 3 and the arrival of *Stunde Null* ended a state of exception, at least officially. Hamburg, in turn, imagined itself to restore the liberal traditions that had been suppressed against its civic will.[3]

After the war, local newspapers annually revisited Hamburg's annihilation in the firestorm of 1943, celebrating the indestructible spirit of a population victimized by both the Nazis and the Allies. Such lore notwithstanding, the end of war was characterized by numerous continuities. A city in ruins reminded the population of the need to defer their aspirations for normality to a distant future. The struggle and strife celebrated by the Nazi regime continued through the years of occupation, only without the celebratory packaging. Even the sirens remained an integral part of life, except that they no longer signaled the approach of enemy aircraft but instead the onset of the daily curfew.[4] Hostilities had ceased but war lingered on. The city was a wasteland, essential goods remained scarce, families were torn apart, and multitudes lived in overcrowded spaces. Millions of soldiers never returned. "They stayed in the war," people would say (*Sie sind im Krieg geblieben*).

Film in postwar Germany provided an important venue for bringing the war to a close. It searched for new beginnings by fixing the past in a particular place: the rubble. Beneath the ashes and debris, the deconstructed city harbored opportunities. With support from the nascent political establishment, inner emigrants and former members of the Nazi avant-garde began to reinvent Hamburg as the center of film production in a democratic, post-fascist Germany. The cultural realm again offered a venue for the political imagination and participation of local players. The debates around *Filmstadt* Hamburg invited cultural elites and emerging political contenders to practice democracy and contest the authority of the occupiers.[5]

The continuities between the early to mid-1930s (described in Chapters 1 and 2) and the postwar era are striking. Rather than offering popular amusement, film once more entered public discourse as a cultural form that promised to bridge local idiosyncrasies and national character as a *sinngebende* (denotative) art form and an expression of a loosely defined, democratically inflected national essence. The former instrument of the Nazi war machine reprised its role as a bearer of Hamburg's national ambitions and international aspirations. Surviving in a coordinated and tightly controlled culture industry, film directors and cineastes reemerged as spokespersons for film in a new democratic era.

Film and film discourse had played a crucial role in the self-understanding and self-representation of local elites during the Nazi period. Accordingly, it is not surprising that plans—first articulated in the summer of 1941—to turn Hamburg into a film production center were revived with fervor during the occupation.[6] With the economy destroyed and the ruined harbor idle, *Filmstadt Hamburg* found support in multiple camps. In terms of personnel, Hamburg was ready to reinvent itself as Germany's new film production center. A considerable contingent of Germany's film industry had moved to Hamburg from Berlin, whose future behind the Iron Curtain remained unclear.[7] The dearth of film stock motivated producers to deal foremost with pressing social questions rather than to waste their raw materials on vacuous entertainment.[8] The British military government was positively disposed toward these ambitions. As well, a German film industry organized according to democratic principles resonated with British goals to foster an economically viable West Germany as a necessary buffer against the Communist East.[9]

In 1941 the plans for *Filmstadt Hamburg* had resonated most strongly with the Hamburg Film Consortium. By 1945 the driving force became German film VIPs living in Hamburg or Munich, restlessly waiting for better times.[10] By 1946 films were being produced, if primarily under open skies or inside a seven-by-fifteen-meter dance hall in the idyllic suburb of Ohlstedt.[11] After monetary reform provided a stable currency, Mayor Brauer approved a project proposed by ex-Tobis director Friedrich Mainz to use the former von Goltz Barracks in Rahlstedt for the location of the *Filmstadt*. Film production would bring jobs, tax revenues, and rental income. Advocates estimated that Hamburg would see an influx of DM 1.6 million annually.[12] The senate approved the DM 7 million for complete construction over the next two years.[13] But the political left shot the project down when the senate presented it to the parliament (*Bürgerschaft*) in April 1949. The ex-Tobis financier Mainz reminded the Communists too much of the earlier Hugenbergization of Ufa.[14] The political left also had different priorities for the DM 7 million earmarked for the *Filmstadt* investment, such as the intractable housing crisis.[15] Hugenbergization or not, they saw *Filmstadt* Hamburg as a prestige project that would serve the vanity of local ambition but hardly help resolve more pressing social questions.[16]

Most important, the proposed *Filmstadt* undercut a central principle of the political left because its success could be guaranteed only through a divided German state. The Christian Democrats and the Free Liberals openly admitted that "Berlin is lost anyway," but to the Social Democrats and the small Communist Party, unification of all zones remained paramount. The political left reasoned that with German unification the old Ufa facilities at Babelsberg used by the Communist-controlled DEFA would undermine the profitability of the Rahlstedt project, all while Hamburg's population continued to live in makeshift shelters.[17] After three of the allied zones formed the Federal Republic of Germany on May 23, 1949, these concerns became moot and Rahlstedt had a shot at profitability. On November 1, Hamburg's senate earmarked DM 3.5 million for construction. Around Christmas, actresses clad in fur coats and stylish gray pants, with painted lips and slim hips, brought color to the rural idyll of Rahlstedt, the home of Walter Koppel's RealFilm, the aspiring local film production company. By the end of 1949, the newspaper *Die Welt* affirmed the diligence and perseverance of the local film advocates, applauding the feat by which Hamburg "became a metropole of the German film."[18] After RealFilm's first production, *Arche Nora* (1947/48), more than ten films were launched from Hamburg's film port. The new industry drew well-known directors, actresses, and actors who eagerly awaited the opportunity to export Germany's new cinematic realism. Continuing along the path set by the Film Consortium in the early 1930s, Hamburg celebrated the former vehicle of wartime propaganda as a "medium with *völkerverbindender Mission* [a mission to promote international understanding]" in the hope of reclaiming the city's exceptional status as Germany's cosmopolitan metropole.[19]

Film proved essential not only for making Nazi Hamburg but also for dismantling it. During the 1930s Hamburg had used film and film discourse to underwrite its own National Socialist credentials with limited success. The efforts to showcase Hamburg's commitment to the National Socialist spirit throughout the 1930s succeeded only when *Grosse Freiheit Nr. 7* (Käutner, 1944) realized the ambitions that had characterized both local cineastes and the wardens of youth who feared that the licentiousness of film would lead to community collapse. Over the course of the war, the methods of discipline and order that the Hamburg administration tried to enact proved to be of little effect. In the aftermath of the 1943 firebombing, Hamburg folded in on itself. Hamburg became a Nazi city at precisely the moment that it no longer needed to convince anyone of its willingness to sacrifice itself in the name of Nazism. The year 1943 signified the ultimate sacrifice. During the postwar occupation and national reorganization, film served as a language to negotiate the unmaking of Nazis, to rehabilitate ordinary Germans, and to celebrate democracy in a collective turn that cleared away the unsavory past together with the rubble.

As I have shown in this book, Hamburg didn't turn into a Nazi city by design. Rather, its conversion came about when cultural visions and social realities upended each other, a change that was imagined, enacted, performed, and ultimately disavowed in film as in everyday life. Hamburg was never the quintessential Nazi city. The plans for *Führerstadt* Hamburg were never realized, the "Greater Hamburg Film" was never completed, and for all the posturing, St. Pauli was never revamped as "an anchor of joy." But as I hope I have demonstrated, cities are rarely quintessentially *anything*, whether modern, ordinary, or Nazi. It is precisely their cultural idiosyncrasies, their social and historical particularities, that are essential to their identities. Hamburg would not have been recognized as prototypically National Socialist by the Nazi regime, German citizens, or scholars at the time (or since). It therefore allows for a nuanced view of the processes and practices that wove National Socialism into the fabric of a particular place.

Following the collapse of the Third Reich, Hamburg tried to expunge from its history its diligent efforts to nazify itself. Its initial ambivalence toward the regime, its cosmopolitan identity, and its liberal history all served to underscore its claim of exceptional status during the Third Reich. After the war, the city's government and citizens subscribed to and eagerly perpetuated the legend that Hamburg had been destroyed by war but barely touched by Nazism, making it an obvious choice to lead a liberal, democratic, outward-looking Germany.

My discussion of Hamburg has shown that taking representations seriously is important and necessary but not sufficient for the story. Understanding what sorts of spaces Nazism produced requires a careful examination of how those representations stood in tension with local histories. This book has mapped these tensions to show how Nazism was imagined in locally specific ways, how it was performed in public discourse, and how it was written onto the urban grid by an army of enforcers and zealots who creatively welded National Socialist maxims onto local histories.

NOTES

Introduction

1. Wildt, *Hitler's Volksgemeinschaft and the Dynamics of Racial Exclusion*; Keller, *Volksgemeinschaft am Ende*; Grossbölting, *Volksgemeinschaft in der Kleinstadt*; Pine, *Hitler's "National Community."*

2. Fritzsche, *Life and Death in the Third Reich.*

3. Roseman, "National Socialism and the End of Modernity," provides a comprehensive overview of these debates and the stakes. See also Roseman, "National Socialism and Modernization"; Fritzsche, "Nazi Modern"; Dickenson, "Biopolitics, Fascism, Democracy"; Frei, "Wie modern war der Nationalismus"; Herf, *Reactionary Modernism*; Bauman, *Modernity and the Holocaust.*

4. See especially *Hamburg im "Dritten Reich"*; Ebbinghaus and Linne, *Kein Abgeschlossenes Kapitel*; Bajohr, *"Arisierung" in Hamburg.*

5. Jochmann and Loose, *Hamburg. Geschichte einer Stadt und ihrer Bewohner.*

6. See Jenkins, *Provincial Modernity.*

7. Eley, *Reshaping the German Right.*

8. Büttner, "Der Aufstieg der NSDAP."

9. Eiber, *Arbeiter und Arbeiterbewegung in der Hansestadt Hamburg in den Jahren 1929-1939.*

10. After Jörg Friedrich's controversial book *The Fire* and the ensuing focus on German suffering and victimization, it is important to highlight not just the complicity of the population at large but the participatory character of National Socialism. For an excellent overview of the public and scholarly debates that followed in the footsteps of Friedrich's original publication in German, *Der Brand*, see Moeller, *War Stories*, and Childers, "'Facilis Descensus Aveni Est': The Allied Bombing of Germany and the Issue of German Suffering."

11. Nossack, *Der Untergang.*

12. *Hamburg im "Dritten Reich,"* 191–224; Jochmann and Loose, *Hamburg. Geschichte der Stadt und ihrer Bewohner*; Ebbinghaus and Linne, *Kein Abgeschlossenes Kapitel*; Ferk, "Judenverfolgung in Norddeutschland"; McElligott, *Contested City.*

13. *Triumph des Willens* (Riefenstahl, 1935).

14. Notable exceptions are Evans, *Death in Hamburg*; Sneeringer, *A Social History of Early Rock 'n' Roll in Germany*; Wackerfuss, *Stormtrooper Families*. There is an excellent German-language literature on Hamburg. In particular, *Hamburg im Dritten Reich*; Ebbinghaus, Kaupen, and Roth, *Kein Abgeschlossenes Kapitel*; Bajohr, *Arisierung in Hamburg*; Führer, *Medienmetropole Hamburg*; Lohalm, *Die Nationalsozialistische Judenverfolgung in Hamburg.*

15. Braun, *Hitlers liebster Bürgermeister.*

16. Neil, *Haunted City.*

17. For the role of infrastructures in making and breaking cities, see Graham and Marvin, *Splintering Urbanism*.

18. In a broader sense the following historians have been crucial in shaping my approach: Fritzsche, *Life and Death in the Third Reich*; Peukert, *Inside Nazi Germany*; Mallmann and Paul, "Omniscient, Omnipotent, Omnipresent?"; Gellately, *Backing Hitler*; Bergerson, *Ordinary Germans in Extraordinary Times*; Wildt, *Volksgemeinschaft als Selbstermächtigung*. For the most useful work on Nazi film propaganda see Welch, *Propaganda and the German Cinema*. The film studies scholarship most influential for the development of my arguments are Rentschler, *The Ministry of Illusion*; Schulte-Sasse, *Entertaining the Third Reich*; Carter, *Dietrich's Ghosts*.

19. Excellent studies on individual cities include *Hamburg im "Dritten Reich"*; Bergerson, *Ordinary Germans in Extraordinary Times*; Hachtmann, *Berlin im Nationalsozialismus*.

20. Richard Sennett notes this absence and faults Hannah Arendt for celebrating the urban condition and not recognizing the violence of the Nazi crowds. Yet Sennett too refrains from integrating the Nazi city into the cannon. Sennett, "The Public Realm"; Sennett, *The Fall of Public Man*.

21. Parker, *Cities, Politics and Power*; Jaskot, *The Architecture of Oppression*.

22. Petsch, *Baukunst und Stadtplanung im Dritten Reich*; Bose et al., "Ein neues Hamburg entsteht"; Holzschuh, *Wiener Stadtplanung im Nationalsozialismus*.

23. Tonkiss, *Cities by Design*.

24. Tooze, *Wages of Destruction*

25. Diehl-Thiele. *Partei und Staat im Dritten Reich*.

26. Drawing attention to competing competencies at the highest administrative levels, Peter Hüttenberger described the Nazi State as a polycratic entity. Hüttenberger, "Nationalsozialistische Polykratie."

27. See in particular Kershaw, *The "Hitler Myth"*; Paul and Mallmann, *Die Gestapo—Mythos und Realität*.

28. Rebentisch, *Führerstaat und Verwaltung im Zweiten Weltkrieg*. Otto and Houwink ten Cate, *Das organisierte Chaos: "Ämterdarwinismus" und "Gesinnungsethik."* A notable exception that extends the investigation of systemic competition to the level of the municipal administration is Gotto, *Nationalsozialistische Kommunalpolitik*. Since the late 1960s historians have begun to fundamentally challenge Hitler's omnipotent role in the Third Reich and to deemphasize his personal intentions as providing the only valid explanation for policy and its execution. See in particular Broszat, *Der Staat Hitlers*; Mommsen, "Hitler's Stellung im nationalsozialistischen Herrschaftssystem"; Mason, "Intention and Explanation." For a definitive summary of these debates see Kershaw, "Hitler: 'Master in the Third Reich' or 'Weak Dictator'?"

29. Peter Fritzsche in *Life and Death in the Third Reich* and in *Germans into Nazis* shows how Germans integrated National Socialism into their own personal lives and details how they reasoned through dissonance that some of the regime's policies produced. Nicholas Stargardt in *The German War* underscores these processes even further by demonstrating how Germans adapted to the war and how it became an overdetermining experience, shaping how Germans understood their own crimes and how they enacted their own defeat. Detlef Peukert's *Inside Nazi Germany* serves as an excellent example of the turn away from superstructures to the everyday practices of National Socialism. Further, Mallmann and Paul, in "Omniscient, Omnipotent, Omnipresent? Gestapo, Society and Resistance," destabilize the image of the "omnipotent supermen in black" and instead argue that repression depended "upon a system of insinuation

and suspicion" of cooperation of Germans that makes the view of the Gestapo as a "foreign institution imposed upon the population" impossible. For a more comprehensive approach to popular consent see Robert Gellately, *Backing Hitler*. For an excellent review of the development and treatment of such questions see Geoff Eley's review "Hitler's Silent Majority? Conformity and Resistance under the Third Reich." Also, Connelly, "The Uses of Volksgemeinschaft," and Bergerson, *Ordinary Germans in Extraordinary Times*, are relevant here.

30. Birdsall, *Soundscapes*; Harris, *Selling Sex in the Reich*; Semmens, *Seeing Hitler's Germany: Tourism in the Reich*; Swett, *Selling Under the Swastika*; Koshar, *Travel Cultures*.

31. Harris, *Selling Sex in the Reich*, 188.

32. Herzog, *Unlearning Eugenics*; Herzog, *Sex After Fascism*.

33. Rentschler, *Ministry of Illusion*; Schulte-Sasse, *Entertaining the Third Reich*; Hake, *Popular Cinema of the Third Reich*; Hake, *German National Cinema*; Carter, *Dietrich's Ghosts*; Ascheid, *Hitler's Heroines*.

34. The magnitude of the Nazi crimes and the *Zivilisationsbruch* of Auschwitz cast questions about Nazism as questions about humanity, about progress, about modernity in general. Adorno, *The Authoritarian Personality*. Historians in contrast looked for continuities in German history that came to be known as the *Sonderweg* of Germany's path to modernity. This provided the dominant frame for understanding Nazism until the publication of Blackbourn and Eley's revision of the *Sonderweg* thesis with *The Peculiarities of German History*. Much like historians, the first work on Nazi film (published originally in 1947) sought to explain the rise of the Nazi regime as a psychosocial phenomenon. Kracauer, *From Caligari to Hitler*.

35. The earliest work in this line is Neumann, *Behemoth*. Numerous later contributions focused on the totalizing nature of the Reich. Bullock, *Hitler: A Study in Tyranny*; Fest, *Das Gesicht des Dritten Reiches*; Bracher, *Die deutsche Diktatur*.

36. See Hull, *Film in the Third Reich*; Leiser, *Nazi Cinema*; Welch, *Propaganda and the German Cinema*; Albrecht, *Der Film im Dritten Reich*; Albrecht, *Nationalsozialistische Filmpolitik*.

37. For pioneering work see Rentschler, *The Ministry of Illusion*, and Schulte-Sasse, *Entertaining the Third Reich*. Their work was in turn inspired by Witte, "Film im Nationalsozialismus." For more recent contributions to this "second wave," see Hake, *Popular Cinema in the Third Reich*; Hake, *German National Cinema*; Carter, *Dietrich's Ghosts*; Bruns, *Nazi Cinema's New Woman*; Ascheid, *Hitler's Heroines*; Reimer, *Cultural History Through a National Socialist Lens*; O'Brien, *Nazi Cinema as Enchantment*.

38. Hake, *Popular Cinema in the Third Reich*.

39. Petro, *Joyless Streets*; Hake, *German National Cinema*; Jacobson, Kaes, and Prinzler, *Die Geschichte des deutschen Films*; von Moltke, *No Place Like Home*. For attention to Nazi cinema's international continuities, see Koepnick, *The Dark Mirror*. The institutional history offered by Klaus Kreimeier, *The Ufa Story*, provides a comprehensive picture of film production in Germany.

40. Storjohann, *Hauptsache: Überleben*, 52, 59.

41. Cresswell, *Place*, 7; Lefebvre, *The Production of Space*.

42. Doreen Massey argues that space does not exist prior to identities or entities but that "the identities/entities, the relations 'between' them and the spatiality which is part of them, are all constitutive." Massey emphasizes "embedded practices" and argues that it is essential to recognize society as both temporal and spatial. Representation (visual or otherwise) generally has space-time as its object. Massey, *For Space*, 10, 27.

43. "Wochenschau und Filme," *Hamburger Zeitung*, August 11, 1943.

Chapter 1

1. Cinema was a nomadic phenomenon first before establishing itself in urban centers. As long as films were few and expensive, it was easier to exchange audiences than fare. St. Pauli's location on the urban fringe, once excluded from Hamburg proper, made for an obvious choice for the traveling exhibitors. See Stark, "Cinema, Society, and the State."

2. Töteberg and Reissmann, *Mach dir ein paar schöne Stunden,* 13–20; Töteberg, *Filmstadt Hamburg,* 12.

3. Töteberg and Reissmann, *Mach dir ein paar schöne Stunden,* 16–17.

4. Töteberg, *Filmstadt Hamburg,* 12.

5. Töteberg and Reissmann, *Mach dir ein paar schöne Stunden,* 16–17.

6. Töteberg and Reissmann, *Mach dir ein paar schöne Stunden,* 20.

7. Töteberg, *Filmstadt,* 12.

8. In the late nineteenth century, Hammerbrook and Barmbek were lightly settled districts of suburban character. By the eve of World War I, they had grown into massive settlements for the urban poor, who lived crowded together under undignified conditions. In 1914 Barmbek alone had a population of 120,000. Compare Jochmann, *Hamburg: Geschichte der Stadt und ihrer Bewohner,* 28.

9. This analysis is based on data contained in the *Kinokatalog* appended to Töteberg and Reissmann, *Mach dir ein paar schöne Stunden,* 175–293. See also Töteberg, *Filmstadt Hamburg,* 55.

10. See Töteberg and Reissmann, *Mach dir ein paar schöne Stunden,* 26–28.

11. Töteberg and Reissmann, *Mach dir ein paar schöne Stunden,* 51.

12. Schauburg Hamm, the largest of the three, had 1,520 seats; the Schauburg Hammerbrook was equipped with 1,451; and Schauburg Barmbek (replacing the Astoria Palast) in its new building provided 1,200. Compare *Kinokatalog* in Töteberg and Reissmann, *Mach dir ein paar schöne Stunden,* 175–293.

13. Töteberg, *Filmstadt Hamburg,* 57.

14. Töteberg and Reissmann, *Mach dir ein paar schöne Stunden,* 55–57. See also "Das größte Theater Europas," *Hamburger Abendblatt,* December 20, 1929; "Der Neue Ufa-Palast," *Hamburgischer Correspondent,* December 21, 1929; "Die Eröffnung des Ufa-Palasts," *Hamburger Nachrichten,* December 22, 1929; STAHH 135-1 Staatliche Pressestelle I-IV 5018. A third and much smaller player on Hamburg's film scene was Emelka, the Munich-based corporation which operated five sizable movie houses, including its flagship, the Emelka Palast, in Eimsbüttel. Compare Reissmann and Töteberg, *Mach dir ein paar schöne Stunden,* 53.

15. Schildt, "Auf Expansionskurs: Aus der Inflation in die Krise," 170–73. Kreimeier, *Ufa Story,* 146–57.

16. As of 1923 the amusement tax was imposed by municipal governments, which in light of the financial crisis sought to infuse the budget with tax increases. In Berlin, for example, a quarter of the ticket price flowed into the treasury. Amusement taxes remained high; in 1930 they were still 10.5 percent of the ticket price. See Schildt, "Auf Expansionskurs," 171; Kreimeier, *The Ufa Story,* 228; Spiker, *Film und Kapital,* 136.

17. See Hake, *German National Cinema,* 51.

18. For a history of Germany's best-known film company see Kreimeier, *The Ufa Story.*

19. After the stock market collapsed, Germany's largest production company began to agitate within SPIO (Spitzenorganisation der Deutschen Filmwirtschaft) for a reorganization of the

German film industry. SPIO, founded in 1923, essentially functioned as a film lobby. See Behn, "Gleichschritt in die 'neue Zeit,'" 340.

20. See Welch, *Propaganda and the German Cinema 1933–1945*; Hull, *Film in the Third Reich*; Stahr, *Volksgemeinschaft vor der Leinwand?*

21. *Handbuch des Films 1935/36*, 136.

22. Regarding the moratorium for cinema construction see Stahr, *Volksgemeinschaft vor der Leinwand*, 60.

23. The Reichsministerium für Volksaufklärung und Propaganda (Reich Ministry for Public Enlightenment and Propaganda, RMVP) was established on March 13, 1933, with Joseph Goebbels at its head. Reichsgesetzblatt I 104, "Erlass über die Errichtung des Reichsministeriums fuer Volksaufklärung und Propaganda," March 13, 1933. Behn, *Das Ufa-Buch*, 340.

24. See Petley, *Capital and Culture*, 51–55.

25. Reichsgesetzblatt 1933 I 82, 483, "Gesetz über die Errichtung einer vorläufigen Filmkammer," July 14, 1933.

26. Behn, 341.

27. Spiker, *Film und Kapital*, 183–87.

28. Spiker, *Film und Kapital*, 199.

29. Führer, "Guckfenster in die Welt," 65–73. The Waterloo was one of five first-run houses. Lessing Theater, Ufa-Palast, Schauburg St. Pauli, and Passage Theater were the remaining four. The minimum prices per theater and seating category were centrally regulated by the Reich's Film Chamber August 12, 1933. Compare Spiker, *Film und Kapital*, 126.

30. "Hamburg- nach Einkommen, Telefon und Kinoplaetzen," *Hamburger Anzeiger*, May 1, 1938, StAHH Gewerbepolizei GN IX F32.

31. *Handbuch des Films 1935/36*, 150, 154; Töteberg and Reissmann, *Mach dir ein paar schöne Stunden*, 168–293.

32. Stahr, *Volksgemeinschaft vor the Leinwand*, 76.

33. See *Statistisches Jahrbuch für die Hansestadt Hamburg 1937/8*, 208. The Greater-Hamburg Law of 1937 redrew the boundaries of the city. See Lohalm, "'Model Hamburg' vom Stadtstaat zum Reichsgau," 131, 140–48. See also "Begründung für gegebenenfalls Rundschreiben," December 15, 1937, StAHH 331-1 Polizeibehörde I, 108.

34. Personal interviews were particularly useful in substantiating the frequency of visits by individuals. Uwe Storjohann, in discussion with the author, September 18, 2006. Kurt Scheffer, in discussion with the author, November 28, 2006. Historians have estimated that those who did go to the movies regularly went at least once every fortnight. In Hamburg, 23 million patrons went to the movies in 1938. In 1942 the city sold 35.2 million tickets, which amounts to 20.7 tickets per inhabitant. Compare Töteberg, *Filmstadt Hamburg*, 18. Stahr maintains that in 1935–36, 36.4 percent of the adult population of Berlin went to the movies at least once a month, 13.45 percent twice a month, and 0.6 percent more than five times a month. Patronage of movie theaters was constantly on the rise since 1937. The average number of visits per Reich citizen increased from 7.6 in 1937–38 to 14.3 in 1942. Stahr, *Volksgemeinschaft*, 175.

35. Bajohr, *"Arisierung" In Hamburg*. For a concise overview of the anti-Jewish policies and their implementation in Hamburg see Bajohr, "Von der Ausgrenzung zum Massenmord," 471–518. Moreover, see Lohalm, *Die Nationalsozialistische Judenverfolgung 1933 bis 1945*.

36. Bajohr, "Von der Ausgrenzung zum Massenmord," 479. Further compare Wildt, *Volksgemeinschaft als Selbstermächtigung*; Bergerson, *Ordinary Germans in Extraordinary Times*; Kaplan, *Between Dignity and Despair*; Confino, *A World Without Jews*.

37. Geschichtswerkstatt St. Pauli. Interview Frau M.

38. Bajohr, "Von der Ausgrenzung zum Massenmord," 499–503.

39. Geschichtswerkstatt St. Pauli. Interview Frau M.

40. Bajohr, *Arisierung in Hamburg,* 15–17.

41. Since the end of the sixteenth century, Jews (Sephardic and Ashkenazi) lived in Hamburg. With the revolution of 1848, Hamburg's Jews attained equality under the law as decreed by the National Assembly in Frankfurt. The emancipation of Jews was not reversed in Hamburg after the revolution failed, and the new Hamburg constitution of 1860 guaranteed Jews full and equal political rights. In large numbers Hamburg's Jews acquired the expensive *Großbürgerrecht* (citizenship). The Hamburger upper classes nonetheless preserved a certain cultural and political distance from Jews. Emancipation facilitated assimilation; the comparably high numbers of mixed marriages in Hamburg is indicative. Hamburg's Jews were predominantly secular. According to a 1927 statistic, of the approximately 20,000 Jews in Hamburg only about 2,800 belonged to Jewish cultural organizations, only 8,000 were part of the German-Israeli community, and only about 1,700 belonged to the association of orthodox Jews in Hamburg. Jews in Hamburg in general were better educated, had higher incomes, and had lower birthrates than the average population in the city. By the turn of the twentieth century, most had left their residences in the Altstadt and Neustadt behind and moved into the posh upper-class districts of Harvestehude and Rotherbaum. Compare Marwedel, *Geschichte der Juden in Hamburg, Altona und Wandsbek*; Herzig and Rohde, *Die Juden in Hamburg 1590–1990*; Krohn, *Die Juden in Hamburg*.

42. Töteberg and Reissmann, 67–70. See also Keller, "Kino Unterm Hakenkreuz," 74–75. For the policies of aryanization in Hamburg see Bajohr, *"Arisierung" In Hamburg*.

43. Töteberg and Reissmann, 67–70.

44. Spiker, *Film und Kapital,* 165–82. For Ufa's nationalization see Kreimeier, *The Ufa Story*, 300.

45. Töteberg and Reismann, *Mach dir ein par schöne Stunden,* 67–70.

46. For the exodus of filmmakers and artists see Brook, *Driven to Darkness*; Wallace, *Exiles in Hollywood*; Koepnick, *The Dark Mirror*; Phillips, *Exiles in Hollywood*.

47. For an excellent overview of the social stratification of Hamburg see Evans, *Death in Hamburg*, in particular, 54–108.

48. Sneeringer, "'Assembly Line of Joys'"; Sneeringer, *A Social History of Early Rock 'n' Roll in Germany*; Manos, *Sankt Pauli*; Barth, *Die Reeperbahn*.

49. Weinhauer, "Handelskrise und Rüstungsboom. Die Wirtschaft," 200. Moreover, see Büttner, *Hamburg in der Staats- und Wirtschaftskrise*.

50. See Jochmann, *Hamburg*; Führer, "Meister der Ankündigung," 432–44. Further, Andreas Walther, *Neue Wege zur Großstadtsanierung*.

51. On prostitution see Harris, *Selling Sex in the Reich*; Herzog, *Sexuality and German Fascism*; Herzog, *Sex after Fascism*; Roos, "Backlash Against Prostitutes' Rights."

52. Semmens, *Seeing in Hitler's Germany*; Baranowski, *Strength Through Joy*; Spode, "Arbeiterurlaub im Dritten Reich."

53. StAHH 135-1 Staatliche Pressestelle I-IV 2077. "St. Pauli wehrt sich gegen seinen Ruf," *Deutsche Allgemeine Zeitung*, May, 25 1935.

54. The consortium's history unfortunately cannot be reconstructed beyond the traces the institution left in the local press, since records regarding its foundations and activities no longer exist. For the plans to beautify St. Pauli, see Johannes Häfker to Mayor Krogmann, January 17, 1938, StAHH 135-1 Staatliche Pressestelle I-IV 2077.

55. See in particular ". . . auf der Reeperbahn, nachts um halb eins," *Hamburger Fremden-blatt,* July 18, 1939, and an impressive number of press reports on the transformation of what was often derogatorily referred to as "St. Slovenly" into "an anchor of joy." Especially, "St. Pauli wehrt sich gegen seinen Ruf," *Deutsche Allgmeine Zeitung,* May 25, 1935, in StAHH 135-1 Staat-liche Pressestelle I-IV 2077.

56. Verschönerung von St. Pauli. Anhang an Schreiben von Johannes Häfker an Mayor Krogmann, January 17, 1938, StAHH 135-1 Staatliche Pressestelle I-IV 2077.

57. See "Das Vergnügungsviertel im neuen Hamburg. Künftiges St. Pauli—schöner als Montmartre," *Hamburger Anzeiger,* March 3, 1939. See also ". . . auf der Reeperbahn, nachts um halb eins," *Hamburger Fremdenblatt,* July 18, 1939, which reports that every establishment will be a sensation. The article further assures readers that even though an amusement district is no finishing school, and certainly nobody here is prudish, certain boundaries of decency and morality will have to be respected. StAHH 135-1 Staatliche Pressestelle I-IV, 2077.

58. StAHH 135-1 Staatliche Pressestelle I-IV, 2077.

59. StAHH 135-1 Staatliche Pressestelle I-IV, 7415. "Bierstreik Hamburg?" *Hamburger 8 Uhr Abendblatt* (February 8, 1932).

60. StAHH 135-1 Staatliche Pressestelle I-IV, 2088.

61. StAHH 135-1 Staatliche Pressestelle I-IV, 2077.

62. See Deutscher Organisationsausschuß des Weltkongresses für Freizeit und Erholung. "Geleitwort des Regierenden Bürgermeisters, Krogmann," 1936.

63. For housing shortages in Hamburg and the Reich see Führer, "Die Machtlosigkeit des 'Maßnahmestaats,'" and Harlander, *Zwischen Heimstätte und Wohnmaschine.*

64. "Die Anpassung and den Publikumsgeschmack Filmschaffende dürfen Kunst nicht mit Künstlichkeit verwechseln," *Film-Kurier,* December 15, 1938.

65. "Ansprache des Reichsministers Dr. Goebbels," *Dokumente der deutschen Politik,* 258–66.

66. "Eine Gegenüberstellung: So war es gestern—und so ist es heute," *Film-Kurier,* April 6, 1938.

67. See "Junge Filmziele," *Hamburger Fremdenblatt,* October 7, 1937.

68. "Der Weg des Films im neuen Reich," *Hamburger Anzeiger,* March 28, 1936.

69. "Junge Filmziele," *Hamburger Fremdenblatt,* October 7, 1937.

70. "Der Weg des Films im neuen Reich," *Hamburger Anzeiger,* March 28, 1936.

71. Ritzheimer, *"Trash," Censorship, and National Identity in Early Twentieth-Century Germany.*

72. "Der Weg des Films im neuen Reich," *Hamburger Anzeiger,* March 28, 1936.

73. "Kein Jude im deutschen Film," *Kölnische Zeitung,* July 26, 1936.

74. "Eine Gegenüberstellung," *Film-Kurier,* April 6, 1938.

75. "Die Anpassung and den Publikumsgeschmack: Filmschaffende dürfen Kunst nicht mit Künstlichkeit verwechseln," *Film-Kurier,* December 15, 1938.

76. "Was will das Publikum auf der Leinwand sehen?," *Film-Kurier,* September 24, 1938.

77. "Die Aufgaben der Avantguard," *Film-Kurier,* December 13, 1938. Emphasis mine.

78. "Deutscher Film dein Feld ist die Welt," *Film-Kurier,* March 13, 1939.

79. Witte, "Film Im Nationalsozialismus: Blendung und Überblendung"; Witte "The Indivisible Legacy of Nazi Cinema"; Rentschler, *Ministry of Illusion;* Reimer, *Cultural History Through a National Socialist Lens.*

80. On the *Jugendfilmstunden* see Welch, *Propaganda and the German Cinema,* 27.

81. Welch, *Propaganda and the German Cinema*, 27.

82. "Filmpublikum Jugend," *Film-Kurier*, November 9, 1938. See also "Jugend wandelt Filmgeschmack," *Hamburger Nachrichten*, October 10, 1937.

83. "Hamburger Jugendfilmstunden beginnen," *Film-Kurier*, October 7, 1938.

84. "Hamburger Jugendfilmstunden beginnen."

85. "Filmpublikum Jugend," *Film-Kurier*, November 9 1938.

86. "Filmpublikum Jugend."

87. "Jugend wandelt Filmgeschmack," *Hamburger Nachrichten*, October 6, 1937.

88. Film als objective Geschichtsschreibung," *Hamburger Tageblatt*, October 5 1937. "Junge Filmziele," *Hamburger Fremdenblatt*, October 7, 1937.

89. "Besuch nicht jugendfreier Filme durch Jugendliche," *Film-Kurier*, February 1, 1939; "Die Aufgaben der Avantguard," *Film-Kurier*, December 13, 1938.

90. "Film als objektive Geschichtsschreibung," *Hamburger Tageblatt*, October 5, 1937. "Junge Filmziele," *Hamburger Fremdenblatt*, October 7, 1937.

91. "Ein Film-Volkstag: Beim Internationalen Filmkongreß," *Film-Kurier*, March 27, 1935. The *Filmvolkstag* did not take place in 1936, since free screenings had already been orchestrated by the Winter Relief Works. See Choy, "Inszenierung der *völkischen* Filmkultur im Nationalsozialismus," 218.

92. "Auch in Hamburg alle Theater gut besucht," *Film-Kurier*, February 28, 1938. Also compare Choy, "Inszenierung der *völkischen* Filmkultur im Nationalsozialismus," 127.

93. "Richtlinien für die Durchführung des Filmvolkstages am Sonntag den 5. März 1939," *Film-Kurier*, February 15, 1939. In 1935, Berlin audiences gained entrance for 10 Pfennigs, whereas everywhere else the token admission amounted to 20 Pfennigs. As of 1938 the *Filmvolkstag* offered admission at 10 Pfennigs throughout the Reich. Compare Choy, "Inszenierung der *völkischen* Filmkultur im Nationalsozialismus," 227.

94. "Filmvolkstag. Überall überfüllte Theater," *Film-Kurier*, February 28, 1938. "Richtlinien für die Durchführung des Filmvolkstages," *Film-Kurier*, February 15, 1939. Rather than ensuring the profitability of local movie houses, the *Filmvolkstag* was a gigantic advertisement campaign for a new consumer product: Nazi film. In the end, the *Filmvolkstag* was financed by participating theaters that were thought to benefit most dramatically from increases in new regulars the *Filmvolkstag* promised to recruit. Yet the Nazi state was quite effective in distributing cost down to individual businesses. Sunday already was the Reich's cinema day par excellence as most patrons went to the movies when they neither could run errands nor had to go to work. The suspension of the regular programming, for which the theater had already paid and promoted, to screen one of last year's favorites did not cogently promise an increase in revenues for individual theaters.

95. Compare "Filmvolkstag: Überall überfüllte Theater" and "Auch in Hamburg alle Theater gut besucht," *Film-Kurier*, February 28, 1938.

96. Geschichtswerkstatt St. Pauli. Interview Frau M.

97. Uwe Storjohann, in discussion with author, September 18, 2006.

98. Uwe Storjohann, in discussion with author, September 18, 2006.

Chapter 2

1. This untranslatable term suggests a mixture of self-reliance, inadvertent obstinacy, and inborn, immutable, and unique qualities of a person, thing, or place. For an original application of *Eigenart* as a theoretical category in an empirical study see Canning, *Languages of Labor and Gender*.

2. For a detailed study on municipal administration in the Third Reich see Gotto, *National-sozialistische Kommunalpolitik*. Also Matzerath, *Nationalsozialismus und kommunale*; Rebentisch, *Führerstaat und Verwaltung im Zweiten Weltkrieg*. For the dissolution of municipal political competencies and an atomization of the administrative apparatus see Noakes, "Oberbürger-meister und Gauleiter"; Fröhlich, "Die Partei auf lokaler Ebene"; Hüttenberger, "Interessenver-tretung und Lobbyismus im Dritten Reich."

3. For the politics of *Gleichschaltung* in Hamburg see Lohalm, "Modell Hamburg."

4. In his speech at the occasion of the inauguration of the Reich Culture Chamber (RKK) Goebbels described the National Socialist revolution as one from below, a process of the genesis of *Volk* out of the German nation, emphasizing the role of art and culture in this particular process as food for the soul of the folk. Compare Goebbels, "Die deutsche Kultur vor Neuen Aufgaben," 131–41.

5. The concept of *"Polykratie"* was first developed as an interpretive tool by Peter Hütten-berger in response to interpretations that the Hitler state appears as the ultimate realization of totalitarianism, with total concentration of power in the hands of the Führer. Instead Hütten-berger argued that "the chaos of competences in the Third Reich cannot solely be explained with the hyper-Machiavellian politics of Hitler, but must be seen as the result of the constant penetration attempts, differentiations, and compromises between individual hegemonic agents." Hüttenberger, "Nationalsozialistische Polykratie," 442. Historians have generally accepted that competing institutions and individuals constituted fluctuating power centers within the Reich that competed with each other over Hitler's favor rather than with Hitler himself. Kershaw's notion of "working toward the Führer" is particularly useful here. Kershaw, "'Working Towards the Führer;" Kershaw, *The "Hitler Myth"*; Kershaw, *Hitler*.

6. Since the film failed to go into production it lacked a firm title. Proposals by film produc-tion companies suggested "Hamburg: Deutschland's Tor zur Welt," "Hamburg von Gestern, Ham-burg von Heute, Hamburg von Morgen," and "Wandlungen einer Stadt," but the final manuscript remained without a title. To underline the self-aggrandizing ambitions of the administration, I am referring to the manuscript discussed as "the Greater-Hamburg Film." For these discussions as well as individual film proposals see StAHH 135-1 Staatliche Pressestelle I-IV 2074.

7. See Neale, "Melodrama and Tears."

8. On the *Heimat* film genre see von Moltke, *No Place Like Home*.

9. It should be noted that usage of the term avant-garde in the context of Nazi film reflects the self-understanding of what film ideologues identified as the New German Film. Conceived in direct opposition to Weimar avant-garde filmmaking, a National Socialist avant-garde, Goeb-bels hoped, would lead cultural production to ideologically compatible and artistically compel-ling heights. National Socialist avant-garde was thought to be at the forefront of expressing the nature of the *Volk* by the use of modern technologies for the great masses in an elating, instruc-tive, and artistically pleasing fashion. It remains doubtful that Goebbels himself had any clear expectations of what this avant-garde culture would look like and hence the term was infused with the various interpretations depending on who was using it. Compare Fulks, "Film Culture and *Kulturfilm*: Ruttmann, the Avant-Garde, and the *Kulturfilm* in Weimar Germany and the Third Reich."

10. Spiker, *Film und Kapital*, 183–87, 199.

11. Spiker, 8.

12. Auszug aus der Niederschrift der Verwaltungsberatung, June 9, 1937. StAHH 135-1 Staatliche Pressestelle I-IV 2074.

13. Lohalm, "'Modell Hamburg,'" 131.

14. On February 2, 1936, the Hamburg-based Kosmos-Film approached Kaufmann and offered its services, invoking discussion concerning the making of a large-scale Hamburg film that had been "going on for a fairly long time." Kosmos-Film to Karl Kaufmann, February 2, 1936, StAHH 135-1 Staatliche Pressestelle I-IV 2074.

15. See, for example, the letter from Skalden Film to Mayor Krogmann asking the city to contribute between 20,000 and 25,000 Reichsmarks in the event that Skalden Film would be entrusted with the production of the Hamburg Film. Skalden Film to Carl Vincent Krogmann, April 28, 1936, StAHH 135-1 Staatliche Pressestelle I-IV 2074.

16. The world congress for leisure and recreation took place in Hamburg in 1937. See *Bericht: Weltkongress für Freizeit und Erholung*.

17. NS institutions such as the official leisure organization *Kraft durch Freude* continuously linked productivity and recreation. See Baranowski, *Strength Through Joy*.

18. See Anlage der Einladung zur Besprechung über den geplanten Film zur Veranschaulichung der Entwicklung Hamburg seit der Machtübernahme von Senator von Allwörden im Auftrag von Governor Kaufmann an diverse behördlichen Stellen, October 25, 1937, StAHH 135-1 Staatliche Pressestellee I-IV 2074.

19. Film companies vying for business did not hesitate to point out that they were already preparing cinematic treatments for other cities. The Berlin-based Infra-Film, for example, pointed out to Otto Hermann that they were currently working on a project entitled "München— gestern, heute, morgen." See Schreiben an die Bildstelle Hansa, February 12, 1938, StAHH 135-1 Staatliche Pressestelle I-IV 2074.

20. See Goergen, "Städtebilder zwischen Heimattümelei und Urbanität," 324–25. Compare also www.filmportal.de, "a free-of-charge internet platform for reliable, in-depth information on German cinema."

21. For a detailed study on the person and responsibilities of governor Karl Kaufmann see Bajohr, "Gaulleiter in Hamburg."

22. Walther Günthers listed 526 films specifically focused on cities or towns in his 1926 catalogue of educational and cultural documentaries. But of those city films, only 25 were recognized as educational and hence, so Jeanpaul Goergen suggests that most of these films did not circulate widely. See Goergen, "Urbanität und Idylle," 152.

23. See Ehmann, "Wie Wirklichkeit erzählen? Methoden des Querschnittfilms," 578. In contrast see Fulks, "Film Culture and *Kulturfilm*," 202. Fulks identifies the film as a prototypical *Industriefilm* rather than a city portrait.

24. Hake, "Urban Spectacle in Walter Ruttmann's *Berlin, Symphony of the Big City*."

25. Goergen, "Urbanität und Idylle." Goergen argues that films depicting cityscapes or landscapes were meant to foster knowledge of and love for the homeland and its idiosyncrasies (151). Between 1933 and 1945 the cultural film production of Ufa delivered only twenty-one city-portrait films, almost all of which were made between 1934 and 1939. See also Goergen, "Städtebilder zwischen Heimattümelei und Urbanität," 324–25.

26. Since 1934, the Reichsfilmkammer made it mandatory for all members who publicly screened feature films to include a *Kulturfilm* with a length of at least 250 meters. In addition, it was required that the respective *Kulturfilm* received one of the following four commendations: artistically, educationally (*volksbildend*), culturally, or state-politically valuable. See Zimmermann, "Der Propaganda-, Kontroll- und Lenkungsapparat," 77.

27. Goergen also illustrates that many city portrait films were films produced on commission of the German *Fremdenverkehrsvereins* and were expected to serve its advancement. See

Goergen," "Urbanität und Idylle," 151. Even Ruttmann continued to produce city-portrait films during the Third Reich in "cinematic tributes to Düsseldorf (1935), Stuttgart (1935), and Hamburg (1938)," but these later compositions never attained the quality of *Berlin*. Fulks, "Film Culture and *Kulturfilm*," 218–19.

28. Fulks claims that the genre of the *Kulturfilm* functioned as a "vessel for that aestheticization of reality constitutive of National Socialism and the repository of what can only be termed a Nazi avant-garde." See Fulks, "Film Culture and *Kulturfilm*," 2. However, National Socialist ideologues would not content themselves with reflections of reality but aspired to utilize the potential of the medium in ways to create a visual alternative that was then to be taken for the reality it supposedly represented.

29. Tooze, *Wages of Destruction*, 222.

30. *Lebensfreude* translates as "groove" or "zest for life."

31. Töteberg, *Filmstadt Hamburg*, 17.

32. See ". . . auf der Reeperbahn nachts um halb eins," *Norddeutsche Nachrichten*, July 18, 1939. The paper reports on Mayor Krogmann's personal investment in returning St. Pauli to some *Ur-status* by restoring the lost romantic that presumably resulted from the particular mix of "*Sehnsucht der Fremden nach fernen Ländern und Meeren*" (longing for foreign country and seas) and beautiful establishments that were, without any uniformity, "artistically beautiful and snug [*künstlerisch schön und anheimelnd*]."

33. For example, the mayor of Wandsbek, Friedrich Ziegler, suggested the inclusion of visual materials from "'the-world-renowned,' the most significant carnival event in Greater Hamburg," as well as the images from the *Sonnabendmarkt* (Saturday night market) with its "life and ado between 11 and 12 o'clock." Oberbürgermeister Ziegler to die Landsbildstelle Hansa, November 23, 1937, StAHH 135-1 Staatliche Pressestelle I-IV 2074. It should be noted, however, that the predominantly protestant Hamburg, unlike Cologne or Mainz, was hardly known for partaking in the Catholic tradition of celebrating carnival.

34. Bajohr, "Die Zustimmungsdiktatur."

35. While national unemployment had been reduced by 57 percent, Hamburg's reductions were far less and also were well below that of other port cities, such as Bremen and Kiel. Wulff, *Arbeitslosigkeit und Arbeitsbeschaffungsmassnahmen in Hamburg*, 96, 145. By the end of 1934, regional statistics still listed 111,872 individuals as unemployed according to the National Socialist publication *Statistisches Jahrbuch für die Freie und Hansestadt Hamburg 1934/35*, 166–67.

36. Compare Wulff, *Arbeitslosigkeit und Arbeitsbeschaffungsmassnahmen in Hamburg 1933-1939*, 158. See also *Statistisches Jahrbuch für die Freie und Hansestadt Hamburg, 1934/35*, 156–58.

37. See Klaus Weinhauer, "Handelskriese und Rüstungsboom: Die Wirtschaft," in *Hamburg im "Dritten Reich*," 203.

38. See Büttner, "Der Aufstieg der NSDAP," 28.

39. Weinhauer, "Handelskriese und Rüstungsboom: Die Wirtschaft," 203.

40. Weinhauer, 202.

41. Weinhauer, 200.

42. Tiess, "Nationalsozialistische Städteplanung: 'Die Führerstädte;'" Bose et al. '. . . *Ein Neues Hamburg Entsteht*,' 20–29; Diefenbach, "Konstanty Gutschow and the Reconstruction of Hamburg"; Necker, *Konstanty Gutschow*.

43. See Bajohr, "Zustimmungsdiktatur," 94–99.

44. See Einladung zur Besprechung über den geplanten Film zur Veranschaulichung der Entwicklung Hamburgs seit der Machtübernahme von Senator von Allwörden im Auftrag von

Gauleiter Kaufmann an diversen behördlichen Stellen, October 25, 1937, StAHH 135-1 Staatliche Pressestlee I-IV 2074.

45. Niederschrift über eine 1. Besprechung mit den Behörden und gemischten wirtschaftlichen Betrieben, betreffend einen Film über die Entwicklung Hamburgs seit der Machtübernahme, am 11. November im Pönix-Saal des Rathauses unter Vorsitz von Senator von Allwörden, November 16, 1937, StAHH 135-1 Staatliche Pressestelle I-IV 2074.

46. Rundschreiben V 5572 des Reichsministers für Volksaufklärung und Propaganda, August 28, 1936, StAHH 135-1 Staatliche Pressestelle I-IV, 2074. It is especially interesting that it was only deemed necessary to inform the bigger cities of the stipulations contained in the circular. See letter of the Reich's Minister for Internal Affairs to all governors, regional administrations, the Reich commissioner for the Saarland, and the government presidents (Oberpräsident und Regierungspräsidenten) in Prussia, October 11, 1936, StAHH 135-1 Staatliche Pressestelle I-IV 2074.

47. Rundschreiben V 5572 des Reichsministers fuer Volksaufklärung und Propaganda, August 28, 1936, StAHH 135-1 Staatliche Pressestelle I-IV 2074.

48. Goebbels curtailed the right of cities to document their own history in film and instead reserved that right for national organs, even though *Kulturfilm*, unlike feature film, did not have to go through the process of obtaining prior approval for film projects. Zimmermann, "Sukzessive Verstaatlichung der Filmindustrie und Entwicklung der Kulturfilm-Produktion," 98. See Bock and Töteberg, *Das Ufa-Buch*.

49. See "Reichsfilmkammer unter Carl Froelich," *Berliner Börsen-Zeitung*, July 1, 1939, in FZH 360. The article illustrates the shift from an economic focus to artistic considerations as tied to the Reich Film Chamber President Oswald Lehnich and his replacement, Carl Froelich.

50. Johannes Eckart explained that "the cultural documentary had the explicit intent to bring valuable instruction and education to the viewer, a tendency which quite naturally contributed to its unpopularity with audiences. Only the filmmaking of the Third Reich succeeded in distancing the cultural documentary from all explicit instruction and strictly separated it from educational film." See "Weltumspannende Kulturfilmarbeit," *Hamburger Nachrichten*, October 7, 1937, StAHH 135-1 Staatliche Pressestelle I-IV 5002.

51. *Ein Mädel von der Reeperbahn* illustrates the presumed danger St. Pauli women pose to society. Stranded after a shipwreck and saved by the lighthouse keeper, the sexy Reeperbahn lass soon represents a formidable threat to the marriage of the lighthouse keeper, who cannot resist her charms. Hochbaum's *Razzia in St. Pauli* centers on the life of a St. Pauli prostitute who falls for the criminal fugitive who promises her a better life. She plans to leave her friend, a local musician, but comes to her senses after the police arrest the fugitive.

52. While the city administration discussed the production of a large-scale, feature-length testimony to the Nazi transformation, three advertisement films about Hamburg were actually made and circulated. On November 12, 1936, *Hamburg und seine Nachbarstadt Altona*, a production of Fremdenverkehrsverein Hamburg e.V, premiered at the Passage Theater. *Das Schöne Hamburg* and *Das schaffende Hamburg*, allegedly screened eight thousand times, were credited with increasing tourism significantly. See "Hebung des Verkehrs in St. Pauli," *Hamburger Tageblatt*, October 12, 1937. In addition, the Consortium St. Pauli-Freiheit planned the production of a specific advertisement film about St. Pauli and its pulsating nightlife. Compare "St. Pauli voran," *Hamburger Fremdenblatt*, October 12, 1937, StAHH 135-1 Staatliche Pressestelle I-IV 2077. See also correspondence between the Hamburg administration and the production company Bundes Film based in Berlin. On April 25, 1938, Bundes Film contacted civil servant Paul Lindemann with

the proposal to produce the advertisement film *Hamburg bei Nacht*. In a second letter, dated May 5, 1938, the company explains that the film will present in hitherto unseen dialogues and images the life (*Eigenleben*) of world port city Hamburg with its international tourism, whose pulsating life is bound to neither time nor light of day. StAHH 135-1 Staatliche Pressestelle I-IV 2077.

53. Bajohr, "Gauleiter in Hamburg," 273.

54. Finanzverwaltung to Karl Kaufmann, November 16, 1934, StAHH 131-4 Senatskanzelei Präsidialabteilung 1934 A90. The letter identifies the film fund of the office of the state (425 RM), the beautification fund (39,549 RM), and the specialty fund (14,669.21 RM) as irreproachable since derived from the sale of *staatsfeindlichen Vermögens* (property of those hostile to the state). Kaufmann was adamant to coordinate the numerous specialty funds of individual senators and bring them under his personal control to enlarge his patronage system. With the establishment of the Hamburger Stiftung (Hamburg Foundation) in 1937, Kaufmann created a fiscal system that was completely independent from the municipal and national budgets. Kaufmann cultivated a system of centralized protectionism that ensured him a cadre of loyal supporters within the administration and beyond. By the end of the war the Stiftung still recorded an account balance of close to 3.2 million Reichsmarks. See balance of "Hamburger Stiftung von 1937," end of March, 1945, April 23, 1945. StAHH 614-2-13 Hamburger Stiftung 1937, 7. Also see Bajohr, "Gauleiter in Hamburg," 279.

55. See "Der Präsident der Reichsfilmkammer über die Aufgaben des Deutschen Films," *Völkischer Beobachter* (Berlin), October 27, 1935, and "Weiter aufwärts mit dem Film," *Film Kurier,* March 4, 1938. Reichminister Goebbels is quoted on establishing "the primacy of art" as the transforming factor in the film industry since 1933.

56. Scholars stressing the power of the Propaganda Ministry, the RFK, and Joseph Goebbels in determining the course of film in the Reich include Albrecht, *Nationalsozialistische Filmpolitik*; Giessen, *Nazi Propaganda Films*; Hoffmann, *The Triumph of Propaganda*; Hull, *Film in the Third Reich*; Leiser, *Deutschland Erwache! Propaganda im Film des Dritten Reichs*; Taylor, *Film Propaganda: Soviet Russia and Nazi Germany*; Welch, *The Third Reich: Politics and Propaganda.*

57. See "Der Präsident der Reichsfilmkammer über die Aufgaben des deutschen Films," *Völkischer Beobachter* (Berlin), October 27, 1935, in FZH 360.

58. Lehnich demanded that "in full consideration of film economic matters, there must be found a new form of film that reflects our [German] nature and spiritual proclivities." In "Der Präsident der Reichsfilmkammer" in FZH 360.

59. Hermann Grieving, Ufa, to Carl Vincent Krogmann, January 7, 1938; C. M. Köhn (Goebbels's liaison to Ufa) to Karl Kaufmann, May 21, 1938, StAHH 135-1 Staatliche Pressestelle I-IV 2074.

60. Bajohr, "Gauleiter in Hamburg," 281. Here Bajohr demonstrates that Kaufmann was so overwhelmed that he tended to throw out letters, correspondence, and other written materials that extended beyond two pages without reading them at all.

61. Bajohr, "Gauleiter," 281.

62. Epoche Gasparcolor Film to Karl Kaufmann, April 12, 1939, StAHH 135-1 Staatliche Pressestelle I-IV 2074.

63. Bose et al., '. . . *Ein Neues Hamburg Entsteht,*' 20–29. In July 1939, after fierce competition, Hitler chose Konstanty Gutschow as the official architect for the reconstruction of the Elbe riverfront and surrounding quarters in St. Pauli.

64. Werner Kark, "Zum ersten Mal: Hamburg im Spielfilm," *Hamburger Tageblatt,* March 10, 1938. For the original proposal for a Hamburg film by Jam Borgestädt, which set

Gauleiter Kaufmann and the mills of the Hamburg administration in motion, see the letter concerning Hamburg-Film, February 2, 1936, StAHH 135-1 Staatliche Pressestelle I-IV 2074.

65. "Hamburg-Dein Film ist da. Hochbaum kehrt zum Experiment zurück," *Hamburger Tageblatt*, September 24, 1938, StAHH 135-1 Staatliche Pressestelle I-IV 5012.

66. In her biography on Arthur Greiser, *Model Nazi,* Epstein describes the model Nazi as one who was "tough, radical, and brooked no compromise" (8). For biographical information on Hochbaum see "Werner Hochbaum," in Bock, *CineGraph*; Holba, "The Enigma of Werner Hochbaum," 99; and Kreimeier, *The Ufa-Story*, 336. Other Hochbaum films include *Razzia in St. Pauli* (1932), *Morgen beginnt das Leben* (1933), *Die Ewige Makse* (1934), *Vorstadtvarieté* (1934), *Schatten der Vergangenheit* (1936), and *Drei Unteroffiziere* (1938/39).

67. Frank S. Nugent, "'The Eternal Mask,' a Drama of Psychoanalysis Opens at the Filmarte—'Hideaway Girl' at the Rialto," *New York Times,* January 13, 1937. The reviewer lauded the film as an "uncommon and an uncommonly fine picture" and exclaimed "it is so seldom that the cinema casts aside its romantic clichés for its proper mantle as an individual art form that this Swiss picture catches us with our guard down and our critical vocabulary rusted. Ordinary superlatives would be ridiculous, comparisons are impossible and that invidious epithet "unique" would not do justice to the occasion."

68. "Werner Hochbaum sprach über den Film," *Hamburger Nachrichten,* September 30, 1938.

69. While Ufa, Terra, Tobis, and Bavaria productions were generally featured in generous advertisement placements in local newspapers and the *Film-Kurier,* the local efforts to promote *Ein Mädchen* went far beyond such standard efforts. In fact, Ufa's advertisement placement was not unusually aggressive, and in contrast to films featuring popular stars the national campaign for *Ein Mädchen* appears rather timid.

70. "Glanzvoller Start in Hamburg: 'Ein Mädchen geht an Land,'" *Film-Kurier,* October 1, 1938.

71. The Lessing Theater was one of the older bourgeois theaters in the inner city on Gänsemarkt and generally the Ufa theater of choice for *Prädikatsfilme* and more explicitly artistic fare. The flagship Ufa-Palast, with more than two thousand seats, generally hosted the premieres of more consumerist and sensationalist films that promised to draw large audiences. Compare Töteberg and Reissmann, *Mach dir ein paar Schöne Stunden,* 223.

72. See "Glanzvoller Start in Hamburg: 'Ein Mädchen geht an Land,'" *Film-Kurier*, October 1, 1938.

73. See "Werner Hochbaum sprach über den Film," *Hamburger Nachrichten*, September 30, 1938.

74. See "Ein glanzvoller Start in Hamburg," *Film-Kurier,* October 1, 1938.

75. See "Der Film von Morgen," *Film-Kurier,* February 22, 1938.

76. Compare "Was will das Publikum auf der Leinwand sehen?," *Film-Kurier,* September 24, 1938.

77. "Erster Vorstoß": ein Mädchen geht an Land," *Hamburger Tageblatt,* October 1, 1938; "Glanzvoller Start in Hamburg: 'Ein Mädchen geht an Land,'" *Film-Kurier,* October 1, 1938.

78. "Die vier Gesellen: festlicher start in Hamburg," *Film-Kurier,* October 3, 1938.

79. See "Hamburg-Dein Film ist da," *Hamburger Tageblatt,* September 24, 1938.

80. Kark, "Zum ersten Mal,"*Hamburger Tageblatt,* March 10, 1938.

81. Kark, "Zum ersten Mal," *Hamburger Tageblatt,* March 10, 1938

82. "Der August in Hamburg," *Film-Kurier,* September 16, 1938.

83. "Der August in Hamburg," *Film-Kurier,* September 16, 1938.

84. "'Erster Vorstoß': ein Mädchen geht an Land," *Hamburger Tageblatt,* October 1, 1938; "Glanzvoller Start in Hamburg: 'Ein Mädchen geht an Land,'" *Film-Kurier,* October 1938.

85. Roschlau, "Ein Mädchen geht an Land," 113.

86. See "'Erster Vorstoß': ein Mädchen geht an Land," *Hamburger Tageblatt,* October 1, 1938; "Glanzvoller Start in Hamburg: 'Ein Mädchen geht an Land,'" *Film-Kurier,* October 1, 1938.

87. Compare the classified ads in *Hamburger Tagblatt* for October and November 1938. For example, at the Schauburg Ham and the Schauburg City, the film played for three days, and nowhere was it prolonged beyond a first week since it was discontinued in the Lessing Theater. In contrast, *Liebe* was prolonged for another week at the Atrium Theater, and since hundreds could not be admitted, the Münzburg Theater added a third and a fourth special screening.

88. "'Hamburger Arbeitsgemeinschaft Film:' Eine Bilanz des guten Willens-Zugleich ein Beitrag zum Thema Filmkulturpropaganda im Reich," *Film-Kurier* Beiblatt, July 2, 1938. See also "Neuaufbau des deutschen Film," *Hamburger Tageblatt,* March 26, 1936. As part of the economic recovery of the German film industry, the *Hamburger Tageblatt* notes the founding of a new organization—the Arbeitsgemeinschaft Film (Film Consortium). Werner Kark was the editor of the party organ *Hamburger Tageblatt,* which since January 1931 was the official party newspaper in the city. Führer, *Medienmetropole Hamburg.*

89. At the national level such consortia include the Reich's Arbeitsgemeinschaft für Raumplanung and the Reichsarbeitsgemeinschaft für Jugendbetreuung. In Hamburg, the Arbeitgemeinschaft St. Pauli-Freiheit, the Arbeitsgemeinschaft Film, and the Arbeitsgemeinschaft für Jugendschutz im Kriege were very different from one another in terms of both purpose and compostion. The Arbeitsgemeinschaft Film seems to have been relatively independent of official government structures. Even though members of the Arbeitsgemeinschaft were party functionaries in St. Pauli, they didn't seem to carry much political weight when it came to the administration. How these bodies functioned as part of the political apparatus remains unclear, as they have not yet received sustained attention from historians.

90. For the history on the Waterloo, see Führer, "Guckfenster in die Welt," 65–73.

91. Führer, "Guckfenster in die Welt," 65–73.

92. Compare "Weiter aufwärts mit dem Film," *Film-Kurier,* March 4, 1938.

93. "Liebeneiner sprach in Hamburg; Durchdrinunge der Materie und Klarheit des Ziels," *Film-Kurier,* November 7, 1938.

94. "Dr. Eckardt in Hamburg: Die Aufgaben der Avantgarde," *Film-Kurier,* December 13, 1938.

95. "Dr. Eckardt in Hamburg: Die Aufgaben der Avantgarde," *Film-Kurier,* December 13, 1938.

96. "Dr. Eckardt in Hamburg: Die Aufgaben der Avantgarde," *Film-Kurier,* December 13, 1938.

97. "Dr. Eckardt in Hamburg: Die Aufgaben der Avantgarde," *Film-Kurier,* December 13, 1938.

98. Hake, *Popular Cinema of the Third Reich,* 173.

99. Hake, *Popular Cinema,* 184–85

100. Two dream sequences as well as vivid depiction of St. Pauli nightlife were cut before the film was released in the rest of the Reich. Compare Roschlau, "Ein Mädchen geht an Land."

101. Hake, *Popular Cinema of the Third Reich,* 182.

102. "'Der grosse Tag von Hamburg': Mit Malbrans Filmleuten beim Schmelingskampf," *Film-Kurier,* April 19, 1938.

103. "Der Film von Morgen," *Film-Kurier*, February 22, 1938.

104. "Hamburg-Dein Film ist da!," *Hamburger Tageblatt*, September 24, 1938.

105. See, for example, Günther Schivark, "Mädchen von Schanghei im Marmorhaus," *Film-Kurier*, September 17, 1938. The author explains, for example, that Loretta Young, "as pretty and shapely she may be, lacks the spiritual depth [*geistiges Format*] to infuse the problematic [. . .] with a deeper meaning."

106. Careful exceptions can be made for films such as *Jud Süss* and *Der Ewige Jude*, since audiences were observed more systematically and repeatedly in order to evaluate the success or failure of such important films of racist propaganda.

107. For an excellent history of the genre of the *Heimatfilm* see von Moltke, *No Place Like Home*, 36.

108. A prominent subgenre of the *Heimatfilm* is the *Bergfilm* or mountain film. For a useful placement of the *Bergfilm* as part of Nazi cinema's contribution to the *Heimatfilm* genre see Rentschler's exploration of Luis Trenker in *Ministry of Illusion*, 73–96. See further von Moltke's detailed discussion of Ganghover's "*Bergheimat*" and its "paradigmatic role in the genrification of the *Heimatfilm*. Von Molkte, *No Place Like Home*, 37, 49.

109. Rentschler defines *Heimat* as "a place, a feeling; a physical space, a province of the psyche; at once something inordinately rich and something irretrievably lost" and suggests that "To contemplate *Heimat* means to imagine an uncontaminated space, a realm of innocence and immediacy" to which the city can only be conceptualized as "other." Rentschler, *Ministry of Illusion*, 74.

110. Von Moltke, *No Place Like Home*, 37.

111. Kristina Söderbaum, also known as the *Reichswasserleiche* (Reich's water corpse), drowned herself in the Neckar River (*Jud Süss*, 1940) and followed her mother into the moor in *Die Goldene Stadt* (1941/42). In each case the loss of virginity would be atoned by the ultimate sacrifice on the altar of racial purity. For a discussion on Söderbaum see Lowry, "Ideology and Excess in Nazi Melodrama."

112. Roschlau convincingly reasons that Erna's suicide would have presented an ending much more to Hochbaum's liking but did not find the support of Ufa dramatic advisors. Roschlau, "Ein Mädchen geht an Land."

113. Stills and a short plot summary were printed in the *Illustrated Film-Kurier*, undated (courtesy of the Film- und Fernsehmuseum, Hamburg). The *Illustrated Film-Kurier* was a program printed for important films and sold in theaters. Undated.

114. "Im Schatten über St. Pauli," *Film-Kurier*, September 24, 1938.

115. In contrast, films such as *Biberpelz, Mustergatte, Was tun, Sybille?, Eine Nacht im Mai, Geheimzeichen LB 17, Rote Orchideen, Maja zwischen zwei Ehen*, and, of course, *Heimat*, received continuous testimonies to their national success in the form of visibly placed advertisements in the *Film-Kurier*, which frequently detailed the number of patrons reached and the number of consecutive weeks the respective film ran in a particular locale. There are no such recurrent Ufa advertisements for *Ein Mädchen*.

116. Max Baumann, "Hamburg—Liebe und Seefahrt," *Hamburger Tageblatt*, October 15, 1938.

117. Große Freiheit is a street in St. Pauli that crosses the Reeperbahn. The Hamburg Hippodrom was a famous nightclub at the time.

118. See Kreimeier, *The Ufa Story*, 408–9; Witte, "Film Im Nationalsozialismus: Blendung Und Überblendung," 119–70; Töteberg, *Filmstadt*, 88–91; Wetzel and Hagemann, *Zensur: Verbotene Deutsche Filme 1933–1945*, 71–74.

119. See in particular Witte, "Film im Nationalsozialismus," 142, 164, 168; Rentschler, *Ministry of Illusion*, 218; Töteberg, *Filmstadt*, 88–91.

120. See Witte, "Film im Nationalsozialismus," 165.

121. Töteberg, *Filmstadt*, 90.

122. Among subversive filmmakers Rentschler lists Helmut Käutner in first place, followed by Reinhold Schünzel and Wolfgang Staudte, but also argues that "aesthetic resistance was part of the system; it provided a crucial function in a larger gestalt." Rentschler, *Ministry of Illusion*, 12, 144.

123. The above formulation is a pun on the phrase *"Die Gnade der späten Geburt,"* or "the grace of the belated birth," used by German Chancellor Helmut Kohl in the Israeli Knesset on January 25, 1984, to assert his personal innocence and that of an entire generation of German politicians. The phrase was originally used by journalist Günter Gaus, who later accused Chancellor Kohl of plagiarism. In Gaus's use the phrase was not meant to provide an excuse but to instead raise questions about how his generation had acted when forced to decide whether to support National Socialism. Only because of "the grace of the late birth" did Gaus's (and Kohl's) generation, so Gaus implied, never have to experience the limits of their moral compass. See "Verschwiegene Entscheidung," *Der Spiegel*, 38 (1986), 47, http://www.spiegel.de/spiegel/print /d-13519977.html. See Gaus, *Die Welt der Westdeutschen*. For a more recent mentioning of the phrase in English literature, see Grossmann, "The 'Goldhagen Effect': Memory, Repetition, and Responsibility in the New Germany," in Eley, *The "Goldhagen Effect": History, Memory, Nazism— Facing the German Past*, 103.

124. Rudolf Mast defines *Große Freiheit Nr. 7* as a declaration of love. See Rudolf Mast, "Im Lagerhaus der Emotion," *nachtkritik.de*, April 23, 2010, https://www.nachtkritik.de/index.php ?option=com_content&view=article&id=4264&Itemid=40.

125. Kreimeier, *The Ufa Story*, 408. Töteberg, *Filmstadt*, 88.

126. Wetzel and Hagemann, *Zensur: Verbotene Deutsche Filme 1933-1945*, 73.

127. Ufa had subsidiaries in the following countries during the war years: Switzerland, France, the Netherlands, Protectorate of Bohemia and Moravia (formerly Czechoslovakia), Hungary, the United States (but exhibitors largely boycotted German films), Belgium, Bulgaria, Denmark, Greece, Italy, Croatia, Norway, Portugal, Romania, Sweden, and Serbia. Films also circulated in Spain, Japan, Croatia, Argentina, and Slovakia, though in the face of mounting pressures. See "Unsere Asulandsbeteiligungen, ihre Lizenserträge im Jahre 43/44, ihre voraussichtliche Entwicklung in 44/45," BArch R 109 II 5.

128. Peter Hagemann, "Große Freiheit Nr. 7," in *Zensur: Verbotene deutsche Film, 1933–45*, 71–74.

129. Hagemann reviews the unsubstantiated rumors concerning Admiral Dönitz. The only verifiable objection came from Karl Kaufmann, yet the nature of his concerns is not recorded. See Hagemann, "Große Freiheit Nr. 7," 71, 73.

130. The *Urlaubstrupp Hafen*, possibly the most prominent example, was a voluntary organization, called to life by Kaufmann, that exempmlified the Nazi ideal of solidarity and community: Lower-level white collar workers (*Angestellte*) and civil servants filled in for harbor workers during their own vacation time, thus providing the possibility for harbor workers to participate in KdF trips. See Bajohr, "Die Zustimmungsdiktatur," 99. On "Gefühlssozialismus" see Bajohr, "Gauleiter in Hamburg," 274, 286.

131. Compare Töteberg, *Filmstadt Hamburg*, 85–90.

132. Cited in Hagemann, "Große Freiheit Nr. 7," 73.

133. The Consortium for Youth Protection in Wartime in Hamburg remarked that *Münchhausen* demonstrated the possibility of being an excellent film had it not been for the inclusion of a number of lewd scenes. See "Geschäftsbericht der Gauarbeitsgemeinschaft für Jugendbetreuung in Hamburg. 1940–1943," StAHH 351-10 Sozialbehörde I VT 38.11. *Münchhausen*, one of the few fantastic films made during the Nazi period, follows the adventures of the liar duke on his travels through time and space. Riding on a cannonball, tasting eternal youth, and achieving victory over his rival, baron Münchhausen's voyage leads through the bed of Catherine the Great and the sultan's harem and makes a short stop on the moon, where the dislocated head of a woman vies for his attention. Compare Rentschler, *Ministry of Illusion,* 193–213.

134. Since the catastrophe of summer 1943, Kaufmann had earned deep respect from the propaganda minster for mastering the situation in Hamburg—after overcoming Kaufmann's initial "shock of reality." Even though Goebbels first thought that Kaufmann's distress after the first and most severe attack was exaggerated and a sign that he was breaking down, Goebbels quickly learned that he had misjudged the situation. Subsequently, he notes in his diary how Kaufmann seems to deal with the constant and destructive attacks on the city without further assistance from the Reich. In December 1944 he even charged Kaufmann to oversee the *Luftschutzbereitschaft* (air-raid readiness) in the Reichsgau Sachsen. Joseph Goebbels, July 29, 1943, August 3, 1943, October 26, 1944, and December 31, 1944, in *Die Tagebücher von Joseph Goebbels*. See Bajohr, "Gauleiter in Hamburg," 292.

135. Goebbels noted in his diary that "Harlan works too much with mysterious choirs and also his dialogue is a bit too sentimental and superficially constructed. I will have to, betimes, take Harlan to task. He currently moves on a path which does not promise especially great chances of success. He has to be brought back down to earth." Goebbels, July 24, 1943, *Die Tagebücher*, 156.

136. Goebbels, December 28,1944, in *Die Tagebücher*, 476.

137. However, Goebbels notes that he spoke to Käutner about slightly problematic things for a new film project on December 16, 1942. Käutner and the minister most likely discussed *Große Freiheit Nr. 7*, which went into production in March 1943, presumably after Käutner made the necessary changes in the manuscript. Goebbels, December 16, 1942, *Die Tagebücher*, 501.

138. In April 2010 one of Hamburg's most prestigious stage theaters, the Thalia Theater, premiered a modern stage adaptation of Käutner's classic. After its initial success in Hamburg in October 1945, *Große Freiheit Nr. 7* quickly attained the status of a cult film. It continues to play on Hamburg's screens together with other "classics," and Hans Albers, the "blond Hans [der blonde Hannes]," as he is lovingly remembered, remains the city's foremost star, a native son. At the precise address that gave the film its title, a dance club opened in April 1993, entertaining patrons in a "Hippodrom" fashion, and repeats night after night the famous song, "Auf der Reeperbahn nachts um halb eins," in front of an audience of *Erlebnistouristen*. See "Es war einmal die Romantik der Matrosen; Luk Perceval konfrontiert im Thalia Käutners 'Große Freiheit Nr. 7' mit der Realität," *Hamburger Abendblatt*, July 6, 2010; "Viermal Kino open air: Das Wunder von Bern, Große Freiheit Nr. 7, African Queen, Soul of A Man," *Hamburger Abendblatt*, August 13, 2004; Matthias Gretzschel, "Der Mythos vom blonden Hans," *Hamburger Abendblatt*, December 17, 2005. See "*Über Uns*," Große Freiheit Nr. 7. Ihr Tanzlokal in Hamburg, http://www.grossefreiheit-nr7.de/ueber-uns.html, accessed July 28, 2010.

139. For claims regarding the film's provocative depiction of women see "Große Freiheit Nr. 7," *Filmzentrale—gesammelte filmkritiken,* http://www.filmzentrale.com/rezis/grosse freiheitnr7ub.htm, accessed July 28, 2010.

140. It has by now been widely accepted that National Socialism was neither antisex nor antipleasure per se, not least because of the pathbreaking contributions by Dagmar Herzog, Elizabeth Heinemann, Julia Roos, and others. See in particular "Sexuality and German Fascism," special issue, *Journal of the History of Sexuality* 11, no. 1/2 (January–April 2002). This newer literature explicitly positions itself against the work of Pini, *Leibeskult und Liebeskitsch*, and Bleul, *Das Saubere Reich*.

141. Ascheid, *Hitler's Heroines*. Ascheid takes seriously the role of female star culture in Nazi Germany and contrasts popular female stars with Nazi ideals of femininity. Unfortunately, Ascheid's analysis of the Nazi ideal of womanhood remains rather one-dimensional.

142. Töteberg, *Filmstadt*, 90.

143. Töteberg, *Filmstadt*, 90.

144. Witte, "Film im Nationalsozialismus," 138; Witte, "The Indivisible Legacy of Nazi Cinema," 23–30.

145. Even though Rentschler identifies *Romanze in Moll* as an example of rare aesthetic resistance, the film found the explicit approval of Goebbels "as an extremely effective, avant-gardist work [*Avantgardistenarbeit*]." Goebbels, January 1, 1943, *Die Tagebücher*, 90. See Rentschler, *Ministry of Illusion*, 218.

146. Witte, "Film im Nationalsozialismus," 146.

147. Hannes explains to the shocked Gisa the mistake everybody seems to make. Here in the German original: "Für eine von der Strasse hat er dich gehalten, für ein Flittchen von die [*sic*] Große Freiheit."

148. ". . . Auf der Reeperbahn, nachts um halb eins," *Hamburger Fremdenblatt,* July 18, 1939, StAHH 135-1 Staatliche Pressestelle I-IV 2007. The article promises that St. Pauli is Hamburg's Montmartre, just more authentic and more beautiful.

Chapter 3

1. *Triumph of the Will* (Riefenstahl, 1935). See Cook, "From Triumph of the Will to Twitter"; Sennett, "Film Propaganda: *Triumph of the Will* as a Case Study"; Marcus, "Reappraising Riefenstahl's *Triumph of the Will*."

2. Speer, *Inside the Third Reich*; Wolf, *Gauforen der Macht*; Schmidt, *Geländebegehung*; Gregor, *Haunted City*; Gregor, "The Illusion of Remembrance"; Macdonald, "Undesirable Heritage"; Hagen and Ostergren, "Spectacle, Architecture and Space at the Nuremberg Party Rallies."

3. Bloxham, "From the International Military Tribunal to the Subsequent Nuremberg Proceedings."

4. Harlander, *Zwischen Heimstätte und Wohnmaschine*, 84; Führer, "Meister der Ankündigung," 437.

5. Kershaw, *Hitler, 1889-1936: Hubris*, 24.

6. Fest, *Hitler: Eine Biographie*, 510. For Hitler's descent into the Viennese underworld see Kershaw, *Hitler, 1989-1936: Hubris*, 27–69.

7. Lörcher, "Reichsplanung," 41.

8. Diefenbach, "Planning for the Mark Brandenburg and for Prague During the Third Reich." It should be noted that the term *Führerstadt* finds representation in the archives only in 1940.

9. Gellately, *Backing Hitler*, 71. For Hamburg see Axel Schildt, "Jenseits von Politik?," 288.

10. For the four-year plan of 1936 see Mason, *Nazism, Fascism, and the Working Class*, 107. In Hamburg the first model bunker was built in April 1933 and since the summer the party

recruited *Blockwarte* in the form of *Luftschutzwarte*. In 1934 Hamburg had its own commissioner for air protection in the person of Senator Alfred Richter, and in the later part of the 1930s, air-raid and darkening drills introduced the population to the use of gas masks and the cellars in which they would spent many nights in the years to come. See Schildt, "Jenseits der Politik?," 287. The *Hamburger Tageblatt* reported repeatedly on air-raid drills, particularly in schools throughout 1938. For the Hitler Youth Law compare Klönne, *Jugend im Dritten Reich*, 27–28, and for conscription see Mason, *Nazism, Fascism and the Working Class*, 117, and Mason, *Social Policy in the Third Reich*, 165. Jill Stephenson, in *Hitler's Homefront*, further differentiates between the various kinds of labor conscription introduced. While men were primarily conscripted into the *Reichsarbeitsdienst* (labor service) or *Landdienst* (service in agriculture), the *Pflichtjahr* (a year of domestic service) was introduced for unmarried women between eighteen and twenty-five. On general labor conscription see also Tooze, *Wages of Destruction*, 261.

11. Niemeyer, "Wo bleibt das Gesetz über die Gesundung der Altstädte?," 89–94.

12. See the reports of individual consortia. "Aufgaben und Arbeitsergebnisse der Raumforschung an deutschen Hochschulen," in *Volk und Lebensraum*, 401–589.

13. Blanck and Bangert, "Köln: Ein städtebaulicher Versuch," 45.

14. Stadverwaltungs-Oberbauamt Labes, Kassel, "Grundsätzliches zur Altstadtsanierung und Altstadterhaltung," *Monatshefte für Baukunst und Städtebau*, June 1936, 61–69.

15. See StAHH 351-10 Sozialbehörde I EF70.15 Band I, in particular the circular from August 1927. Also, Roos, "Backlash Against Prostitutes' Rights."

16. Niemeyer, "Wo bleibt das Gesetz über die Gesundung der Altstädte?"

17. For a critical evaluation of antiurbanism in Imperial Germany, see Lees, *Cities Sin, and Social Reform in Imperial Germany*. Further, see Ritzheimer, *"Trash," Censorship, and National Identity in Early Twentieth-Century Germany*.

18. Harlander, *Zwischen Heimstätte und Wohnmaschine*, 84; Führer, "Meister der Ankündigung," 437.

19. Walther, *Neue Wege zur Großstadtsanierung*, 4.

20. Walther, *Neue Wege zur Großstadtsanierung*, 4.

21. Walther, *Neue Wege zur Großstadtsanierung*, 4.

22. Walther, *Neue Wege zur Großstadtsanierung*, 4.

23. Walther, *Neue Wege zur Großstadtsanierung*, 19.

24. Lidbetter, *Heredity and the Social Problem Group*. Lidbetter entered the service of the poor law authority in 1898 and had been intimately involved in poor relief in London until the publication of his book, where he advanced arguments about the hereditary inferiority of social problem groups. While not negating negative environmental effects he insisted on the heredity of certain defects. Walther, *Neue Wege zur Großstadtsanierung*, 7.

25. Much of Walther's treatise is concerned with defining these terms.

26. Walther, *Neue Wege zur Großstadtsanierung*, 6.

27. Walther, *Neue Wege zur Großstadtsanierung*, 5–6.

28. For Alfred Rosenberg's mysticism, see Piper, *Alfred Rosenberg*, 198, 202, 226–31.

29. Feder, *Die Neue Stadt*, 24. Feder was installed as *Reichskommissar für das Siedlungswesen* (Reich commissioner for settlement) in March 1934. For Feder the city "with its haste, its noise, its often questionable entertainment, its dangers and its squalor" spelled the death of the nation. But already by August, Feder was forced into retirement. See Harlander, *Zwischen Heimstätte und Wohnmaschine*, 60.

30. Scranton, *Learning to Die in the Anthropocene,* takes on a wicked problem of our own time (53).

31. For the relationship between the Nazi state and the working classes, see Mason, *Social Policy in the Third Reich,* and Mason, *Nazism, Fascism, and the Working Class*; also, Alf Lüdtke, *Eigen-Sinn: Fabrikalltag, Arbeitererfahrungen und Politik.* For Hamburg see Grüttner, *Arbeitswelt and der Wasserkante.*

32. Foucault, *Discipline and Punish.* Scott, *Seeing Like a State.*

33. Necker, *Konstanty Gutschow,* 209.

34. Tiess, "Nationalsozialistische Städteplanung," 27.

35. Krogmann. *Es ging um Deutschland's Zukunft,* 322. Hitler suggested that "Hamburg habe so etwas Amerikanisches, und es wäre durchaus falsch nur Häuser im Stile des Braunen Hauses zu bauen."

36. Bose et al., 33–34. See also "Hamburg to Erect 60-Story Building," *New York Times,* June 11, 1937.

37. On Hamburg's parks see "Die Stadt im Grünen," in *Führer durch Hamburg,* 54. Krogmann, *Es ging um Deutschlands Zukunft,* 22.

38. See Bose et al., ". . . *Ein Neues Hamburg Entsteht,*" 20–29. Yet it is not until the *Generalbebauungspläne* of 1940–41 and 1944 that plans attained concrete form first in light of the impressive military victories and later in the context of destroyed cities. Bose et al., ". . . *Ein Neues Hamburg Entsteht,*" 55–61. Diefenbach, "Konstanty Gutschow and the Reconstruction of Hamburg."

39. Necker, *Konstanty Gutschow,* 167–68.

40. Lefebvre, *The Production of Space.*

41. Necker, *Konstanty Gutschow,* 229–30.

42. Necker, *Konstanty Gutschow,* 234.

43. "Generalbauinspektor für die Reichshauptstadt Albert Speer," 14.

44. See Bose et al., ". . . *Ein neues Hamburg entsteht,*" 5.

45. Kaufmann, quoted in Necker, *Konstanty Gutschow,* 259.

46. Necker, *Konstanty Gutschow,* 261. Pahl-Weber, "'Die Ortsgrjppe als Siedlungszelle.' Ein Vorschlag zur Methodik der großstadtischen Stadterweiterung von 1940."

47. On March 29, 1934, Hitler's *Erlass zum deutschen Siedlungswesen* (RGBl. I, 295) established a Reich commissioner for settlement (*Reichskommissar für das Siedlungswesen*) who answered to both the Reich economic minister (Hjalmar Schacht, 1934–37) and the Reich labor minister (Franz Seldte, 1933–45). Harlander, *Zwischen Heimstätte und Wohnmaschine.* See further Ludorf, "Luftschutz durch Städtebau," 59–60. To protect the population from demoralization and the productive capacity of the Reich from destruction, Ludorf demanded the creation of dispersed and spacious cities. For existing towns and cities he suggested a disaggregation by way of green corridors and open spaces. Petsch, *Baukunst und Stadtplanung im Dritten Reich,* 192.

48. Mächler, "Die Großstadt als Kultur- und Raumproelm und die Grenzen ihrer Größe," 63. Martin Mächler was an architect and urban planner, fascinated by Berlin and actively involved in its urban development since the 1920s. Even though his monograph *Demodynamik* was burned by the National Socialists in 1934, he remained an active and respected authority on spatial planning throughout the Nazi period and beyond. Compare biographical entry in Munziger-Archiv https://www.munzinger.de/search/accept?accept-code=-336828491092602405&netto=12.9, retrieved July 1, 2009.

49. Gottfried Feder's concept of the New City (*Neue Stadt*) was first published in 1939.

50. Killus, "Der Totalitätsgedanke im Neuen Städtebau," 85–88.

51. The idea of *Gartenstadt* was by no means particular to National Socialism. The Garden City Association was founded on June 10, 1899, based on concepts developed by Ebenezer Howard, who is credited with the urban utopia of the Garden City in reaction to the nineteenth-century city. The garden city movement originated in Great Britain and found ample support in Germany in the 1920s. Sennett, *Garden Cities in Theory and Practice*; Parsons and Schuyler, *From Garden City to Green City*; Buder, *Visonaries and Planners*; Unwin, *Nothing Gained by Overcrowding*. For Germany in the 1920s see Migge, *Deutsche Binnenkolonisation*.

52. Frank and Frank, "Die Gartenstadt Klein-Borstel in Hamburg"; Fleige, "Städtebau—Gestern und Heute." See Sennett. *Garden Cities in Theory and Practice*; Lidbetter, *Heredity and the Social Problem Group*.

53. Schivelbusch, *The Culture of Defeat*.

54. On women of lesser means, see Davis, *Home Fires Burning*.

55. For a history of the legends that were collapsed into "stab in the back," see Barth, *Dolchstoßlegenden und politische Desintegration*. Barth illustrates that broader trends and structural developments prepared the ground for claims that explained the defeat of 1918 as the result of treason and sabotage *during* the war. Moreover, Barth uncovers the legend of the "stab in the back" as a displaced and multifaceted indictment of the inner weakness of the home front. See also Stibbe, *Germany 1914–1933*.

56. This argument is made explicitly by Wildt throughout *Volksgemeinschaft als Selbstermächtigung*. Moreover Bergerson's study on everyday life in Hildesheim illustrates that mundane practices such as exchanging greetings articulated and refined local ideas of *Volksgemeinschaft*. Bergerson, *Ordinary German in Extraordinary Times*.

57. For a link between moral or cultural decline and defeat in the memories of intellectuals of the Weimar Republic, compare Barth, *Dolchstoßlegenden und politische Disintegration*, in particular 422, 432, 454. Also, Barnouw, *Weimar Intellectuals and the Threat of Modernity* and Rickels, "The Demonization of the Home Front: War Neurosis and Weimar Cinema."

58. "RFK-Anordnungen über die Programmlänge," *Film-Kurier*, October 26, 1939.

59. "Aufruf; An alle deutschen Filmteahterbesitzer: Jedes deutsche Filmtheater soll nach Möglichkeit ausserhalb der normalen Spielzeit Sonderveranstaltungen durchführen," *Film-Kurier*, September 30, 1939.

60. "In Hamburg: Vorbildliche Kameradschaft der Theaterbesitzer," *Film-Kurier*, October 5, 1939.

61. "Der Film im Dienste der nationalen Erziehung," *Film-Kurier*, November 6, 1939.

62. "Aufruf; An alle deutschen Filmtheaterbesitzer: Jedes deutsche Filmtheater soll nach Möglichkeit außerhalb der normalen Spielzeit Sonderveranstaltungen durchführen," *Film-Kurier*, September 30, 1939.

63. Ritzheimer, *'Trash,' Censorship and National Identity in Early Twentieth-Century Germany*; Lees, *Cities, Sin, and Social Reform in Imperial German*.

64. Storjohann, *"Hauptsache: Überleben" Eine Jugend im Krieg*, 82.

65. For most of the 1930s, the *Verwahrlosungs* discourse was limited to prostitution and its control. The city of Hamburg actively transformed itself into the guardian of prostitutes willing to submit or unable to resist regulation, monitoring their health and confining their whereabouts with the goal of guaranteeing STD-free sexual access for German soldiers. See StAHH, 351-10 Sozialbehörde I EF70.21. Further see letter by chief criminal inspector, October 10, 1933, StAHH 351-10 Sozialbehörde I, EF70.15 Band I. Also, "Der Kampf gegen die Prostitution," *Hamburger Fremdenblatt*, September 8, 1933.

66. Quoted in Ian Kershaw, *Hitler, 1936-1945: Nemesis*, 187.

67. Schreiben vom Amt für Volkswohlfahrt, an die Arbeitsgemeinschaft für Jugendschutz im Kriege, August 8, 1940, StAHH 354-5 Jugendbehörde I 343c.

68. Führsorgerinnen (female social workers) and Oberführsorgerinnen (supervising female social workers) constituted the field staff of the social welfare office. See internal memo from September 30, 1939, StAHH 351-10 Sozialbehörde I VG30.70.

69. Compare various Stimmungsberichte der Kreisdienststellen, November 1939. StAHH 351-10 Sozialbehörde I VG30.70.

70. Niederschrift über die Sitzung betr. Verwahrlosung der Jugend als Begleiterscheinung des Krieges. February 2, 1940, StAHH 354-5 Jugendbehörde. I. 343c.

71. The Swing Kids or Swing Youth first came to the notice of the authorities in 1938. According to the Hitler Youth report, close to five hundred adolescents gathered in a back room of the bougie Kaiserhof in Altona on February 3, 1940, to listen to English-language swing and jazz records. A month later, again as the result of a tip from the Hitler Youth, forty Gestapo and criminal police officers cracked down on various gatherings of Swing Youths in Hamburg, closing down the premises and meticulously recording the names, ages, and addresses of 408 young people. While the Anglophile attire as well as the English music scandalized local authorities, it was the Gestapo who interpreted the unfamiliar dance moves to tunes like the "Tiger Rag," the predominantly English conversations, and the fashion statements of umbrellas, tweed jackets, and lipstick as *staatsfeindlich*. Gauleiter Kaufmann was more worried about the city gaining a negative reputation in Berlin than about the organized subversion of National Socialist ideology by swing-dancing (mostly middle class) adolescents. Gauarbeitsgemeinschaft für Jugendbetreuung, "Arbeitskreis zur Bekämpfung von Jugendkriminalität und Jugendgefährdung," February 2, 1943, StAHH 361-2 Oberschulbehörde VI 1541; Schreiben an Gebietsführer Kohlmeyer vom HJ Streifendienst February 8, 1940, StAHH 354-5 Jugendbehörde I 343c; Aktennotiz: Razzia im Curio-Haus, March 2, 1940, and letter from Hitler Youth leader Nygaard to Kohlmeyer March 6, 1940, StAHH 354-5 Jugendbehörde I 343c.

72. See StAHH 351-10 Sozialbehörde I-IV VT38.11, Niederschrift der Aussprache über Jugenschutz im Kriege, March 7, 1940.

73. See StAHH 351-10 Sozialbehörde I VT38.11, Niederschrift der Aussprache über Jugenschutz im Kriege, March 7, 1940. In the summer of 1942 the regime ordered the organization of Gau Consortia for the Supervision of Youth, mandating the reorganization of existing consortia in the Gaue Niederrhein, Moselland, Nordsee, Hamburg, and Niederschlesien. See Deutscher Gemeindetag Nr. III 1806/42. Letter to the regional youth departments, July 25, 1942, StAHH 351-10 Sozialbehörde I VZ38.10.

74. Runderlass der Reichsführung SS Chef der Deutschen Polizei, March 18, 1940, StAHH 351-10 Sozialbehörde I VT 38.11.

75. Kollmeier, 86. Niederschrift der 2. Sitzung der Arbeitsgemeinschaft für Jugendschutz im Kriege, April 4, 1940, StAHH 351-10 Sozialbehörde VT 38.11. See Runderlerlaß der Reichsführung SS und Chef der Deutschen Polizei, April 25, 1940, StAHH 351-10 Sozialbehörde I, VT38.11.

76. StAHH 351-10 Sozialbehörde I-IV VT38.11 Niederschrift der Aussprache über Jugenschutz im Kriege March 7, 1940.

77. See Niederschrift über die Sitzung des Arbeitskreises zur Bekämpfung von Schmutz und Schund, July 31, 1940. StAHH 351-10 Sozialbehörde I-IV VT38.11.

78. Niederschrift über die Sitzung des Arbeitskreises zur Bekämpfung von Schmutz und Schund, July 31, 1940, StAHH 351-10 Sozialbehörde I-IV VT38.11.

79. Niederschrift über die Sitzung des Arbeitskreises zur Bekämpfung von Schmutz und Schund, July 31, 1940, StAHH 351-10 Sozialbehörde I VT 38.11.

80. The fight against trashy publications was, however, continued in certain provinces of the Reich even though the Reich's chamber for literature refused to ban or take out of circulation the identified materials. See protocol from the Rheinprovinz regarding the measures against youth endangerment during the war especially due to pornographic literature (Nacktliteratur) attached to Niederschrift über die Sitzung des Arbeitskreises zur Bekämpfung von Schmutz und Schund, July 31, 1940, StAHH 351-10 Sozialbehörde I VT 38.11. Also, Niederschrift über die 2. Sitzung des Arbeitskreises zur Prüfung und Schmutz und Schund August 7, 1940. Listed publications included *Mocca, Die Muskete*, unnamed crime novellas, and Nacktkulturliteratur, as well as novellas such as *Ich zwinge dich zu deinem Glück, Unterbrochene Hochzeitsreise, Ein Kuss Madame, Ernst heiratet eine Theory*, and *Barbara im Liebesfeuer* See Niederschrift über die 6. Sitzung der Arbeitsgemeinschaft für Jugendschutz im Kriege, September 27, 1940, StAHH 351-10 Sozialbehörde I VT 38.11.

81. Letter from Sieverts to Prof. Mulzer, October 14, 1940, in StAHH 351-10 Sozialbehörde I VZ38.10

82. Niederschrift über die 2. Sitzung des Arbeitskreises zur Bekämpfung von Schmutz und Schund, August 7, 1940, StAHH 351-10 Sozialbehörde I VT 38.11. The workshop reports that responses to a survey indicate that in the city 18.5 percent of adolescents go to the movies weekly, 51.3 percent occasionally, and 30.2 percent never. There is no record of the survey and many of the observations are mostly likely taken from Alois Funke's book on the endangerment of youths due to cinema, published in 1934, as the workshop participants had hardly enough time to collect a significant number of responses in a week's time. It seems that the attendance rate in 1940 was much higher as cinema attendance between 1934 and 1940 increased significantly overall, and it is implausible that the numbers from 1934 would still be accurate in 1940.

83. Funke, *Film und Jugend.*

84. Niederschrift über die 2. Sitzung des Arbeitskreises zur Bekämpfung von Schmutz und Schund, August 7, 1940, StAHH 351-10 Sozialbehörde I VT 38.11.

85. Niederschrift über die 2. Sitzung des Arbeitskreises zur Bekämpfung von Schmutz und Schund, August 7, 1940, StAHH 351-10 Sozialbehörde I VT 38.11.

86. Niederschrift über die 2. Sitzung des Arbeitskreises zur Bekämpfung von Schmutz und Schund, August 7, 1940, StAHH 351-10 Sozialbehörde I VT 38.11.

87. This seems to be based on Funke again. The workshop participants name neither films nor individuals that had to endure the horrific effects of film viewing. Funke, *Film und Jugend.*

88. Abschrift aus der Zeitschrift "Deutsche Justiz" Nr. 10 v. 6, March 1936, StAHH 351-10 Sozialbehörde I, EF70.21. See Harris, *Selling Sex in the Reich.*

89. Timm, "Prostitution, Venereal Disease, and Militarized Masculinity," 238. For a general overview of prostitution policies in the Third Reich see Roos, "Backlash against Prostitutes Rights: Origins and Dynamics of Nazi Prostitution Policies," and Harris, *Selling Sex in the Reich.*

90. On March 7, Party Comrade Eckhardt (Sicherheitsdienst) reported on his conversation with the Reichsführer SS, Heinrich Himmler, regarding the question of youth dilapidation, during which Himmler supposedly suggested outsourcing the sexual functions currently filled by adolescent girls to professional prostitutes which were subjected to mandatory medical examinations. Niederschrift über die Aussprache über Jugendschutz im Kriege, March 7, 1940. StAHH 351-10 Sozialbehörde I-IV VT38.11.

91. Timm, "Prostitution, Venereal Disease, and Militarized Masculinity," 227.

92. Harris, *Selling Sex in the Reich*, 155–67; Timm, "Prostitution, Venereal Disease, and Militarized Masculinity," 238. See also Roos, "Backlash against Prostitutes' Rights," 87.

93. See StAHH 351-10 Sozialbehörde I GF33.10 Band I.

94. Timm, 247.

95. Auszug aus dem Kurzbericht der Kreisstellenleiter und Oberfürsorgerinnen, July 1941, Kreistelle 3b. StAHH 354-5 Jugendbehörde I 343b.

96. Timm, "Prostitution, Venereal Disease, and Militarized Masculinity," 255.

97. Complaints about individual films to the RFK were not uncommon. BArch R 109 II 5 registers a complaint about the Heinz Rühmann film *Der Engel mit dem Seitenspiel*. In BArch NS 18/ 348 we find complaints about *Die Feuerzangenbowle, Ich liebe Dich*, and a complaint by the Gauleiter of Sudentenland about *Die goldene Stadt*.

98. See Geschäftsbericht der Gauarbeitsgemeinschaft für Jugendbetreuung in Hamburg, 1940–1943. StAHH 351-10 Sozialbehörde I VT 38.11.

99. Yet the monthly reports of "Übertretungen der Jugendschutzverordnung" sent to Berlin lists between thirty and forty cases of adolescents violating the particular stipulations with regards to moviegoing. For example, from the introduction of the police ordinance in mid-March to the end of April, 1940, were reported forty cases of adolescents in movie theaters after 9:00 P.M., out of which thirty were male. In contrast, 189 adolescents were found in violation of the ban of youth from public restaurants and more than 600 individuals visited public dances. Yet the Reich Youth Leader could slouch back in his chair by mid-July when he received the report for June, which listed no violation of the dance prohibition. See StAHH 354-5 Jugendbehörde I 343c. Schreiben an den Jugendführer des Deutschen Reichs, July 16, 1940. The Consortium for the Protection of Youth in Wartime, however, was quite comfortable assuming that the number of unreported cases was much higher.

100. Auszüge aus den Kurzberichten, November 8, 1942, in StAHH 351-10 Sozialbehörde I VZ38.10.

101. Auszüge aus den Kurzberichten, November 8, 1942, in StAHH 351-10 Sozialbehörde I VZ38.10.

102. Solmitz Tagebücher, 1938-1940, October 19, 1939, FZH 11 S. 12.

103. Hamburg's first postwar mayor, Rudolf Petersen, gave a deposition according to which the persecution of Jews in Hamburg took place in a more moderate form. Compare Bajohr, "Von der Ausgrenzung zum Massenmord," 478 (especially annotation 19). For Hamburg's liberal *Sonderweg* see Bajohr, "Gauleiter in Hamburg," 267–95, in particular 268 and annotations 4 and 6. Also Axel Schildt, "Von der Kaufmann-Legende zur Hamburg-Legende." Heffters Vortrag 'Hamburg und der Nationalsozialismus' in der Hamburger Universität am 9. November 1950," 10–46.

104. For these numbers and a more in-depth discussion of the deportations of Jews from Hamburg see Bajohr, "Von der Ausgrenzung zum Massenmord: Die Verfolgung der Hamburger Juden 1933-1945," 505–9.

105. Stargardt, *The German War*, 373.

106. Nossack, *The End*, 14–16; Stargardt, *The German War*, 375.

107. Stargardt, 380. Compare Fritzsche, *Life and Death in the Third Reich*, 225–307.

108. See "In Zwei Kriegsmonaten 21 Filme begonnen," *Film-Kurier*, November 2, 1939.

109. See "Überall im Reich starker Filmtheaterbesuch. Unsere Korrespondenten berichten über den 1. Monat des Abwehrkampfes," in *Film-Kurier*, October 5, 1939. Also compare Stahr, *Volksgemeinschaft vor der Leinwand*, 174.

110. Schreiben an Reichsminister vom Filmintendant Hinkel, October 27, 1944 and Schreiben und Anlage betreffend der Umwandlung von Sprechtheatern, October 6, 1944, in BArch R 109 III 13. Also, Wiederherstellung von fliegergeschädigten Lichtspieltheatern, March 12, 1945. BArch R 109 III 19. The rise in visits to the movies, however, clearly predated the war. In 1934 Hamburg alone counted 11,989,899 ticket sales, and three years later in 1937 that number nearly doubled as the city registered 21,772,138 movie patrons. For statistical information on theater attendance see StAHH A2-2 Statistisches Jahrbuch 1934–35 and Statistisches Jahrbuch 1937–38.

111. For prosed rationing of moviegoing see Schildt, 296. Stephenson demonstrates in her study of Würtemberg during the Second World War that such amenities as the cinema were often unavailable in small village communities. See Stephenson *Hitler's Home Front*, 20, 34.

112. Obvious exceptions include Leni Riefenstahl's *Triumph of the Will* (1935) and *Olympia* (1938).

113. *Die Goldene Stadt* (Harlan, 1942), *Die Große Liebe* (Hansen, 1941/2), *Damals* (Hansen, 1942/3).

114. *Mutterliebe* (Ucicky, 1939), *Die Reise nach Tilsit* (Harlan, 1939), *Opfergang* (Harlan, 1942/44), *. . . reitet für Deutschland* (Rabenalt, 1940/41).

115. *Bismarck* (Liebeneiner1940), *Friedrich Schiller* (Maisch, 1940), *Der Große König* (Harlan 194042), *Rembrandt* (Steinhoff, 1942), *Carl Peters* (Selpin, 1940/41), *Die Degenhardts* (Klinger, 1943/44), *Die Rothschildts* (Waschneck, 1940).

116. Hake, *Popular Cinema of the Third Reich*. Hake has convincingly argued that Nazi cinema was a popular cinema that shared much in its social function, mode of address, and reception with other popular cinemas of the time.

117. It should be noted that none of these films was considered suitable for minors; they were either not approved for adolescents or explicitly prohibited for audiences under 18 years.

118. The first quotation is from Rentschler, *Ministry of Illusion*, 196, the second from Schulte-Sasse, *Entertaining the Third Reich*, 303.

119. Rentschler, *Ministry of Illusion*, 194.

120. Rentschler, *Ministry of Illusion*, 193. Shooting took place in Berlin, Babelsberg, Bodenwerder, and Venice between April and December 1942. Compare Kreimeier, *Die Ufa-Story*, 386.

121. Here Veit Harlan's epic *Kolberg* appears as the last effort to mobilize the cinematic apparatus to proclaim the belief that willpower alone can reverse adverse material preconditions.

122. Schulte-Sasse argues that "*Münchhausen's* raison d'être is to celebrate cinema." See *Entertaining the Third Reich*, 302. Rentschler suggests that *Münchhausen* was a testament to the war with the "German cinema's own past as well as with Hollywood competitors." See *Ministry of Illusion*, 212.

123. See Schulte-Sasse, *Entertaining the Third Reich*, 303.

124. Schulte-Sasse, *Entertaining the Third Reich*, 307.

125. Advertisement, *Hamburger Tageblatt*, September 11, 1943.

126. "Hamburger Alltag," *Hamburger Zeitung*, August 7, 1943.

127. Rentschler, *Ministry of Illusion*, 195.

128. Quoted in Rentschler, *Ministry of Illusion*, 193.

129. Auszug aus Berichten der Kreisdienststellen und Obefürsorgerinnen. Kreisstelle 4a, December 1, 1939, StAHH354-5 Jugendbehörde I 343b.

130. See Auszüge aus den Berichten der Kreisdienstellenleiter. Kreis 3b, February 25, 1942. See also Bericht der Oberführsorgerinnen Stand März 42, für Kreisdienststelle 2a, February 25,

1942, in StAHH 354-5 Jugenbehörde I 343b. Regarding incidents of dodging Hitler Youth service see also February 2, 1943, Gauarbeitsgemeinschaft für Jugendbetreuung, in StAHH 361-2 Oberschulbehörde VI 1541.

131. Kollmeier, *Ordnung und Ausgrenzung*; Kater, *Hitler Youth*; Brandenburg, *Die Geschichte der HJ*; Klönne, *Jugend im Dritten Reich*.

132. DTA Emmendingen 1454/I *Liebebriefe auf KZ Wache*. September 2, 1944, 39.

133. Necker, *Konstanty Gutschow*, 286.

Chapter 4

1. Borchert, "Die Küchenuhr," 201–4.

2. Büttner, "'Gomorrha' und die Folgen: Der Bombenkrieg," 616.

3. Büttner, "'Gomorrha' und die Folgen: Der Bombenkrieg," 616. See also Nossack, *Der Untergang: Hamburg 1943*. Valuable description in an otherwise controversial and problematically decontextualized book, Friedrich, *The Fire: The Bombing of Germany*.

4. Büttner, "'Gomorrha' und die Folgen: Der Bombenkrieg," 617.

5. Boberach, "SD-Berichte zu Inlandfragen," August 2, 1943, 5560.

6. Boberach, "SD-Berichte zu Inlandfragen," August 2, 1943, 5560.

7. See Familienfürsorge Uhlenhorst. Lagebericht nach dem Stande von Ende September 1943, September 29, 1943, StAHH 351-10 Sozialbehörde I VG30.70. In contrast, Hans-Erich Nossack's eyewitness account reminds us of the protracted rescue efforts that for weeks would retrieve burned and suffocated bodies that had been trapped in collapsed buildings or bunkers. Addressing the rumors regarding the dead, he asked, "Why are we trying to lie to the dead? Why doesn't anyone say, we cannot count them?" See Nossack, *Der Untergang*, 98–99.

8. Nossack, *Der Untergang*, 99–100.

9. "Lebensmittelgeschäfte, Gaststätten offenhalten!," *Hamburger Zeitung*, July 29, 1943, and "Die Hamburger Verpflegungstätten," *Hamburger Zeitung*, August 3, 1943.

10. Lagebericht der Familienfuersorge im Stadtteil Eimsbüttel, September 1943, StAHH 351-10 Sozialbehörde I VG30.70.

11. Lagebericht der Familienfuersorge im Stadtteil Eimsbüttel, September 1943, StAHH 351-10 Sozialbehörde I VG30.70.

12. Sebald, *On the Natural History of Destruction*, 51.

13. Fritzsche, *Life and Death in the Third Reich*, 225–307.

14. Nossack, *The End*, 12.

15. Nossack, *The End*, 14, 15.

16. Nossack, *The End*, 23.

17. Nossack, *The End*, 22–23.

18. Stargartdt, *The German War*, 377

19. Stargardt, *The German War*, 376–77.

20. Shandley, *Rubble Film*; Baer, *Dismantling the Dream Factory*; Fischer, "Wandering in/to the Rubble-Film"; Shandley, "Rubble Canyons"; Wilms and Rasch, *German Postwar Films*; compare to earlier, rather short descriptions of the rubble film in Göttler, "Westdeutscher Nachkriegsfilm: Land der Väter," 178.

21. Halbjahresbericht Kreisdienststelle 2a, September 26, 1940, StAHH 351-10 Sozialbehörde I VG30.70.

22. Sozialverwaltung Kreisdienststelle 2b. Bericht für die Zeit vom 1 April 1940, September 30, 1940, StAHH 351-10 Sozialbehörde I VG30.70.

23. In early May 1941 heavy air strikes against the city shattered the hope that war was to be quick and relatively painless. See reports of Oberführsorgerinnen from Kreisdienstelle 1a, 3a, 4a, May 27, 1941, StAHH 351-10 Sozialbehörde I VG30.70, and Kurzbericht Kreisdienstelle 2a, November 24, 1941, StAHH 351-10 Sozialbehörde I VG30.70.

24. Auszüge aus den Kurzberichten. Kreisdienstelle 3a, November 25, 1941, StAHH 351-10 Sozialbehörde I VG30.70.

25. "The reports of the last six months stood under the great impact of the dramatic developments in the East. This heated struggle tore deep and painful wounds here as well. Suffering and grief are great, as great and as unrelenting is the stern determination for ultimate victory. Until now, 48 of our men fell in the Russian campaign, whose loved-ones are receiving welfare support." Halbjahresbericht Kreisdienstelle 10, September 29, 1941, StAHH 351-10 Sozialbehörde I VG30.70.

26. Halbjahresbericht Kreisdienststelle 7, October 1940, StAHH 351-10 Sozialbehörde I VG30.70.

27. See Vierteljahresbericht der Leiter und Oberfürsorgerinnen der Kreisdienststellen. Stand Dezember 1941, 351-10 Sozialbehörde I VG 30.68 Band 4.

28. Führer, "Meister der Ankündigung;" Harlander, *Zwischen Heimstätte und Wohnmaschine.*

29. See Vierteljahresbericht der Leiter und Oberfürsorgerinnen der Kreisdienststellen. Stand Dezember 1941, 351-10 Sozialbehörde I VG 30.68 Band 4. See also Berichte der Oberfürsorgerinnen 2a, August 28, 1942, 351-10 Sozialbehörde I UG 30.92.

30. Letter from Herwarth von Schade, August 1, 1943, StAHH 731 Zeitgeschichtlich Sammlungen 14c.

31. "Die Sonderzuteilungen für alle!," *Hamburger Zeitung,* July 27, 1943. Everybody received 30 grams of coffee (*Bohnenkaffee*), sweets as of August 2, and a half bottle of liquor for everyone eighteen and older. In addition, tobacco was promised. Letter from Herwarth von Schade, August 1, 1943, StAHH 731 Zeitgeschichtlich Sammlungen 14c. See also Storjohann, "*Hauptsache: Überleben,*" 148.

32. Storjohann, "*Hauptsache: Überleben,*" 148.

33. Friedrich, *The Fire,* 220–25; also 72–74. The Millennium Raid on Cologne on May 30, 1942, is generally seen as the beginning of a different kind of air war. In the aftermath of the thousand-bomber raid, firefighters from Cologne and surrounding cities managed to keep the fires in check by pumping tons of river water through pipes into the city. Subsequent raids, especially beginning in 1943, were more effective in wreaking the intended havoc.

34. Statistik über Luftangriffe auf Hamburg, June 30, 1943, July 31, 1943, August 31, 1943, StAHH 331-1 Polizeibehörde I 1537.

35. The immediate reports by Nazi authorities list 30,500 dead. Scholars have since estimated that between 34,000 and 40,000 people died as a result of the bombing. Büttner, "'Gomorrha' und die Folgen," 618, and Friedrich, *The Fire,* 166. Der Polizeipräsident der Stadt Hamburg an das Reichspropagandaamt, December 1943, StAHH 331-1 Polizeibehörde I 1537.

36. Lagebericht der Familienfürsorge im Ortsamt Eppendorf, in der Ortstelle Breitenfelderstrasse 35, September 29, 1943, StAHH 351-10 Sozialbehörde I VG30.70.

37. Lagebericht der Familienfürsorge im Ortsamt Eppendorf, in der Ortstelle Breitenfelderstrasse 35, September 29, 1943, StAHH 351-10 Sozialbehörde I VG30.70. See also "Die ärztliche Versorgung," *Hamburger Zeitung,* July 29, 1943.

38. On August 25, 1943, the first issue of the *Hamburger Zeitung* was printed at 11 P.M., reporting on the first night of Operation Gomorrah. Until August 21, 1943, the *Hamburger*

Zeitung, an emergency cooperative of Hamburg-based dailies replacing the *Hamburger Tageblatt*, *Hamburger Fremdenblatt*, and *Hamburger Anzeiger*, was distributed by the Gaupropaganda Office to the citizens of Hamburg free of charge.

39. "Wochenschau und Filme," *Hamburger Zeitung*, August 11, 1943.

40. "Wochenschau und Filme," *Hamburger Zeitung*, August 11, 1943.

41. "Wochenschau und Filme," *Hamburger Zeitung*, August 11, 1943.

42. Töteberg and Reissmann, *Mach dir ein paar schöne Stunden*, 85.

43. For the following films see advertisement in *Hamburger Tageblatt*, August 26, 1943.

44. "Wochenschau und Filme," *Hamburger Zeitung*, August 11, 1943.

45. König, *Volkswagen, Volksempfänger, Volksgemeinschaft*. Particularly relevant here is Tooze, *Wages of Destruction*, 147–65.

46. "So wirtschaftet die Hausfrau in England" in *Hamburger Tageblatt*, February 19, 1939, which ridicules the British housewife for her dependence on canned foods and her inability to be self-sufficient. "Macht der Zucker dick?," in "Die Frau," *Hamburger Tageblatt*, February 10, 1939. The paper warns the German housewife against the dangers of canned foods (American style) while lauding the natural qualities of sugar. The *Hamburger Tageblatt* regularly printed recipes and instructions to German women as prewar food rationing became a fact of everyday life. See "Speisequark und Milcheiweisspulver: Zwei wichtige 'Rohstoffe' der modernen Ernährung in vielfältiger Verwendung," in *Hamburger Tageblatt*, February 11, 1939. The gloss by Fischer, "Edamer – Bezugscheinfrei" in *Hamburer Fremdenblatt*, September 11, 1940, ridicules a fictional Herr Plisch for buying two gigantic rounds of Edamer cheese from his local deli, which appeared to be unregulated because, as Plisch finds out soon enough, they are window dressings made from wood. In the absence of basic consumer goods, Nazi ideologues reminded the war-weary population of the power inherent in the "little things." See Schmidt, "Von der Macht der kleinen Dinge," 113–16.

47. Büttner. "'Gomorrah' und die Folgen," 613–32, and Brunswig, *Feuersturm Über Hamburg*. For the advertisement of *Ich vertraue dir meine Frau an*, see *Hamburger Zeitung*, August 26, 1943.

48. Nossack, *Der Untergang*, 85.

49. Nossack, *Der Untergang*, 102.

50. Stargardt, *The German War*, 383.

51. Büttner, "'Gomorrha' und die Folgen," 628. By the end of September much of the shipyard was operational, and even though the city's industrial output in 1943 could not match that of the previous year, it exceeded it in 1944. See also "Die Wiederaufnahme der Arbeit," *Hamburger Zeitung*, August 3, 1943. For the deterioration of the general mood see also Friedrich, *The Fire*, 98. Here Friedrich discusses the investigations by US occupying forces into the reactions of bomb victims and explains that the accumulation of experiences tended to dull the effect of shock that accompanied the first attack.

52. Boberach, "SD-Berichte zu Inlandfragen," May 4, 1944, and May 18, 1944, 6509, 6535.

53. "Ab morgen neue Lebensmittelkarten," *Hamburger Zeitung*, August 15, 1943.

54. "Die Verteilung des Wohnraumes an Berufstätige," *Hamburger Tageblatt*, August 26, 1943. Büttner, "'Gomorrah' und die Folgen," 630.

55. On June 6, 1944, Allied forces invaded occupied France, and they liberated Paris on August 24. For reactions to Italy's surrender see Boberach, "SD-Berichte zu Inlandfragen," July 29, 1943, 5540. "According to available reports, the resignation of the Duce [Mussolini] shocked the population . . . almost the entire population in all parts of the Reich was of the opinion that 'fascism had obviously been done in.'"

56. Wette, Bremer, Vogel, *Das letzte halbe Jahr*, 392. Workers, who were the last to make it to the already understocked stores, demanded more rigorous prosecution of favoritism and secret deals (*Schiebereien*). For illicit dealings see Boberach, *Meldungen aus dem Reich.* "The population reacted with skepticism to the Minister's claims that bartering and smuggling remained the exception" (6539). Instead, "there was doubt in the mind of the population that certain individuals receive more than 50 times the amount of sugar allotted to the 'normal consumer' [*Normalverbraucher*] due to connections, relations, or friendship. Especially business men and innkeepers are scrutinized for signs of favoritism" (6713).

57. Letter from Else Behncke to her husband, December 28, 1944, DTA 1454 I Liebesbriefe auf KZ Wache. Briefe-Tagebücher von Hugo und Else Behncke Mai 1944 bis Kriegsende, 101.

58. For those who could not afford exorbitant prices—bread was apparently sold for up to RM 400—and who had no connections or wares to trade, the last week of a food allocation period was indeed a Horst Wessel week: Since nothing was available any longer, people ate only in spirit. See Wette, Bremer, Vogel, *Das letzte halbe Jahr*, 403.

59. Goebbels, July 14, 1943, in *Die Tagebücher von Joseph Goebbels*, 99–100.

60. Rolf Giessen calculates the total costs for *Kolberg* at RM 8.8 million . See Giesen, *Nazi Propaganda*, 171.

61. The production of *Kolberg* drew substantial numbers of soldiers from the front to obtain the necessary extras for the film only months before the Reich mobilized the *Volkssturm* in September 1944. Veit Harlan claimed in his memoirs that he requested 6,000 horses and 187,000 Wehrmacht soldiers for the making of the film. Drawing on the memory of Heinz Pehlke, the assistant cameraman, Giessen offers a more realistic estimate of about 5,000 extras, of which about 2,000 were sailors. Giesen, *Nazi Propaganda Films*, 171–72.

62. Beauftragte für den Vierjahresplan. Reichskommissar für die Preisbildung. Runderlass Nr. 38/44 vom 20 Aug 1944 Betr. Vereinfachung der Eintrittspreisbildung der Filmtheater für die Dauer des Krieges, StAHH 371-16 Behörde für Wirtschaft und Verkehr 1852.

63. Amt für Preisbildung und Preisüberwachung. Bericht, November 22, 1944, StAHH 371-16 Behörde fuer Wirtschaft und Verkehr 1852.

64. For a history of the *Volkssturm* and its significance see Yelton, *Hitler's Volkssturm.*

65. Schreiben der UFA Theater-Betriebs-GmBH und Amt für Preisbildung und Preisüberwachung, Hamburg. Betrifft: Lessing-Theater, March 23, 1945, StAHH 371-16 Behörde für Wirtschaft und Verkehr 1852.

66. Aktenvermerk zum Prüfungsauftrag vom 16 Feb 1945, Ergänzungsprüfung, March 30, 1945, StAHH 371-16 Behörde für Wirtschaft und Verkehr 1852.

67. Stargardt, 371.

68. Bericht des Reichsbeauftragten für die deutsche Filmwirtschaft an Reichsfilminten-danten. Betreff: Wiederherstellung von fliegergeschädigten Lichtspieltheatern, March 12, 1945, BArch 109 III 19.

69. Cited in Wette, Bremer, Vogel, *Das letzte halbe Jahr*, 396.

70. Wette, Bremer, Vogel, *Das letzte halbe Jahr*, 401.

71. Wette, Bremer, Vogel, *Das letzte halbe Jahr*, 390

72. Goebbels, *Die Tagebücher.*

73. Bekanntmachung des Polizeipräsident Betr. Einmarsch der Besatzungstruppen in Hamburg, May 3, 1945, StAHH 331-1 Polizeibehörde 340.

74. Bekanntmachung des Polizeipräsident Betr. Einmarsch der Besatzungstruppen in Hamburg, 3 May 1945, StAHH 331-1 Polizeibehörde 340.

75. In a legendary move, Hamburg's foremost National Socialist "saved" the city from further destruction by handing it over to the British rather than defending it. Kaufmann's racism, corruption, and hunger for power notwithstanding, the political elites in Hamburg described Kaufmann as an "island of relative reason" and claimed that his personality saved them from "participating in actions" or from gaining "knowledge of such plans and actions" that were tried at Nuremberg. The *Hamburger Freie Presse* even asserted that Kaufmann had had no knowledge of the atrocities at Neugengamme Concentration Camp. See "Auch Kaufmann wußte nichts," *Hamburger Freie Presse*, April 10, 1946. For a more comprehensive discussion of the Kaufmann legend and an excellent study of his personal and political career see Bajohr, "Gauleiter in Hamburg," 267–95.

76. Compare Wildt, *Am Beginn der "Konsumgesellschaft,"* 36–37. Wildt illustrates that the experience of want and deprivation in the immediate postwar period must be seen in light of a much longer trajectory of want and need since the First World War. Wildt argues against the notion that the fall of Stalingrad and the destruction of German cities in 1943 presented one of two end points framing a period of "extra-ordinariness" that lasted until the monetary reform of 1948. Instead he suggests that neither the notion of "orderliness" before the war nor celebrated immediate effects of monetary reform on everyday life withstand more careful historical investigation.

77. Senator Friedrich Frank, "Karten Klarheit und Karten Wahrheit wollen wir haben," *Hamburger Echo*, March 7, 1947, StAHH 135-1 Staatliche Pressestelle V IRIb. The senator writes against the seemingly pervasive presumptions that the "rape of the calorie" set in after the collapse of the Reich. Instead he assures the readership that the deterioration of food provisions had already started during the war, but apparently only in a democratic Germany can frustration about it be expressed.

78. Szodrzynski, "Die 'Heimatfront' zwischen Stalingrad und Kriegsende," 639.

79. Jahn, ed., *Stalingrad Erinnern*; Moeller, review of Peter Jahn, 697–99. Moeller points to the significance of Stalingrad as a symbol of the victim status of German soldiers at the hands of their own murderous government. Also see Moeller, *War Stories*.

80. The Bizone was established between the British and American occupation zones, effective as of January 1, 1947. Compare "Ab 1.1.47 Wirtschaftliche Zusammenlegung der britschen und amerikanischen Zone!," *Hamburger Freie Presse*, December 4, 1946. See also Benz, *Von der Besatzungsherrschaft zur Bundesrepublik*.

81. Weisbrod, *Von der Währungsreform zum Wirtschaftswunder*.

82. The Bundesrepulik Deutschland (BDR) was established on May 23, 1949, the Deutsche Demokratische Republik (DDR) on October 7, 1949.

83. See in particular the contributions in Giles, *Stunde Null*; also Braun, Gerhardt, Holtman, *Die lange Stunde Null*.

84. Kommando der Schutzpolizei. Betr: Anordnung der Britischen Militärvewaltung, May 6, 1945, StAHH 331-1 Polizebehörde 340.

85. Kommando der Schutzpolizei. Betr: Anordnung der Britischen Militärvewaltung, May 6, 1945, StAHH 331-1 Polizebehörde 340.

86. Anordnungen der Militärverwaltung, May 6, 1945, StAHH 331-1 Polizeibehörde I, 340.

87. Öffentliche Bekanntmachungen für die Zivilbevölkerung, May 15 1945, StAHH 131-14 Verbindunsstelle der Militärregierung VI 1.

88. Der Kommandeur der Schutzpolizei and Kameraden der Schutzpolizei, Verwaltungspolizei, und Kriminalpolizei, May 29, 1945, StAHH 331-1 Polizeibehörde I, 340.

89. Elementary schools resumed operations on August 6, 1945. Öffentliche Bekanntmachungen aus dem Hamburger Nachrichten-Blatt vom Donnerstag, den 2. August 1945, StAHH
131-14 Verbindunsstelle der Militärregierung VI 1.

90. Bekanntmachungen der Militaerregierung aus dem Hamburger Nachrichten-Blatt vom
24. Juli 1945, StAHH 131-14 Verbindunsstelle der Militaerregierung VI 1.

91. STAHH 131-14 Verbindungsstelle zur Militärregierung III 1 Band 6.

92. Stüber, *Kampf gegen den Hunger 1945-1950*, 108. The German Interregional Food
Allocation Committee set the daily ration at 1,550 calories; in comparison, the average daily
rations in summer 1944 hovered around 2,000 calories according to American calculations.
The *New York Times* reported that "Germans, at the time of their surrender, were regularly
getting twice as much meat as Britons got throughout the war, living reasonably well off the
stocks in stores and warehouses, which are being doled out by the Military Government much
in a continuance of the German rationing system." See "'Starving' in Reich is put up to U.S.,"
New York Times, May 17, 1945. See further Weinreb, *Modern Hungers: Food and Power in
Twentieth-Century Germany*.

93. Judt, *Postwar*, 21.

94. Tooze, *Wages of Destruction*, 544–45. Jews were the first population group designated
for starvation under the Hunger Plan. Except for three hundred thousand Jews designated as
workers, Polish Jews no longer received any official rations in August 1942. Rations for non-
Jewish Poles were supposed to be cut off in March 1943 but could be sustained at a ridiculously
low level due to an exceptional harvest the previous fall.

95. Judt, *Postwar*, 21–22.

96. Wildt, *Am Beginn der "Konsumgesellschaft,"* 31.

97. "Wiedereröffnung der Hamburger Kinos," *Hamburger Nachrichtenblatt*, July 26, 1945,
372-3 Gewerbepolizei Gen IX F 32.

98. *Das Bad auf der Tenne* (1942/43), *Ich vertraue dir meine Frau an* (1942/43), *Der Engel
mit dem Saitenspiel* (1944), and *Gefährtin meines Sommers* (1942/43) were the first four films
to play in Hamburg after the collapse of the Reich. The first British film, *Rembrandt*, started
at the refurbished Waterloo Theater on September 20, 1945. Compare Bericht: Eröffnung des
"Waterloo-Theater," 376-2 Gewerbepolizei Spz IX F 13.

99. "Wiedereröffnung der Hamburger Kinos," *Hamburger Nachrichtenblatt*, July 26, 1945,
372-3 Gewerbepolizei Gen IX F 32.

100. Gabriele Clemens convincingly argues that the "projection of Britain" was the main
goal of British cultural policy in occupied Germany. Instructing Germans in British-style
democracy and simultaneously using cultural media to present the British nation in favorable
and sympathetic ways, the British policy was one of mediation (33–38). Clemens, *Britische Kulturpolitik*. A similar argument is advance by Welch, "Priming the Pump of German Democracy."

101. Feherenbach, *Cinema in Democratizing Germany*, 54; Clemens, *Britische Kulturpolitik
in Deutschland*, 130.

102. Moeller, *War Stories*, 5.

103. "Hunger als Schuld und Schicksal," *Hamburger Freie Presse*, April 10, 1946.

104. "Demokratie—recht verstanden," *Hamburger Freie Presse*, April 6, 1946.

105. "Demokratie—recht verstanden," *Hamburger Freie Presse*, April 6, 1946.

106. "Kollektivschuld," *Hamburger Freie Presse*, May 4, 1946.

107. "Man kann ein hungerndes Volk nicht zur Demokratie erziehen," *Hamburger Freie
Presse*, June 8, 1946.

108. Fehrenbach, *Cinema in Democratizing Germany*, 5.

109. Huebener, "The French Cultural Program in Germany," 425.

110. Familienfürsorge Kreis 1. Amt Innenstadt. Lagebericht für Monat Oktober, November 13, 1945, StAHH 354-5 Jugendbehörde II Ablage 22. 7.1981 1.

111. Familienfürsorge Kreis 1. Amt Innenstadt. Lagebericht für Monat Oktober, November 13, 1945, StAHH 354-5 Jugendbehörde II Ablage 22. 7.1981 1.

112. Sozialabteilung Innenstadt. Familienfürsorge. Lagebericht für die Monate Juli, August und September 1947, StAHH 354-5 Jugendbehörde II Ablage 22. 7.1981 1.

113. Sozialabteilung Innenstadt. Fürsorgerinnendienst. Lagebricht über die Monate Oktober November, Dezember 21 Jan 48, StAHH 354-5 Jugendbehörde II Ablage 22. 7.1981 1.

114. Sozialabteilung Innenstadt, Familienfuersorge. Lagebericht für die Monate Janaur bis März 1947, 15 April 1947, StAHH 354-5 Jugendbehörde II Ablage 22. 7.1981 1.

115. See Weinreb, "Matters of Taste," 105.

116. West Germans continued to equate the suffering of expellees, POWs, and bomb victims with that endured by the victims of the Nazi regime. Compare Moeller, *War Stories*.

117. Joseph, "Our Film Program in Germany: How Far Was it a Success?" Against discontent from industry representatives, the article asserts the importance of the involvement of government agencies in educating the German public. The Americans, the article claims, are doing the best possible job of all occupation powers in deploying film as a means of instruction.

118. McLaughlin, "U.S. Now Operates Reich Movie Studio," *New York Times*, August 5, 1945; Egan, "OWI Will Drive Home the Truth to Germans," *New York Times*, April 15, 1945; "Film Education Urged," *New York Times*, March 24 1945; "Bestiality of the Nazis," *Manchester Guardian*, May 2, 1945; "Nazi Camp Films," *Manchester Guardian*, April 26, 1945.

119. "A more liberal policy in Germany," *Manchester Guardian*, June 30, 1945.

120. The first news agency was formed a month after the war's end; it consisted of a mixed team of British military personal and civilians. "Freedom of Mind in Germany," *Manchester Guardian*, February 15, 1947.

121. "A more liberal policy in Germany," *The Manchester Guardian*, June 30, 1945.

122. McLaughlin, "U.S. Now Operates Reich Movie Studio," *New York Times*, August 5, 1945; Hill, "British to Show German Motion Pictures in Zone Despite Delay in American Area," *New York Times*, July 29, 1945.

123. Fehrenbach, *Cinema in Democratizing Germany*, 56–58.

124. Theaters in the French Zone also started on German reruns, introducing foreign films later. Clemens, *Britische Kulturpolitik in Deutschland*, 130.

125. "U.S. Zone Revives Film Competition," *New York Times*, December 9, 1947. Compare Clemens, *Britische Kulturpolitik in Deutschland*, 132, 241. As of October 1948 the distribution system was extended to the French Zone as well.

126. Clemens, *Britische Kulturpolitik in Deutschland*, 241.

127. Clemens, *Britische Kulturpolitik*, 133.

128. For the creation of Ufa Film GmbH (Ufi) compare Spiker, *Film und Kapital*, 194. Ufi reorganized all major German film companies under the aegis of a state monopoly. This giant trust included the previously state-dominated companies, Ufa, Tobis, Terra, and Bavaria, plus Berlin-Filmkunst, Prag-Film AG, Wien-Film, Continental Films, Deutsche Zeichenfilm, Mars-Film, and Berliner Künstlerbühnen. Ufi also absorbed the entire distribution sector, studios, Deutsche Filmtheater GmbH, and Ufa-Theater Betriebs GmbH. Ufi even controlled newsreel production and distribution. See Spiker, *Film und Kapital*, 226.

129. Clemens, *Britische Kulturpolitik,* 133.

130. Clemens, *Britische Kulturpolitik,* 235. The Russians were generally more lenient when it came to popular entertainment and apparently did not impose a general ban on movie exhibition. Compare Gladwin Hill, "British to Show German Motion Pictures in Zone Despite Delay in American Area," *New York Times,* July 29, 1945.

131. Roland, "The Film Scene in Germany," *New York Times,* January 6, 1946. Schmidt, "Germany's Muddled Film Situation," *New York Times,* June 22, 1947. Among the famous hiding out in Munich or American-occupied Germany were Hans Albers, Erich Engel, Emil Jannings, Von Bolvari, Harlad Braun, Willy Forst, Ilse Werner, and Ferdinand Marian. Zarah Leander, at first, returned to her native Sweden.

132. These were *Die Mörder sind unter uns, In jenen Tagen, Sag die Wahrheit* (Weiss, Studio-45, 1946) and *Zwischen Gestern und Morgen* (Braun, NDF, 1947). Compare Chronik 1946–47 in Jacobson, Kaes, and Prinzler, *Die Geschichte des Deutschen Films,* 535. Also Larsen, "The Emergence of a New Film Industry." See further the appendix on films produced between 1945 and 1949 in Fay, "The Business of Cultural Diplomacy," 329.

133. "German Film Growth Decried by U.S. Aide," *New York Times,* January 18, 1947.

134. Arthur J. Rank was a British media magnate who in 1937 formed the Rank Organization, a vertically integrated film company that not only effectively dominated British film production but also controlled a large number of exhibition outlets. See Eyles, *Odeon Cinemas 2*; "British Lords Commend Rank, Film Czar, for Efforts to Compete with Hollywood," *New York Times,* February 24, 1944; "British Film Group Plans to Invade World Market," *New York Times,* February 11, 1944.

135. Der Bürgermeister der Hansestadt Hamburg an Information Control Unit, Hansestadt Hamburg, December 20, 1946, StAHH 131-14 Verbindungstelle der Militaerregierung III2 Band 9.

136. Der Bürgermeister der Hansestadt Hamburg an Information Control Unit, Hansestadt Hamburg, December 20, 1946, StAHH 131-14 Verbindungstelle der Militaerregierung III2 Band 9.

137. Der Bürgermeister der Hansestadt Hamburg an Information Control Unit, Hansestadt Hamburg, December 20, 1946, StAHH 131-14 Verbindungstelle der Militaerregierung III2 Band 9.

138. Der Bürgermeister der Hansestadt Hamburg an Information Control Unit, Hansestadt Hamburg, December 20, 1946, StAHH 131-14 Verbindungstelle der Militaerregierung III2 Band 9.

139. *Brief Encounter* was nominated for three Oscars in 1947, and David Lean won the Grand Prix at the Cannes Film Festival in 1946. Even though Celia Johnson did not receive an Oscar, she won the New York Film Critics Circle Award for best actress in 1946. Compare "*Brief Encounter,*" Awards, *Internet Movie Database,* http://www.imdb.com/title/tt0037558/awards.

140. Laurence Olivier won the Honorary Award for outstanding achievement as an actor, producer, and director of this film at the 1947 Academy Awards. Compare *Henry V*, Awards, *Internet Movie Database* http://www.imdb.com/title/tt0036910/awards.

141. Lüth, "Zensur auf Umwegen," *Hamburger Freie Presse,* July 7, 1948.

142. Lüth, "Zensur auf Umwegen," *Hamburger Freie Presse,* July 7, 1948.

143. "General Angriff auf die Trümmer," *Hamburger Freie Presse,* April 3, 1946; "Die Todesmühlen," *Hamburger Freie Presse,* April 3, 1946; "Demokratie—recht verstanden," *Hamburger*

Freie Presse, April 6, 1946; "Kollektivschuld," *Hamburger Freie Presse,* May 4, 1946; and "Briefe an die Redaktion: Zur Schuldfrage," *Hamburger Freie Presse,* April 3, 1946.

144. Quoted in Ebsworth, *Restoring Democracy in Germany,* 21.

145. "Demokratie—recht verstanden," *Hamburger Freie Presse,* April 6, 1946.

146. "Demokratie—recht verstanden," *Hamburger Freie Presse,* April 6, 1946.

147. Still in 1944 Goebbels identifies Käutner as the greatest German film artist, the true avant-garde of German film. See Goebbels, *Die Tagebücher,* 476. Film scholars and historians, however, have consistently stressed Käutner's inner emigration and his political distance from the regime. Witte, "Film im Nationalsozialismus," 138, and Witte, "The Indivisible Legacy of Nazi Cinema," 23–30. See also Rentschler's discussion of Käutner's *Romanze in Moll,* in *Ministry of Illusion,* 218.

148. Töteberg, *Filmstadt Hamburg,* 110–13.

149. Töteberg, *Filmstadt Hamburg,* 110–13.

150. "Zur Gründung des Wirtschaftsverbandes der Filmtheater e.V. (Brit. Zone)," *Film-Echo,* May 1947, 26.

151. Tötegerg, *Filmstadt,* 110–11.

152. Scholars have described Käutner's *In jenen Tagen* as a fraudulent attempt to grapple with German guilt and have compared it (unfavorably) to Wolfgang Staudte's *Die Mörder sind unter uns.* See Göttler, "Westdeutscher Nachkriegsfilm," 178. Göttler argues that Käutner, rather than offering a tentative and suggestive exploration of what it *might* have been like, clearly affirmed "this is how it was." For the premier see "'In jenen Tagen' Helmut-Käutner-Film-Uraufführung in Hamburg," *Rhein-Neckar-Zeitung,* June 24, 1947, StAHH 135-1 Staatliche Pressestelle V. IJ VIII a.

153. See in particular Göttler, "Westdeutscher Nachkriegsfilm," 171–210; Weckel, "The Mitläufer in Two German Postwar Films." Both Göttler and Weckel describe *Die Mörder* as exceptions to German unwillingness to explore questions of guilt rather than victimhood. Robert Moeller suggests that guilt and victimhood were mutually exclusive categories in postwar Germany and identifies Staudte's film as one that raised difficult questions about war guilt. Moeller, *War Stories.*

154. See König, *Volkswagen, Volksempfaenger, Volksgemeinschaft;* Tooze, *Wages of Destruction,* 152, 156.

155. See Moeller, *War Stories,* 49–50. Also Weckel and Wolfrum *"Bestien und "Befehlsempfänger": Frauen und Männer in NS-Prozessen nach 1945.*

156. Lüth, "Zensur auf Umwegen," *Hamburger Freie Presse,* July 7, 1948.

157. "Kollektivschuld," *Hamburger Freie Presse,* May 4, 1946.

158. Joseph von Baky directed the first postwar German film made by an American licensed studio and Hans Albers played the lead role in *Und über uns der Himmel* (1947) without invoking references to their last common venture, *Münchhausen* (1943), a film made in celebration of the twenty-fifth anniversary of Ufa.

159. Veit Harlan was facing charges for crimes against humanity in Hamburg. After a seven-week show trial Harlan was acquitted for lack of evidence. The Hamburg jury court felt unable to determine whether the anti-Semitic hate film *Jud Süss* had been able to injure a Jewish sense of honor or led to later crimes against Jews. See "Ein Umstrittenes Urteil: Veit Harlan freigesprochen," *Der Neue Film,* April 1949.

160. "Germans Boo British Film," *Manchester Guardian,* November 16, 1946.

161. For example, when movie theaters first opened in the US Zone, Germans "almost mobbed the theater in the hope of seeing *Gone With the Wind*" and accordingly were more than disappointed when treated to an hour and fifteen minutes of "rotten propaganda" that was subsequently described as "the worst show I've ever paid to see." McLaughlin, "Munich Germans Score Film Fare," *New York Times,* August 5, 1945; Schmidt, "Our Movies Leave Germans Hostile," *New York Times,* July 23, 1946.

Epilogue

1. Rau, "Holsteinische Landesstadt oder Reichsstadt?"

2. See "Auch Kaufmann wußte nichts," *Hamburger Freie Presse,* April 10, 1946. Bajohr, "Gauleiter in Hamburg," 267–95.

3. Agamben, *State of Exception.*

4. Auszug aus den Bekanntmachungen der Brit. Militärregierung aus dem Hamburger Nachrichten-Blatt vom 13. November 1945, StAHH 331-1 Polizeibehörde 340.

5. I borrowed the phrase "practicing democracy" from Anderson, *Practicing Democracy.*

6. "Hamburg als Filmproduktionstätte," *Film-Kurier,* August 13, 1941.

7. "Kann Hamburg Filmstadt Sein? Ein Praktiker nimmt das Wrot zu einer viel diskutierte Frage," *Neue Hamburger Presse,* October 17, 1945, StAHH 135-1 Staatliche Pressestelle V IJVIIIb.

8. "Und was sagt die Film-Section?," *Hamburger Freie Presse,* August 10, 1948, StAHH 135-1 Staatliche Pressestelle V IJVIIIb.

9. Deighton, "Cold-War Diplomacy."

10. "Kann Hamburg Filmstadt sein? Ein Praktiker nimmt das Wort zu einer viel diskutierte Frage," *Neue Hamburger Presse,* October 17, 1945, StAHH 135-1 Staatliche Pressestelle V IJVIIIb.

11. Käutner shot *In jenen Tagen,* the first film made by a British-licensed film company, without any studio resources—all takes were shot outdoors. In contrast, the Real-Film *Arche Nora* was shot in the Ohlstedt dancehall, which was used as a makeshift studio. Since wide-angle takes were out of the question, the film relied on extreme close-ups and tableaus. See "Hamburg doch eine Filmstadt?," *Die Welt,* August 12, 1947, StAHH 135-1 Staatliche Pressestelle V IJVIIIb.

12. "Hamburg projektiert Filmindustrie," *Hamburger Echo,* March 29, 1949, StAHH 135-1 Staatliche Pressestelle V IJVIIIb.

13. "Filmstadt Hamburg wird Wirklichkeit," *Die Welt,* March 29, 1949, StAHH 135-1 Staatliche Pressestelle V IJVIIIb.

14. In 1927, Alfred Hugenberg, media mogul and then leader of the German National People's Party (DNVP) acquired the majority shares in Germany's largest film production company, Universum Film AG (Ufa). Hugenberg, who was sympathetic to the Nazi cause, made his media empire available to Hitler and the NSDAP as politics of a national opposition gained traction and thus it was crucial to Hitler's electoral successes in the early 1930s. Hugenberg also served in Hitler's first cabinet but soon outlived his usefulness to Reich Chancellor Hitler after the Nazi Party had absorbed most of the DNVP's members and successfully cemented its power and dismantled Weimar democracy. Kreimeier, *Ufa Story.*

15. "Filmstadt Hamburg wird Wirklichkeit," *Die Welt,* March 29, 1949, StAHH 135-1 Staatliche Pressestelle V IJVIIIb.

16. "Millionen-Filmprojekt vorläufig abgelehnt," *Hamburger Volkszeitung,* April 14, 1949, StAHH 135-1 Staatliche Pressestelle V IJVIIIb.

17. "Millionen-Filmprojekt vorläufig abgelehnt," *Hamburger Volkszeitung,* April 14, 1949, StAHH 135-1 Staatliche Pressestelle V IJVIIIb. For the importance of unification to the Social Democrats compare Moeller, *War Stories,* 23.

18. "Optimisten in Rahlstedt," *Die Welt,* December 3, 1949, StAHH 135-1 Staatliche Pressestelle V IJ VIIIb.

19. "Kulturfilm vereint Nationen," *Hamburger Allgemeine Zeitung,* May 9, 1949.

BIBLIOGRAPHY

Archives

Bundesarchiv Berlin (BArch)
Bundesarchiv Filmarchiv (BAF)
Deutsche Kinnemathek Berlin
Deutsches Tagebucharchiv Emmendingen (DTA)
Staatsarchiv Hamburg (StAHH)
Forschungsstelle für Zeitgeschichte in Hamburg (FZH)
Stadtteilarchiv Barmbek
Stadtteilarchiv Eimsbüttel (Galerie Morgenland)
Stadtteilarchiv Ottensen
Stadtteilarchiv St. Pauli
Zeitzeugenbörse Hamburg
Film- und Fernsehmuseum Hamburg

Published Primary Sources

Bericht. Weltkongress für Freizeit und Erholung. Berlin: Verlag Freude und Arbeit, 1937.

Blum, O. *Städtebau.* 2nd ed. Berlin: Julius Springer, 1937.

Boberach, Heinz, ed. *Meldungen aus dem Reich. Die geheimen Lageberichte des Sicherheitsdienstes der SS, 1938–1945.* 17 vols. Berlin: Pawlag Verlag Herrsching, 1984.

Bockenmühl, Eric. *Volksgemeinschaft der Tat: Geschichten vom Hilswerk "Mutter und Kind," vom "Winterhilfswerk" and von "Kraft Durch Freude."* Halle: Carl Marhold Verlag, undated.

Buchert, Gerhart. *Der Marshallplan. Ein Weg in die Zukunft.* Frankfurt a.M.: Wolfgang Metzner, 1949.

Daitz, Werner. *Lebensraum und gerechte Weltordnung: Grundlagen einer anti-Atlantikcharta.* Amsterdam: De Amsterdamsche Keurkamer, 1943.

Dresler, Adolf. *Deutsche Kunst und entartete "Kunst"; Kunstwerk und Zerrbild im Spiegel der Weltanschauung.* Munich: Deutscher Volksverlag, 1938.

Fairbanks, Douglas. *Hitler's Shadow over South America.* Brooklyn: Free German Movement, 1941.

Feder, Gottfried. *Die neue Stadt. Versuch der Begründung einer neuen Stadtplanungskunst aus der sozialen Struktur der Bevölkerung.* Berlin: Julius Springer, 1939.

Fleige, Kurt. "Städtebau-Gestern und Heute." *Monatshefte für Baukunst und Städtebau* 9 (September 1941): 229–30.

Frank, Hermann, and Paul Frank. "Die Gartenstadt Klein-Borstel in Hamburg." *Monatshefte für Baukunst und Städtebau* 11 (November 1941): 317–24.

Funke, Alois. *Film und Jugend: Eine Untersuchung über die psychischen Wirkungen des Films im Leben der Jugendlichen.* Munich: Ernst Reinhardt, 1934.

Goebbels, Joseph. "Ansprache des Reichsministers Dr. Goebbels vor den Filmschaffenden in der Krolloper am 10. Februar 1934." In *Der Aufbau des Deutschen Führerstaates. Das Jahr 1934. Dokumente der deutschen Politik,* edited by Paul Meier-Benneckenstein, 258–66. Vol. II. Berlin: Junker und Dünnhaupt, 1936.

———. *Die Tagebücher Von Joseph Goebbels.* Edited by Elke Fröhlich. Munich: Saur, 1993.

———. *Die Zeit ohne Beispiel. Reden und Aufsätze aus den Jahren 1939/40/41.* Munich: Zentralverlag der NSDAP, 1941. Heiber, Helmut, ed. *Goebbels-Reden.* Vol. 1: 1932–1939. Düsseldorf: Droste, 1971.

Handbuch des Films 1935/36. Berlin: Hoppenstedt & Co., 1936.

Heiss, Fridrich. *Bei uns in Deutschland. Ein Bericht.* Berlin: Volk und Reich Verlag, 1938.

Hiller, Friedrich. *Deutscher Kampf um Lebensraum.* Leipzig: Armanen Verlag, 1933.

Hinkel, Hans, ed. *Handbuch der Reichskulturkammer.* Berlin: Deutscher Verlag für Politik und Wirtschaft, 1937.

Hitler, Adolf. *Der Führer vor dem ersten Reichstag Großdeutschlands. Reichstagsrede vom 30. Januar 1939.* Munich: Zentralverlag der NSDAP, 1939.

———. "Reden des Führers." n.p., 1936.

Hitler over Latin America: Why the Embargo Against Spain Must Be Lifted Now! New York: Lawyers Committee on American Relations with Spain, 1937.

Huebener, Theodore. "The French Cultural Program in Germany." *French Review* 24, no. 5 (April 1951): 421–25.

Kerr, Harrison. "Information Control in the Occupied Areas." *Notes* Second Series 4, no. 4 (September 1947): 431–35.

Killus, Heinz. "Der Totalitätsgedanke im neuen Städtebau." *Monatshefte für Baukunst und Städtebau* 4 (April 1940): 85–88.

Klemperer, Victor. *LTI: Notizbuch eines Philologen.* Berlin: Aufbau-Verlag Berlin, 1947.

"Die Kongreßstadt Hamburg." In *Amtlicher Führer zum Weltkongress für Freizeit und Erholung, Hamburg 23-3- Juli 1936.* Deutscher Organisationsasuschuß des Weltkongresses für Freizeit und Erholung, 1936.

Köttgen, Arnold. *Deutsche Verwaltung.* 2nd ed. Berlin: Weidemannsche Verlagsbuchhandlung, 1937.

Krogmann, Carl Vincent. *Es ging um Deutschlands Zukunft: 1932-1939. Erlebtes täglich diktiert von dem früheren regierenden Bürgermeister von Hamburg.* Leoni am Starnberger See: Druffel-Verlag, 1976.

Krüger, Herbert "Der Raum als Gestalter der Innen- und Aussenpolitik." In *Reich, Volksordnung, Lebensraum.* Vol. I. Darmstadt: L. C. Wittich Verlag, 1941.

Landesamt, Statistisches, ed. *Statistisches Jahrbuch für die Freie und Hansestadt Hamburg, 1934/35.* Hamburg: Komissionsveralg von Lütcke & Wulff, 1935.

———. *Statistisches Jahrbuch für die Hansestadt Hamburg 1937/1938.* Hamburg: Lütcke & Wulff, 1939.

Larson, Egon. "The Emergency of a New Film Industry." *Hollywood Quarterly* 3, no. 4 (Summer 1948): 387–94.

Leidmann, Eva. *Ein Mädchen geht an Land.* Berlin: Schützen-Verlag, 1944.

Ley, Robert. *Ein Volk erobert die Freude.* Verlag der Deutschen Arbeitsfront GmbH, 1937.

Lidbetter, Ernest James. *Heredity and the Social Problem Group*. London: Edward Arnold & Co., 1933.

Ludorf, Stadtrat A. D. "Luftschutz durch Städtebau." *Monatshefte für Baukunst und Städtebau* 5 (May 1935): 59–60.

Mächler, Martin. "Die Großstadt als Kultur- und Raumproblem und die Grenzen ihrer Größe." *Monatshefte für Baukunst und Städtebau* 6 (June 1939): 63.

Mann, Klaus. "What's Wrong with Anti-Nazi Films?" "File and Exile." Special issue, *New German Critique* 89 (Spring-Summer 2003): 173–82.

Marshall, S. L. A. *Blitzkrieg: Its History, Strategy, Economics, and the Challenge to America*. New York: William Morrow, 1940.

Meier-Benneckenstein, Paul, and Axel Friedrichs, eds. *Dokumente der deutschen Politik. Der Aufbau des deutschen Führerstaates. Das Jahr 1934*. Vol. 2. Berlin: Junker und Dünnhaupt, 1936.

Meyer, Konrad, ed. *Volk und Lebensraum: Forschungen im Dienste von Raumordnung und Landesplanung*. Berlin: Kurt Vowinckel Verlag, 1938.

Migge, Berecht. *Deutsche Binnenkolonisation: Sachgrundlagen des Siedlungswesen*. Edited by Deutsche Gartenstadt-Gesellschaft. Berlin: Deutscher Kommunal-Verlag, 1926

"Neutrality, Peace Legislation and Our Foreign Policy. Hearings before the Committee on Foreign Relations United States Senate." Washington, DC: Government Printing Office, 1939.

Noack, Viktor. "Die Umgestaltung des Gängeviertels in Hamburg." *Bauen, Siedeln, Wohnen* 23–24 (1934): 390ff.

Nossack, Hans Erich. *Der Untergang: Hamburg 1943*. 1948. Hamburg: Ernst Kabel Verlag, 1981.

———. *The End: Hamburg 1943*. Translated by Joel Agee. Chicago: University of Chicago Press, 2004.

Petersen, Käthe. "Entmündigung Geistesschwacher Prostituierter." *Zeitschrift für psychische Hygiene* 15, no. 4/6 (January 1943): 67–76.

Schlange-Schöningen, Hans. *Im Schatten des Hungers: Dokumentarisches zur Ernährungspolitik und Ernährungswritschaft in den Jahren 1945–1949*. Hamburg: Paul Parey, 1955.

Schubert, Werner, ed. *Akademie für Deutsches Recht 1933–1945. Protokole der Ausschüsse*. Berlin: De Gruyter, 2001.

Seasbury, William Marston. *The Public and the Motion Picture Industry*. New York: Macmillan, 1926.

Sennett, A. R. *Garden Cities in Theory and Practice. Being an Amplification of a Paper on the Potentialities of Applied Science in a Garden City. Read before Section F of the British Association*. Vol. I. London: Bemrose and Sons Ltd., 1905.

Silverman, Dore. "The Film in Germany." *Sight and Sound* 18, no. 70 (Summer 1949): 66ff.

Speer, Albert. *Inside the Third Reich: Memoirs by Albert Speer*. Translated by Richard and Clara Winston. New York: Macmillan, 1970.

———, ed. *Neue deutsche Baukunst*. Berlin: Volk und Reich, 1943.

Starcke, Gerhard. *Die Deutsche Arbeitsfront*. 1940.

Storjohann, Uwe. *"Hauptsache: Überleben" Eine Jugend im Krieg 1936–1945*. 1993. 2nd ed. Hamburg: Dölling und Galitz Verlag, 1994.

Tretz, Karl Wilhelm. "Zwei Jahre NS-Gemeinschaft 'Kraft durch Freude.'" *Unser Wille und Weg: Monatsblätter der Reichspropagandaleitung* (January 1936): 23–25.

Turrou, Leon. *Nazi Spies in America*. New York: Random House, 1939.

Unwin, Sir Raymond. *Nothing Gained by Overcrowding. How the Garden City Type of Development May Benefit Both Owner and Occupier*. London: P. S. King & Sons, 1912.

Verband Hamburgischer Verkehrsvereine E.V., ed. *Führer durch Hamburg*. Hamburg, 1927.

von Schirach, Baldur. *Die Hitler-Jugend. Idee und Gestalt*. Berlin: Zeitgeschichte Verlag, 1934.

Walther, Andreas. *Neue Wege zur Großstadtsanierung*. Stuttgart: Verlag von W. Kohlhammer, 1936.

Wehner, Gerhard. *Die rechtliche Stellung der Hitler-Jugend*. Dresden: Verlag M. Dittert, 1939.

Wette, Wolfram, Ricarda Bremer, and Detlef Vogel, eds. *Das letzte halbe Jahr: Stimmungserichte der Wehrmachtspropaganda 1944/45*. Essen: Klartext, 2001.

Wollenberg, H. H. "From Adolf Hitler to Stewart Granger." *Sight and Sound* 18, no. 70 (Summer 1949): 63–65.

———. "New from Germany." *Sight and Sound* 15, no. 57 (Spring 1946): 22–23.

———. "The Revival of the German Film." *Sight and Sound* 16, no. 62 (Spring 1947): 9–11.

Secondary Sources

Abel, Richard. *The Ciné Goes to Town: French Cinema 1896–1914*. Berkeley: University of California Press, 1994.

———, ed. *Silent Film*. New Brunswick: Rutgers University Press, 1996.

Adorno, Theodor W., et al. *The Authoritarian Personality*. New York: Norton, 1950.

Agamben, Giorgio. *State of Exception*. Chicago: University of Chicago Press, 2005.

Albrecht, Gerd. *Der Film im Dritten Reich. Eine Dokumentation*. Karlsruhe: Schauburg, 1979.

———. *Nationalsozialistische Filmpolitik. Eine soziologische Untersuchung über die Spielfilme des Dritten Reichs*. Stuttgart: Ferdinand Enke, 1969.

Allen, William Sheridan. *The Nazi Seizure of Power: The Experience of a Single German Town, 1922–1945*. 2nd and revised ed. New York: F. Watts, 1984.

Alpers, Benjamin. "This Is the Army: Imagining a Democratic Military in World War II." *Journal of American History* 85, no. 1 (June 1998): 129–63.

Ambler, Charles. "Mass Media and Leisure in Africa." *International Journal of African Historical Studies* 35, no. 1 (2002): 119–36.

———. "Popular Films and Colonial Audiences: The Movies in Northern Rhodesia." *American Historical Review* 106, no. 1 (February 2001): 81–105.

Ames, Eric. "Herzog, Landscape, and Documentary." *Cinema Journal* 48, no. 2 (Winter 2009): 49–69.

Amin, Ash, and Nigel Thrift. *Cities: Reimagining the Urban*. Cambridge: Polity, 2002.

Applegate, Celia. *A Nation of Provincials: The German Idea of Heimat*. Berkeley: University of California Press, 1990.

Ascheid, Antje. *Hitler's Heroines: Stardom and Womanhood in Nazi Cinema*. Philadelphia: Temple University Press, 2003.

Asper, Helmut G. *"Etwas Besseres als den Tod . . ." Filmexil in Hollywood. Porträts, Filme, Dokumente*. Marburg: Schüren, 2002.

Bachrach, Susan D. *Deadly Medicine: Creating the Master Race*. Washington, DC: United States Holocaust Memorial Museum, 2004.

Baer, Hester. *Dismantling the Dream Factory: Gender, German Cinema, and the Postwar Quest for a New Film Language*. New York: Berghahn Books, 2009.

Bahr, Ehrhard. "The Anti-Semitism Studies of the Frankfurt School: The Failure of Critical Theory." *German Studies Review* 1, no. 2 (May 1978): 125–38.

Bajohr, Frank. *"Arisierung" In Hamburg: Die Verdrängung der jüdischen Unternehmen 1933–1945*. Hamburg: Christians, 1997.

———. "Gauleiter in Hamburg. Zur Person und Tätigkeit Karl Kaufmanns (1900–1969)." *Vierteljahreshefte für Zeitgeschichte* 43 (1995): 267–95.

———, ed. *Nordeutschland im Nationalsozialismus*. Hamburg: Ergebnisse Verlag, 1993.

———. "Die Zustimmungsdiktatur: Grundzüge nationalsozialistischer Herrschaft in Hamburg." In *Hamburg im "Dritten Reich,"* edited by FZH. Göttingen: Wallstein Verlag, 2005.

Bajohr, Frank, Werner Johe, and Uwe Lohalm, eds. *Zivilisation und Barbarei: Die widersprüchlichen Potentiale der Moderne*. Hamburg: Christians, 1991.

Baranowski, Shelley. *Strength Through Joy: Consumerism and Mass Tourism in the Third Reich*. Cambridge, UK: Cambridge University Press, 2004.

Barclay, David E., and Elisabeth Glaser-Schmidt, eds. *Transatlantic Images and Perceptions: Germany and America since 1776*. Washington, DC: German Historical Institute, 1997.

Barnouw, Dagmar. *Weimar Intellectuals and the Threat of Modernity*. Bloomington: Indiana University Press, 1988.

Bartels, Ulrike. *Die Wochenschau im Dritten Reich: Entwicklung und Funktion eines Massenmediums unter besonderer Berücksichtigung völkisch-nationaler Inhalte*. Frankfurt a.M.: Peter Lang, 2004.

Barth, Ariane. *Die Reeperbahn: Der Kampf um Hamburgs sündige Meile*. Hamburg: Spiegel-Buchverlag, 1999.

Barth, Boris. *Dolchstoßlegenden und politische Desintegration. Das Trauma der deutschen Niederlage im Ersten Weltkrieg 1914–1933*. Düsseldorf: Droste, 2003.

Barth, Erwin. *Joseph Goebbels und die Formierung des Führer-Mythos 1917–1934*. Erlangen: Palm & Enke, 1999.

Baudry, Jean-Louis. "The Apparatus: Metapsychological Approaches to the Impression of Reality in Cinema." In *Narrative, Apparatus, Ideology: A Film Theory* Reader, edited by Philip Rosen. New York: Columbia University Press, 1986. 299–318.

———. "Ideological Effects of the Basic Cinematographic Apparatus." In *Narrative, Apparatus, Ideology: A Film Theory* Reader, edited by Philip Rosen. New York: Columbia University Press, 1986. 286–98.

Behn, Manfred. "Gleichgeschaltet in Die 'Neue Zeit.'" In *Das Ufa-Buch. Kunst und Krisen. Stars und Regisseure. Wirtschaft und Politik*, edited by Hans Michael Bock and Michael Töteberg. Frankfurt a.M.: Zweitausendeins, 1992.

Benamou, Catherine L. *It's All True: Orson Welles's Pan-American Odyssey*. Berkeley: University of California Press, 2007.

Bender, Otto. *Swing unterm Hakenkreuz in Hamburg: 1933–1943*. Hamburg: Christians, 1993.

Benjamin, Walter. "The Work of Art in the Age of Mechanical Reproduction." In *The Nineteenth-Century Visual Culture Reader,* edited by Vanessa R. Schwartz and Jeannene M. Przyblski. New York: Routledge, 2004.

Benninghaus, Christina, and Deborah Laurie Cohen. "Mother's Toil and Daughters' Leisure: Working Class Girls and Time in 1920s Germany." *History Workshop Journal* 50 (2000): 45–72.

Benz, Wolfgang. *Von der Besatzungsherrschaft zur Bundesrepublik: Stationen einer Staatsgründung 1946–1949*. Frankfurt a.M.: Fischer, 1984.

———. *Herrschaft und Gesellschaft im Nationalsozialistischen Staat: Studien zur Struktur- und Mentalitätsgeschichte*. Frankfurt a.M.: Fischer, 1990.

Bergerson, Andrew. *Ordinary Germans in Extraordinary Times: The Nazi Revolution in Hildesheim*. Bloomington: Indiana University Press, 2004.

Berghahn, Volker R. "Hamburg im Frühjahr 1945: Stimmungsberichte aus den letzten Wochen des Zweiten Weltkrieges." *Geschichts- und Heimatblätter* 8/9 (December 1969): 193–211.

Berman, Marshall. *All That Is Solid Melts into Air: The Experience of Modernity.* New York: Simon and Schuster, 1982.

Bessel, Richard. *Germany 1945: From War to Peace.* London: Simon & Schuster, 2009.

———, ed. *Life in the Third Reich.* New York: Oxford University Press, 1987.

———. *Nazism and War.* New York: Modern Library, 2004.

Bingham, John. *Weimar Cities: The Challenge of Urban Modernity in Germany, 1919–1933.* New York: Routledge, 2008.

Birdsall, Carolyn. *Nazi Soundscapes: Sound, Technology and Urban Space in Germany, 1933–1945.* Amsterdam: Amsterdam University Press, 2012.

Birdwell, Michael. *Celluloid Soldiers: The Warner Bros Campaign against Nazism.* New York: New York University Press, 1999.

Blackbourn, David, and Geoff Eley. *The Peculiarities of German History.* Oxford: Oxford University Press, 1984.

Blank, Ralf. *Hagen im Zweiten Weltkrieg: Bombenkrieg, Kriegsalltag und Rüstung einer westfälischen Großstadt.* Essen: Klartext, 2008.

Blessing, Benita. *The Antifascist Classroom: Denazification in Soviet-Occupied Germany, 1945–1949.* New York: Palgrave Macmillan, 2006.

Bleuel, Hans Peter. *Das saubere Reich. Theorie und Praxis des sittlichen Lebens im Dritten Reich.* Bern: Scherz, 1972.

Block, Marcelline, ed. *Situating the Feminist Gaze and Spectatorship in Postwar Cinema.* Newcastle: Cambridge Scholars Publishing, 2008.

Bock, Hans-Michael. *Die Tobis, 1928–1945.* Hamburg: Verlag Edition Text und Kritik, 2003.

Bock, Hans-Michael, Wolfgang Jacobsen, and Jörg Schöning, eds. *Alliierte für den Film: Arnold Pressburger, Gregor Rabinowitsch und Die Cine-Allianz.* Hamburg: Edition Text + Kritik, 2004.

Bloxham, Donald. "From the International Military Tribunal to the Subsequent Nuremberg Proceedings: The American Confrontation with Nazi Criminality Revisited." *History* (2013), 567–91.

Bönisch, Georg, and Klaus Wiegrefe, eds. *Die 50er Jahre: Vom Trümmerland Zum Wirtschaftswunder.* Munich: DTV, 2006.

Bordwell, David, Janet Staiger, and Kristin Thompson, eds. *The Classical Hollywood Cinema: Film Style and Mode of Production to 1960.* New York: Columbia University Press, 1985.

Bose, Michael, et al. *". . . Ein neues Hamburg entsteht." Planen und Bauen von 1933–1945.* Hamburg: VSA, 1986.

Bracher, Karl Dietrich. *Die deutsche Diktatur: Entstehung, Struktur, Folgen ses Nationalsozialismus.* Berlin: Ullstein, 1979.

Bracher, Karl Dietrich, Manfred Funke, and Hans-Adolf Jacobson, eds. *Deutschland 1933–1945. Neue Studien zur Nationalsozialistischen Herrschaft.* Düsseldorf: Droste, 1992.

Brandelmeier, Thomas. "Lachkultur im Kino vom Fin-De-Siècle bis zum Ersten Weltkrieg." In *Die Modellierung des Kinofilms. Zur Geschichte des Kinopgrogramms zwischen Kurzfilm und Langfilm 1905/06–1918,* edited by Corinna Müller and Harro Segeberg. Munich: Wilhlem Fink Verlag, 1998.

Brandenburg, Hans-Christian. *Die Geschichte der HJ.* Cologne: Verlag für Wissenschaft und Politik Berend von Nottbeck, 1982.

Braun, Hans, Uta Gerhardt, and Everhart Holtman, eds. *Die lange Stunde Null: Gelenkter sozialer Wandel in Westdeutschland Nacch 1945*. Baden Baden: Nomos, 2007.

Braun, Matthias Klaus. *Hitlers Liebster Bürgermeister: Willy Liebel (1897–1945)*. Nürnberg: Verlag Ph. C. W. Schmidt, 2012.

Breckman, Warren. "Disciplining Consumption: The Debate About Luxury in Wilhelmine Germany, 1890–1914." *Journal of Social History* 24, no. 3 (Spring 1991): 485–505.

Brewer, Stewart. *Borders and Bridges: A History of US-Latin American Relations*. Westport: Praeger Security International, 2006.

Bridenthal, Renate, Atina Grossmann, and Marion Kaplan, eds. *When Biology Became Destiny: Women in Weimar and Nazi Germany*. New York: Monthly Review Press, 1984.

Broe, Dennis. *Film Noir, American Workers, and Postwar Hollywood*. Gainesville: University of Florida Press, 2009.

Brook, Vincent. *Driven to Darkness: Jewish Émigré Directors and the Rise of Film Noir*. New Brunswick: Rutgers University Press, 2009.

Brooker, Will, and Deborah Jermyn, eds. *The Audience Studies Reader*. London: Routledge, 2003.

Brooks, Peter. *The Melodramatic Imagination: Balzac, Henry James, Melodrama and the Mode of Excess*. New Haven: Yale University Press, 1995.

Broszat, Martin. *Der Staat Hitlers*. Munich: DTV, 1969.

Browning, Christopher. *Ordinary Men: Reserve Police Battalion 101 and the Final Solution in Poland*. New York: Harper Perennial, 1992.

Bruns, Jana F. *Nazi Cinema's New Woman*. Cambridge, UK: Cambridge University Press, 2009.

Brunswig, Hans. *Feuersturm über Hamburg: Die Luftangriffen auf Hamburg im Zweiten Weltkrieg und ihre Folgen*. 3rd ed. Stuttgart: Motorbuch Verlag, 1979.

Buchholz, Wolfgang. "Die nationalsozialistische Gemeinschaft 'Kraft durch Freude.' Freizeitgestaltung und Arbeiterschaft im Dritten Reich." PhD diss., Ludwig-Maximilians-Universität zu München, 1976.

Buder, Stanley. *Visionaries and Planners: The Garden City Movement and the Modern Community*. Oxford: Oxford University Press, 1990.

Bullock, Alan. *Hitler: A Study in Tyranny*. London: Odhams Press, 1952.

Burleigh, Michael, and Wolfgang Wippermann. *The Racial State: Germany 1933–1945*. Cambridge, UK: Cambridge University Press, 1991.

Burns, James. *Flickering Shadows: Cinema and Identity in Colonial Zimbabwe*. Athens: Ohio University Press, 2002.

Büttner, Ursula. "Der Aufstieg der NSDAP." In *Hamburg im "Dritten Reich,"* edited by FZH. Göttingen: Wallstein, 2005. 27–65.

———. "'Gomorrha' und die Folgen. Der Bombenkrieg." In *Hamburg im "Dritten Reich,"* edited by FZH. Göttingen: Wallstein, 2005. 613–32.

———. *Hamburg in der Staats- und Wirtschaftskrise*. Hamburg: Christians, 1982.

Candy, Susan. *America's Nazis: A Democratic Dilemma: A History of the German American Bund*. Menlo Park, CA: Markgraf Publications Group, 1990.

Canning, Kathleen. *Gender History in Practice: Historical Perspectives on Bodies, Class, and Citizenship*. Ithaca: Cornell University Press, 2005.

———. *Languages of Labor and Gender: Female Factory Work in Germany 1850–1914*. Ann Arbor: University of Michigan Press, 2002.

———. "The Politics of Symbols, Semantics, and Sentiments in the Weimar Republic." *Central European History* 43, no. 4 (2010). 567–80.

Carter, Erica. *Dietrich's Ghosts: The Sublime and the Beautiful in Third Reich Film*. London: BFI, 2004.

Castells, Manuel. *The Informational City: Information Technology, Economic Restructuring, and the Urban-Regional Process*. Oxford: B. Blackwell, 1989.

Chakrabarty, Dipesh. *Provincializing Europe: Postcolonial Thought and Historical Difference*. Princeton: Princeton University Press, 2000.

Chambers, John Whiteclay II, and David Culbert, eds. *World War II, Film, and History*. New York: Oxford University Press, 1996.

Chickering, Roger. *The Great War and Urban Life in Germany. Freiburg, 1914–1918*. Cambridge, UK: Cambridge University Press, 2007.

———. *Imperial Germany and the Great War, 1914–1918*. Cambridge, UK: Cambridge University Press, 1998.

Childers, Thomas. "'Facilis Descensus Aveni Est': The Allied Bombing of Germany and the Issue of German Suffering." *Central European History* 38, no. 1 (2005): 75–105.

Choy, Yong Chan. "Inszenierung der *völkischen* Filmkultur im Nationalsozialismus: 'Der Internationale Filmkongress in Berlin 1935.'" PhD diss., Technische Universität Berlin, 2006.

Clemens, Gabriele. *Britische Kulturpolitik in Deutschland, 1945–1949: Literatur, Film, Musik und Theater*. Stuttgart: Franz Steiner, 1997.

Clinefelder, Joan L. *Artists for the Reich: Culture and Race from Weimar to Nazi Germany*. New York: Berg, 2005.

Confino, Alon. *The Nation as a Local Metaphor: Württemberg, Imperial Germany, and National Memory, 1871–1918*. Chapel Hill: University of North Carolina Press, 1997.

———. "The Warm Sand of the Coast of Tantura: History and Memory in Israel after 1948." *History & Memory* 27, no. 1 (Spring/Summer 2015): 43–82.

———. *A World Without Jews: The Nazi Imagination from Persecution to Genocide*. New Haven: Yale University Press, 2014.

Connelly, John. "Nazis and Slavs: From Racial Theory to Racist Practice." *Central European History* 32, no. 1 (1999): 1–33.

———. "The Uses of Volksgemeinschaft: Letters to the NSDAP Kreisleitung in Eisenach." *Journal of Modern History* 68, no. 4 (Dec 1996): 899–930.

Conrad, Sebastian. "Entangled Memories: Versions of the Past in Germany and Japan, 1945–2001." *Journal of Contemporary History* 38, no. 1 (2003): 85–99.

Courtis, Scott. "The Taste of a Nation: Training the Senses and Sensibility of Cinema Audience in Imperial Germany." *Film History* 6, no. 4 (1994): 445–69.

Crane, Susan. "Memory, Distortion and History in the Museum." In "Producing the Past: Making Histories Inside and Outside the Academy." Theme issue, *History and Theory* 36, no. 4 (1997): 44–63.

Cresswell, Tim. *Place: A Short Introduction*. Oxford: Blackwell Publishing, 2004.

Crew, David F. "*Alltagsgeschichte*: A New Social History 'from Below'?" *Central European History* 22, no. 3 (September/December 1989): 394–407.

———. *Germans on Welfare: From Weimar to Hitler*. New York: Oxford University Press, 1998.

———, ed. *Nazism and German Society*. New York: Routledge, 1994.

Davidson, John, and Sabine Hake, eds. *Framing the Fifties: Cinema in Divided Germany*. New York: Berghahn Books, 2007.

Davis, Belinda. *Home Fires Burning: Food, Politics, and Everyday Life in World War I Berlin*. Chapel Hill: University of North Carolina Press, 2000.

Davis, Diane E., and Nora Libertun de Duren. *Cities & Sovereignty: Identity Politics in Urban Space*. Bloomington: Indiana University Press, 2011.

Davis, Mike. *Ecology of Fear: Los Angeles and the Imagination of Disaster*. New York: Vintage, 1998.

de Certeau, Michel. *The Writing of History*. Translated by Tom Conley. New York: Columbia University Press, 1988.

de Lauretis, Teresa. "Through the Looking Glass." In *Narrative, Apparatus, Ideology: A Film Theory Reader*, edited by Philip Rosen. New York: Columbia University Press, 1986.

Deak, Istvan. *Weimar Germany's Left-Wing Intellectuals: A Political History of the Weltbühne and Its Circle*. Berkeley: University of California Press, 1968.

Dean, Martin. *Robbing the Jews: The Confiscation of Jewish Property in the Holocaust, 1933–1945*. New York: Cambridge University Press, 2008.

Dear, Michael. *Landscapes of Despair: From Deinstitutionalization to Homelessness*. Princeton: Princeton University Press, 1987.

Decker, Thomas. *The Modern City Revisited*. London: Spon Press, 2000.

DeCoste, F. C., and Bernard Schwartz, eds. *The Holocaust's Ghosts: Writings on Art, Politics, Law, and Education*. Edmonton: University of Alberta Press, 2000.

Deichmann, Ute. *Biologists Under Hitler*. Cambridge, MA: Harvard University Press, 1996.

Deighton, Anne. "Cold-War Diplomacy: British Policy Towards Germany's Role in Europe, 1945–9." In *Reconstruction in Post-War Germany: British Occupation Policy and the Western Zones, 1945–1955*, edited by Ian D. Turner. Oxford: Berg, 1989. 15–34.

DeJean, Joan E. *How Paris Became Paris: The Invention of the Modern City*. New York: Bloomsbury, 2014.

Dewar, Margaret, and June Manning Thomas, eds. *The City After Abandonment*. Philadelphia: University of Pennsylvania Press, 2013.

Dick, Bernhard F. *The American World War II Film*. Lexington: University of Kentucky Press, 1985.

Dickinson, Edward Ross. *German Child Welfare: From the Empire to the Federal Republic*. Cambridge, MA: Harvard University Press, 1996.

Diehl-Thiele, Peter. *Partei Und Staat Im Dritten Reich*. Munich: Beck, 1969.

Dimendberg, Edward. "Down These Seen Streets a Man Must Go." In "Film and Exile." Special issue, *New German Critique* 89 (Spring/Summer 2003): 113–43.

Doenecke, Justus D., and John E. Wilz. *From Isolation to War, 1931–1941*. 2nd ed. Arlington Heights: Harlan Davidson, 1991.

Doherty, Thomas. *Projections of War: Hollywood, American Culture, and World War II*. New York: Columbia University Press, 1993.

———. "This Is Where We Came In: The Audible Screen and the Voluble Audience of Early Sound Cinema." In *American Movie Audiences: From the Turn of the Century to the Early Sound Era*, edited by Melvyn Stokes and Richard Maltby. London: BFI, 1999.

Dräger, Horst. *Die Gesellschaft für Verbreitung von Volksbildung: Eine historische-problemgeschichtliche Darstellung*. Stuttgart: Klett, 1975.

Dubiel, Helmut, and Alfons Söllner, eds. *Wirtschaft, Recht und Staat im Nationalsozialismus: Analysisen des Instituts für Sozialforschung, 1939–1942*. Frankfurt a.M.: Europäische Verlagsanstalt, 1981.

Dülffer, Jost, Jochen Thies, and Josef Henke. *Hitler's Städte. Baupolitik im Dritten Reich. Eine Dokumentation*. Cologne: Böhlau, 1978.

Düwel, Jörn, and Niels Gutschow. *Städtebau in Deutschland im 20.Jahrhundert*. Stuttgart: Teubner, 2001.

Dyer, Richard, Ann E. Kaplan, and Paul Willemen. *American Cinema and Hollywood: Critical Approaches*. Oxford: Oxford University Press, 2000.

Ebbinghaus, Angelika, ed. *Opfer und Täterinnen. Frauenbiographien des Nationalsozialismus*. Frankfurt: Fischer, 1997.

Ebbinghaus, Angelika, Heidrun Kaupen-Hass, and Karl-Heinz Roth, eds. *Heilen und Vernichten im Mustergau Hamburg: Bevölkerung und Gesundheitspolitik im Dritten Reich*. Hamburg: Konkret Literatur Verlag, 1984.

Ebbinghaus, Angelika, and Karsten Linne, eds. *Kein abgeschlossenes Kapitel: Hamburg im "Dritten Reich."* Hamburg: Europäische Verlagsanstalt, 1997.

Ebsworth, Raymond. *Restoring Democracy in Germany: The British Contribution*. London: Stevens & Sons, 1961.

Ehmann, Antje. "Wie Wirklichkeit Erzählen? Methoden des Querschnittfilms." In *Geschichte des dokumentarischen Films in Deutschland*, Vol. II, edited by Klaus Kreimeier, Antje Ehmann and Jeanpaul Goergen, Stuttgart: Philipp Reclam, 2005. 576–600.

Eiber, Ludwig. *Arbeiter und Arbeiterbewegung in der Hansestadt Hamburg in den Jahren 1929–1939: Werftarbeiter, Hafenarbeiter, Seeleute. Konformität, Opposition. Widerstand*. Frankfurt a.M.: Peter Lang, 2000.

Eitzen, Dirk. "When Is a Documentary?: Documentary as Mode of Reception." *Cinema Journal* 35, no. 1 (Autumn 1995): 81–102.

Eley, Geoff. *A Crooked Line: From Cultural History to the History of Society*. Ann Arbor: University of Michigan Press, 2005.

———, ed. *The "Goldhagen Effect": History, Memory, Nazism—Facing the German Past*. Ann Arbor: Michigan University Press, 2000.

———. "Hitler's Silent Majority? Conformity and Resistance under the Third Reich." *Michigan Quarterly Review* 42, no. 2–3 (Spring 2003): 389–425.

———. *Labour History-Social History-Alltagsgeschichte: Experience, Culture, and the Politics of the Everyday. A New Direction for German Social History?* Ann Arbor: University of Michigan Press, 1989.

———. *Nazism as Fascism: Violence, Ideology, and the Ground of Consent in Germany 1930–1945*. London: Routledge, 2013.

———. "Nazism, Politics and the Image of the Past: Thoughts on the West German Historikerstreit 1986–1987." *Past & Present* 121 (November 1988): 171–208.

Eley, Geoff, and Atina Grossman. "Watching Schindler's List." In "Memories of Germany." Special issue, *New German Critique* 71 (Spring/Summer 1997): 41–62.

Eley, Geoff, and Jan Palmowski, eds. *Citizenship and National Identity in Twentieth-Century Germany*. Stanford: Stanford University Press, 2008.

Elsaesser, Thomas. *Fassbinder's Germany: History, Subject, Identity*. Amsterdam: Amsterdam University Press, 1996.

———. *Filmgeschichte und frühes Kino: Archälogie eines Medienwandels*. Munich: Edition Text + Kritik, 2002.

———. *Weimar Cinema and After. Germany's Historical Imaginary*. London: Routledge, 2000.

Engel, Kathrin. *Deutsche Kulturpolitik im besetzten Paris, 1940–1944: Film und Theater*. Munich: Oldenbourg, 2003.

Evans, Richard J. *Death in Hamburg: Society and Politics in the Cholera Years*. New York: Penguin, 2005.

———. "'Red Wednesday' in Hamburg: Social Democrats, Police, and *Lumenproletariat* in the Suffrage Disturbances of 17 January 1906." *Social History* 4, no. 1 (Jan 1979): 1–31.

———. *The Third Reich at War: How the Nazis Led Germany from Conquest to Disaster.* New York: Allen Lane, 2008.

Eyles, Allen. *Odeon Cinemas 2: From J. Arthur Rank to the Multiplex.* London: Cinema Theater Association, 2005.

Faber, David. *Munich, 1938: Appeasement and World War II.* New York: Simon & Schuster, 2008.

Fay, Jennifer. "The Business of Cultural Diplomacy: American Film Policy in Occupied Germany, 1945–1949." PhD diss., University of Wisconsin–Madison, 2001.

Feherenbach, Heide. *Cinema in Democratizing Germany: Reconstructing National Identity after Hitler.* Chapel Hill: University of North Carolina Press, 1995.

Ferk, Gabriele. "Judenverfolgung in Norddeutschland." In *Norddeutschland im Nationalsozialismus,* edited by Frank Bajohr. Hamburg: Ergebnisse, 1993. 280–309.

Fest, Joachim C. *Das Gesicht des Dritten Reiches: Profil einer totalitären Herrschaft.* Munich: R. Piper, 1963.

Fischer, Jaimey. "Wandering in/to the Rubble-Film: Filmic Flânerie and the Exploded Panorama after 1945." In "Focus on Film." Special issue, *German Quarterly* 78, no. 4 (Fall 2005): 461–80.

Forschungstelle für Zeitgeschichte in Hamburg, ed. *Hamburg im "Dritten Reich."* Göttingen: Wallstein Verlag, 2005.

Foschepoth, Josef, and Rolf Steiniger. *Die britische Deutschland- und Besatzungspolitik.* Paderborn: F. Schöningh, 1985.

Fox, Jo. *Film Propaganda in Britain and Nazi Germany: World War II Cinema.* Oxford: Berg, 2007.

Frei, Norbert. *Adenauer's Germany and the Nazi Past: The Politics of Amnesty and Integration.* New York: Columbia University Press, 2002.

Freund-Widder, Michaela. *Frauen unter Kontrolle: Prostitution und ihre staatliche Bekämpfung in Hamburg vom Ende des Kaiserreichs bis zu den Anfängen der Bundesrepublik.* Berlin: LIT Verlag, 2003.

Friedrich, Jörg. *The Fire: The Bombing of Germany, 1940–1945.* New York: Columbia University Press, 2006.

Frieser, Karl-Heinz. *Blitzkrieg Legend: The 1940 Campaign in the West.* Annapolis: Naval Institute Press, 2004.

Fritzsche, Peter. *Germans into Nazis.* Cambridge, MA: Harvard University Press, 1997.

———. *An Iron Wind: Europe Under Hitler.* New York: Basic Books, 2016.

———. *Life and Death in the Third Reich.* Cambridge, MA: Belknap Press of Harvard University Press, 2008.

Führer, Karl Christian. "Guckfenster in die Welt. Das 'Waterloo'-Kino in Hamburg in den Jahren der NS-Herrschaft." In *Zeitgeschichte Hamburg,* edited by FZH. Hamburg: FZH, 2005.

———. "Die Machtlosigkeit des 'Maßnahmestaats.' Wohnungsmarkt und öffentliche Wohnraumbewirtschaftung." In *Kein abgeschlossenes Kapitel: Hamburg im "Dritten Reich,"* edited by Angelika Ebbinghaus and Karsten Linne. Hamburg: Europäische Verlagsanstalt, 1997.

———. *Medienmetropole Hamburg: Mediale Öffentlichkeit 1930–1960.* Hamburg: Dölling und Galitz Verlag, 2008.

———. "Meister der Ankündigung: Nationalsozialistische Wohungsbaupolitik." In *Hamburg im "Dritten Reich,"* edited by FZH. Göttingen: Wallstein, 2005.

Fulks, Barry A. "Film Culture and *Kulturfilm:* Walter Ruttmann, the Avant-Garde, and the *Kulturfilm* in Weimar Germany and the Third Reich." PhD diss., University of Wisconsin, 1982.

Fyne, Robert. *The Hollywood Propaganda of World War II*. Metuchen: Scarecrow Press, 1994.

Gaines, Jane, ed. *Classical Hollywood Narrative: The Paradigm Wars*. Durham: Duke University Press, 1992.

Gardner, Gerald. *The Censorship Papers: Movie Censorship Letters Form the Hays Office, 1934–1968*. New York: Dodd, Mead, 1987.

Gellately, Robert. *Backing Hitler: Consent and Coercion in Nazi Germany*. Oxford: Oxford University Press, 1998.

Gemünden, Gerd. "Brecht in Hollywood: 'Hangman Also Die' and the Anti-Nazi Film." In "German Brecht, European Readings." Special issue, *TDR* 43, no. 4 (Winter 1999): 65–76.

———. *Continental Strangers: German Exile Cinema, 1933–1951*. New York: Columbia University Press, 2014.

Geyer, Michael. "Insurrectionary Warfare: The German Debate about a Levée En Masse in October 1918." *Journal of Modern History* 73, no. 3 (2001): 459–527.

Giesen, Rolf. *Nazi Propaganda Films: A History and Filmography*. Jefferson: McFarland, 2003.

Giles, Geoffrey J., ed. *Stunde Null: The End and the Beginning Fifty Years Ago*. Washington, DC: German Historical Institute, 1997.

Gillard, David. *Appeasement in Crisis: From Munich to Prague, October 1938-March 1939*. New York: Palgrave Macmillan, 2007.

Gillette, Howard Jr. *Camden After the Fall: Decline and Renewal in a Post-Industrial City*. Philadelphia: University of Pennsylvania Press, 2005.

Gilman, Sander L. "Is Life Beautiful? Can the Shoah Be Funny? Some Thoughts on the Reception of Recent and Older Films." *Critical Inquiry* 26, no. 2 (Winter 2000): 279–308.

Gleber, Anke. *The Art of Taking a Walk: Flânerie, Literature, and Film in Weimar Culture*. Princeton: Princeton University Press, 1999.

Gledhill, Christine, ed. *Home Is Where the Heart Is: Studies in Melodrama and the Woman's Film*. London: BFI, 1990.

Glensk, Evelyn. *Die Aufnahme und Eingliederung der Vertriebenen und Flüchtlinge in Hamburg 1945–1953*. Hamburg: Verlag für Hamburgische Geschichte, 1994.

Godmilow, Jill, and Ann-Louise Shapiro. "How Real Is the Reality in Documentary Film?" In "Producing the Past: Making Histories Outside the Academy." Theme issue, *History and Theory* 36, no. 4 (December 1997): 80–101.

Goergen, Jeanpaul. "Städtebilder zwischen Heimattümelei und Urbanität." In *Die Geschichte des dokumentarischen Films in Deutschland*, edited by Peter Zimmermann and Kay Hoffmann. Vol. III. Stuttgart: Philipp Reclam, 2005.

———. "Urbanität und Idylle. Städtefilme zwischen Kommerz und Kulturpropaganda." In *Geschichte des dokumentarischen Films in Deutschland*, edited by Klaus Kreimeier, Antje Ehmann and Jeanpaul Goergen. Vol. II. Stuttgart: Philipp Reclam, 2005. 151–72.

Goldstein, Cora Sol. *Capturing the German Eye: American Visual Propaganda in Occupied Germany*. Chicago: Chicago University Press, 2009.

Göttler, Fritz. "Westdeutscher Nachkriegsfilm: Land der Väter." In *Die Geschichte des deutschen Films*, edited byWolfgang Jacobson, Anton Kaes, and Hans Helmut Prinzler. Stuttgart: Verlag J. B. Metzler, 1993.

Gotto, Bernhard. *Nationalsozialistische Kommunalpolitik: Administrative Normalität und Systemstabiliserung durch die Augsburger Stadtverwaltung, 1933–1945*. Munich: Oldenburg Verlag, 2006.

Grabbe, Joachim. *Als in Eimsbüttel die Straßenbahn noch fuhr. Eine Kindheit und Jugend in den 50er Jahren*. 2nd ed. Hamurg: Dölling und Galitz Verlag, 2004.

Graham, Stephen and Simon Marvin. *Splintering Urbanism: Networked Infrastructures, Technological Mobilities and the Urban Condition*. London: Routledge, 2001.

Graml, Herman. *Die Allierten und die Teilung Deutschlands: Konflikte und Entscheidungen, 1941-48*. Frankfurt a.M.: Fischer, 1985.

Gräser, Marcus. *Der blockierte Wohlfahrtsstaat*. Göttingen: Vandehoeck & Rupprecht, 1995.

Gregor, Neil. *Haunted City: Nuremberg and the Nazi Past*. New Haven: Yale University Press, 2008.

———. "A Schicksalsgemeinscahft? Allied Bombing, Civilian Morale, and Social Dissolution in Nuremberg, 1942–1945." *Historical Journal*. 43, no. 4 (2000) 1051–70.

Grobecker, Kurt, Hans-Dieter Loose, and Erik Verg, eds. *. . . Mehr als ein Haufen Steine*. Hamburg 1945–1949. Hamburg: Ernst Kabel, 1981.

Grossbölting, Thomas. *Volksgemeinschaft in Der Kleinstadt : Kornwestheim Und Der Nationalsozialismus*. Stuttgart: Verlag W. Kohlhammer, 2017.

Grossmann, Atina. *Jews, Germans, and Allies: Close Encounters in Occupied Germany*. Princeton: Princeton University Press, 2007.

Grover, Warren. *Nazis in Newark*. New Brunswick: Transaction Publishers, 2003.

Grünbacher, Armin. *The Making of German Democracy: West Germany During the Adenauer Era, 1945-65*. New York: Manchester University Press, 2010.

Grüttner, Michael. *Arbeitswelt an der Wasserkante: Sozialgeschichte der Hamburger Hafenarbeiter, 1886–1914*. Göttingen: Vandenhoeck & Rupprecht, 1984.

Haarmann, Hermann, ed. *Heimat, liebe Heimat: Exil und innere Emigration (1933–1945)*. Berlin: Bostelmann & Siebanhaar, 2004.

———, ed. *Berlin Im Kopf—Arbeit am Berlin-Mythos: Exil und Innere Emigration 1933 Bis 1945*. Berlin: B&S Siebenhaar Verlag, 2008.

Hachtmann, Rüdiger. *Berlin im Nationalsozialismus: Politik und Gesellschaft 1933–1945*. Göttingen: Wallstein, 2012.

Haerendel, Ulrike. *Kommunale Wohnungspolitik im Dritten Reich: Siedlungsbauideologie, Klainhausbau und 'Wohnraumarisierung am Beispiel Münchens*. Munich: Oldenburg Verlag, 1999.

Haff, Peter. "Technology as a Geological Phenomenon: Implications for Human Well-Being." In *A Stratigraphical Basis for the Anthropocene*, edited by C. N. Waters, et al. London: Geological Society of London, 2013.

Hake, Sabine. *German National Cinema*. London: Routledge, 2002.

———. *Popular Cinema of the Third Reich*. Austin: University of Texas Press, 2001.

———. *Topographies of Class: Modern Architecture and Mass Society in Weimar Berlin*. Ann Arbor: University of Michigan Press, 2008.

———. "Urban Spectacle in Walter Ruttmann's *Berlin, Symphony of the Big City*." In *Dancing on the Volcano: Essays on the Culture of the Weimar Republic*, edited by Thomas W. Kniesche and Stephen Brockmann. Columbia,: Camden House, 1994.

Hall, David S. *Film in the Third Reich*. New York: Simon and Schuster, 1973.

Hall, Stuart. "Encoding /decoding." In *Culture, Media, Language: Working Papers in Cultural Studies*. London: Hutchinson, 1980.

Die Hamburger Speicherstadt. Berlin: Ernst & Sohn, 1990.Hannigan, John. *Fantasy City: Pleasure and Profit in the Postmodern Metropolis*. New York: Routledge, 1998.

Hansen, Miriam. *Babel and Babylon: Spectatorship in American Silent Film*. Cambridge, MA: Harvard University Press, 1991.

———. "Cooperative Auteur Cinema and Oppositional Public Sphere: Alexander Kluge's Contribution to Germany in Autumn." Double Issue on New German Cinema." Special issue, *New German Critique* 24–25 (Autumn 1981/Winter 1982): 36–56.

———. "Early Silent Cinema. Whose Public Sphere?" In "The Origins of Mass Culture. The Case of Germany, 1871–1918." Special issue, *New German Critique* 29 (Spring/Summer 1983): 147–84.

———. "Schindler's List is Not 'Shoah': The Second Commandment, Popular Modernism and Public Memory." *Critical Inquiry* 22, no. 2 (Winter 1996): 292–312.

Haridakis, Paul M., Barbara S. Hugenberg, and Stanley T. Wearden, eds. *War and Media: Essays on News Reporting, Propaganda, and Popular Culture.* Jefferson: McFarland, 2009.

Harlander, Tilman. *Zwischen Heimstätte und Wohnmaschine: Wohnungsbau und Wohngspolitik in der Zeit des Nationalsozialismus.* Basel: Birkhäuser, 1995.

Harris, Victoria. *Selling Sex in the Reich: Prostitutes in German Society, 1914–1945.* Oxford: Oxford University Press, 2010.

Harvey, David. "Contested Cities: Social Process and Spatial Form." In *The City Reader*, edited by Richard T. LeGates and Frederic Stout. 3rd ed. London: Routledge, 2003. 227–34.

———. "Globalization and the 'Spatial Fix.'" *Geographische Revue* 2 (2001): 23–30.

———. "The Spatial Fix." *Antipode* 13, no. 3 (1981): 1–12.

Harvey, Elizabeth. *Youth and the Welfare State in Weimar Germany.* Oxford: Clarendon Press, 1993.

Heineman, Elizabeth. "Sexuality and Nazism: The Doubly Unspeakable?" *Journal of the History of Sexuality* 11, no. 1/2 (January/April 2002).

Heins, Laura. *Nazi Film Melodrama.* Urbana: University of Illinois Press, 2013.

Helmer, Stephen D. *Hitler's Berlin: The Speer Plans for Reshaping the Central City.* Ann Arbor: UMI Research Press, 1985.

Herbert, Ulrich. "'Die guten und die schlechten Zeiten.' Überlegungen zur diachronen Analyse lebensgeschichtlicher Interviews." In *"Die Jahre weiß man nicht, wo man die heute hinsetzen soll." Faschismus Erfahrungen im Ruhrgebiet*, edited by Lutz Niethammer. 2nd ed. Berlin: J. H. W. Dietz, 1986. 67–96.

———. "Good Times, Bad Times." *History Today* 36, no. 2 (February 1986): 42–48.

Herf, Jeffrey. *Divided Memory: The Nazi Past in the Two Germanys.* Cambridge, MA: Harvard University Press, 1997.

———. *Reactionary Modernism: Technology, Culture, and Politics in Weimar and the Third Reich.* Cambridge, UK: Cambridge University Press, 1986.

Herzig, Arno, Dieter Langewiesche, and Arnold Sywottek, eds. *Arbeiter in Hamburg. Unterschichten, Arbeiter und Arbeiterbewegung seit dem ausgehenden 18 Jahrhundert.* Hamburg: Verlag für Erziehung und Wissenschaft, 1983.

Herzig, Arno, and Saskia Rohde, eds. *Die Juden in Hamburg 1590–1990.* Hamburg: Dölling und Galitz Verlag, 1991.

Herzog, Dagmar. "Hubris and Hypocrisy, Incitement and Disavowal: Sexuality and German Fascism." *Journal of the History of Sexuality* 11, no. 1/2 (January/April 2002).

———. *Sex after Fascism: Memory and Morality in Twentieth-Century Germany.* Princeton: Princeton University Press, 2003.

———, ed. *Sexuality and German Fascism.* New York: Berghahn Books, 2005.

———. *Unlearning Eugenics: Sexuality, Reproduction and Disability in Post Nazi Europe.* Madison: University of Wisconsin Press, 2018.

Hilton, Stanley E. *Hitler's Secret War in South America, 1939–1945: German Military Espionage and Allied Counterespionage in Brazil.* Baton Rouge: Louisiana State University Press, 1981.

Hobsbawm, Eric, and Terence Ranger. *The Invention of Tradition*. New York: Cambridge University Press, 1983.

Hochmuth, Ursel, and Gertrud Meyer. *Streiflichter aus dem Hamburger Widerstand 1933-1945*. Frankfurt a.M: Röderberg, 1980.

Höffkes, Karl. *Hitlers Politische Generale: Die Gauleiter des Dritten Reiches: Ein biographisches Nachschlagewerk*. Tübingen: Grabert-Verlag, 1986.

Hoffmann, Hilmar. *The Triumph of Propaganda: Film and National Socialism, 1933-1945*. Translated by John Broadwin and Volker R. Berghahn. Frankfurt a.M: Berghahn Books, 1997.

———. *Und die Fahne führt uns in die Ewigkeit*. Frankfurt: Fischer, 1988.

Hoffmann, Kay. "Bollwerk im Westen und Vorstoß nach Osten." In *Die Geschichte des dokumentarischen Films in Deutschland*, edited by Peter Zimmermann and Kay Hoffmann. Vol. III. Stuttgart: Philipp Reclam, 2005.

Holba, Herbert. "The Enigma of Werner Hochbaum." *Sight and Sound* 45, no. 2 (Spring 1976): 98–103.

Holzbach, Heidrun. *Das "System Hugenberg." Die Organisation Bürgerlicher Sammlungspolitik Vor Dem Aufstieg Der Nsdap*. Stuttgart: Deutsche Verlags-Anstalt, 1981.

Hong, Young-Sun. *Welfare, Modernity, and the Weimar State, 1919-1933*. Princeton: Princeton University Press, 1998.

Huchzermeyer, Marie. *Cities with "Slums": From Informal Settlement Eradication to a Right to the City in Africa*. Claremont: University of Cape Town Press, 2011.

Hull, David Stewart. *Film in the Third Reich*. 1969. New York: Touchstone, 1973.

Hüttenberger, Peter. *Die Gauleiter: Studie zum Wandel des Machtgefüges in der NSDAP*. Stuttgart: Deutsche Verlagsanstalt, 1969.

———. "Nationalsozialistische Polykratie." *Geschichte und Gesellschaft: Zeitschrift für historische Sozialwissenschaft* 2 (1976): 417–42.

Ingrao, Charles W., and Franz A. J. Szabo, eds. *The Germans and the East*. West Lafayette: Purdue University Press, 2008.

Jacobs, Lewis. "World War II and the American Film." *Cinema Journal* 7 (Winter 1967/68): 1–21.

Jacobson, Wolfgang, Anton Kaes, and Hans Helmut Prinzler, eds. *Die Geschichte des deutschen Films*. Stuttgart: Metzler, 1993.

Jahn, Peter, ed. *Stalingrad Erinnern: Stalingrad im deutschen und russischen Gedächtnis*. Berlin: Ch. Links, 2003.

Jancovich, Mark, Lucy Faire, and Sarah Stubbings, eds. *The Place of the Audience: Cultural Geographies of Film Consumption*. London: BFI, 2003.

Jarausch, Konrad H., and Michael Geyer. *Shattered Past: Reconstructing German Histories*. Princeton: Princeton University Press, 2003.

Jaskot, Paul B. *The Architecture of Oppression: The SS, Forced Labor and the Nazi Monumental Building Economy*. New York: Routledge, 2000.

Jener, Robert E. *FDR's Republicans: Domestic Political Realignment*. Lanham: Lexington Books, 2010.

Jenkins, Jennifer. *Provincial Modernity: Local Culture and Liberal Politics in Fin-De-Siècle Hamburg*. Ithaca: Cornell University Press, 2003.

Jochmann, Werner, and Hans Dieter Loose, eds. *Hamburg. Geschichte einer Stadt und ihrer Bewohner. Vol. II: Vom Kaiserreich bis zur Gegenwart*. Hamburg: Hoffmann & Campe, 1985.

Johe, Werner. *Die unfreie Stadt: Hamburg 1933-1945*. Hamburg: Landeszentrale für politische Bildung, Hamburg, 1991.

Johnson, Ronald Wayne. *The German-American Bund 1924–1941*. PhD diss., University of Wisconsin–Madison, 1967.

Jones, Larry Eugene. *German Liberalism and the Dissolution of the Weimar Party System, 1918–1933*. Chapel Hill: University of North Carolina Press, 1988.

Jones, William David. *The Lost Debate: German Socialist Intellectuals and Totalitarianism*. Urbana: University of Illinois Press, 1999.

Judt, Tony. *Postwar: A History of Europe since 1945*. 2005. New York: Penguin, 2006.

Jung, U., and M. Loiperdinger, eds. *Geschichte des dokumentarischen Films in Deutschland. Kaiserreich 1895–1918*. Vol. 1. Stuttgart: Reclam, 2005.

Kaes, Anton. "The Debate About the Cinema: Charting a Controversy (1909–1929)." In "Weimar Film Theory." Special issue, *New German Critique* 40 (Winter 1987): 7–33.

———, ed. *Kino-Debatte. Literatur und Film*. Tübingen: DTV, 1978.

Kantsteiner, Wulf. "Finding Meaning in Memory: A Methodological Critique of Collective Memory Studies." *History and Theory* 41, no. 2 (May 2002): 179–97.

Kaplan, Marion A. *Between Dignity and Despair: Jewish Life in Nazi Germany*. Oxford: Oxford University Press, 1998.

Kater, Michael. *Gewagtes Spiel: Jazz im Nationalsozialismus*. Cologne: Kiepenrheuer & Witsch, 1995.

Keller, Gerti. "Kino unterm Hakenkreuz. Das Beispiel Hamburg." Magisterarbeit, Universität Hamburg, 1993.

Keller, Sven. *Volksgemeinschaft Am Ende : Gesellschaft Und Gewalt 1944/45*. Munich: Oldenbourg Verlag, 2013.

Kempowski, Walter. *Das Echolot: Barbarossa '41: Ein kollektives Tagebuch*. Munich: Knaus, 2002.

Kershaw, Ian. *The "Hitler Myth": Image and Reality in the Third Reich*. Oxford: Oxford University Press, 1989.

———. *Hitler, 1889–1936. Hubris*. New York: W. W. Norton, 1999.

———. *Hitler, 1936-45: Nemesis*. New York: W. W. Norton, 2000.

Kißener, Michael, and Joachim Scholtyseck, eds. *Die Führer der Provinz: NS-Biographien aus Baden und Württemberg*. 1997. Konstanz: UVK, 1999.

Kitchen, Martin. *Nazi Germany: A Critical Introduction*. Gloucestershire: Tempus, 2004.

Klee, Ernst. *Das Personenlexikon zum Dritten Reich: Wer war was vor und nach 1945*. Frankfurt: Fischer, 2005.

Klemperer, Victor. *Lti, Notizbuch Eines Philologen*. Berlin: Aufbau-Verlag, 1947.

Klessmann, Christoph. *Die doppelte Staatsgründung*. Göttingen: Vandenhoeck & Rupprecht, 1982.

Klönne, Arno. *Gegen den Strom: Bericht über Jugendwiderstand im Dritten Reich*. Hanover: O. Goedel, 1960.

———. *Jugend Im Dritten Reich*. Cologne: Eugen Dietrich Verlag, 1982.

Knopp, Daniel. *NS-Film Propaganda: Wunschbild und Feindbild in Leni Riefenstahls "Triumph des Willen" und Veit Harlans "Jud Süß."* Marburg: Tectum, 2004.

Koepnick, Lutz, ed. *The Dark Mirror: German Cinema Between Hitler and Hollywood*. Berkeley: University of California Press, 2002.

———. "Komik Als Waffe? Charlie Chaplin, Ernst Lubitsch und Das Dritten Reich." In *Mediale Mobilmachung II: Hollywood, Exil und Nachkrieg*, edited by Harro Segeberg. Munich: Fink, 2006.

Kollmeier, Katrin. *Ordnung und Ausgrenzung. Die Disziplinarpolitik der Hitler-Jugend*. Göttingen: Vandehoeck & Rupprecht, 2007.

König, Wolfgang. *Volkswagen, Volksempfänger, Volksgemeinschaft. "Volksprodukte" im Dritten Reich: Vom Scheitern einer nationasozialistischen Konsumgesellschaft.* Paderborn: Ferdinand Schöningh, 2004.

Koonings, Kees, and Dirk Kruijt, eds. *Mega-Cities: The Politics of Urban Exclusion and Violence in the Global South.* London: Zed Books, 2009.

Kopitzsch, Franklin, and Dirk Brietzke, eds. *Hamburgische Biografie.* 4 vols. Göttingen: Wallenstein, 2001.

———, eds. *Hamburgische Biografie 3. Personenlexikon.* Vol. III. Göttingen: Wallenstein, 2006.

Köpke, Wulf, and Bernd Schmelz, eds. *Hamburgs Tor zur Welt: 125 Jahre Museum für Völkerkunde Hamburg.* Hamburg: Museum für Völkerkunde Hamburg, 2004.

Koppes, Clayton, and Gregory Black. *Hollywood Goes to War: How Politics, Profits and Propaganda Shaped World War II Movies.* London: Free Press, 1987.

Koshar, Rudy, ed. *Germans at the Wheel: Cars and Leisure Travel in Interwar Germany.* New York: Berg, 2002.

———. *German Travel Cultures.* New York: Berg, 2000.

———. *Social Life, Local Politics, and Nazism: Marburg, 1880–1935.* Chapel Hill: University of North Carolina Press, 1986.

Koven, Seth. *Slumming: Sexual and Social Politics in Victorian London.* Princeton: Princeton University Press, 2004.

Kracauer, Siegfried. *From Caligari to Hitler. A Psychological History of the German Film.* Revised and expanded edition. Edited by Leonardo Quaresima. Princeton: Princeton University Press, 2004.

———. *The Mass Ornament: Weimar Essays.* Translated and edited by Thomas Y. Levin. Cambridge, MA: Harvard University Press, 1995.

Krebbedies, Frank. *Außer Kontrolle. Jugendkriminalität in der NS-Zeit und der Frühen Nachkriegszeit.* Düsseldorf: Klartext, 2000.

Kreimeier, Klaus. *The Ufa Story: A History of Germany's Greatest Film Company, 1918–1945.* New York: Hill and Wang, 1996.

Kreimeier, Klaus, A. Ehmann, and J. Goergen, eds. *Geschichte des dokumentarischen Films in Deutschland. Weimarer Republik 1918–1933.* Vol. 2. Stuttgart: Reclma, 2005.

Krogmann, Carl Vincent. *Es ging um Deutschlands Zukunft: 1932–1939. Erlebtes, täglich diktiert von dem früheren regierenden Bürgermeister von Hamburg.* Leoni am Starnberger See: Druffel-Verlag, 1976.

Krohn, Helga. *Die Juden in Hamburg: Die politische, soziale und kulturelle Entwicklung einer jüdischen Großstadtgemeinde nach der Emanzipation, 1948–1918.* Hamburg: Hans Christians Verlag, 1974.

Larkin, Brian. "The Politics and Poetics of Infrastructure." *Annual Review of Anthropology* 42 (July 2013): 237–43.

Larsson, Lars Olof. *Die Neugestaltung Der Reichshauptstadt: Albert Speers Generalbebauungsplan für Berlin.* Stockholm: Almqvist & Wiksell International (distr.), 1977.

Laurie, Clayton D. *The Propaganda Warriors. America's Crusade against Nazi Germany.* Lawrence: University Press of Kansas, 1996.

Lees, Andrew. *Cities, Sin, and Social Reform in Imperial Germany.* Ann Arbor: University of Michigan Press, 2002.

Lefebvre, Henri. *The Production of Space.* Translated by Donald Nicholson-Smith. Oxford: Blackwell, 1991.

Lehmann, Axel. *Der Marshall-Plan und das neue Deutschland: Die Folgen amerikanischer Besatzungspolitik in Dden Westzonen*. Münster: Waxman, 2000.

Leiser, Erwin. *Nazi Cinema*. Translated by Gertrud Mander and David Wilson. New York: Collier, 1975.

Lesch, Paul. *Heim ins Ufa-Reich? NS-Filmpolitik und die Rezeption deutscher Filme in Luxemburg 1933–1944*. Trier: Wissenschaftlicher Verlag Trier, 2002.

Lilla, Joachim. *Die Stellvertretenden Gauleiter und die Vertretung der Gauleiter der NSDAP im "Dritten Reich."* Koblenz: Bundesarchiv, 2003.

Lindner, Burkhardt. "Die Spuren von Auschwitz in der Maske des Komischen. Chaplins Great Dictator und Monsieur Veroux." In *Lachen über Hitler. Auschwitz-Gelächter,* edited by Margrit Fröhlich, Hanno Loewy, and Heinz Steinert. Munich: Edition Text + Kritik, 2003. 83–106.

Linton, Derek S. *Who Has the Youth, Has the Future: The Campaign to Save Young Workers in Imperial Germany*. Cambridge, UK: Cambridge University Press, 1991.

Loewy, Ronny. "Der Lächerlichkeit preisgegeben. Nazis in den anti-Nazi Hollywood Filmen." In *Lachen über Hitler. Auschwitz-Gelächter,* edited by Margrit Fröhlich, Hanno Loewy, and Heinz Steinert. Munich: Edition Text & Kritik, 2003. 125–32.

Lohalm, Uwe. "An der inneren Front. Fürsorge für die Soldatenfamilie und 'rassenhygenische' Krankenpolitik." In *Hamburg im "Dritten Reich,"* edited by FZH, 444–67. Göttingen: Wallstein, 2005.

———. "Für eine leistungsbereite und 'erbgesunde' Volksgemeinschaft: Selektive Erwerbslosen- und Familienpolitik." In *Hamburg im "Dritten Reich,"* edited by FZH. Göttingen: Wallstein, 2005. 379–431.

———. "'Modell Hamburg.' Vom Stadtstaat zum Reichsgau." In *Hamburg im "Dritten Reich,"* edited by FZH. Göttingen: Wallstein, 2005. 122–53.

———. *Die nationalsozialistische Judenverfolgung 1933 bis 1945: Ein Überblick: Hamburg im Dritten Reich*. Hamburg: Landeszentrale für Politische Bildung, 1999.

———. *Völkischer Radikalismus: Die Geschichte des Deutschvölkischen Schutz-und Trutz-Bundes, 1919–1923*. Hamburg: Leibniz, 1970.

Lower, Wendy. *Nazi Empire-building and the Holocaust in Ukraine*. Chapel Hill: University of North Carolina Press, 2005.

Lowry, Stephen. "Ideology and Excess in Nazi Melodrama." In "Nazi Cinema." Special issue, *New German Critique* 74 (1998): 125–49.

———. *Pathos und Politik. Ideologie in Spielfilmen des Nationalsozialismus*. Tübingen: Niemeyer, 1991.

Lüdtke, Alf. *Alltagsgeschichte: Zur Rekonstruktion historischer Erfahrungen und Lebensweisen*. Frankfurt: Campus, 1989.

———. "'Coming to Terms with the Past:' Illusions of Remembering, Ways of Forgetting." *Journal of Modern History* 65, no. 3 (1993): 542–72.

———. *Eigen-Sinn: Fabrikalltag, Arbeitererfahrungen und Politik. Vom Kaiserreich bis in den Faschismus*. Hamburg: Ergebnisse Verlag, 1993.

Lüdtke, Alf, Inge Marßolek, and Adelheid von Saldern, eds. *Amerikanisierung: Traum und Alptraum im Deutschland des 20. Jahrhunderts*. Stuttgart: Franz Steiner, 1996.

Lust, Gunter. *The Flat Foot Floogee . . . , treudeutsch, treudeutsch: Erlebnisse eines Hamburger Swingheinis*. Hamburg: Olling und Galitz, 1992.

Luthöft, Hans-Jürgen. *Der Nordische Gedanke in Deutschland, 1920–1940*. Stuttgart: Ernst Klett, 1971.

Maack, Benjamin. "Der (M)Untergang." *SpiegelOnline*, January 28, 2009, http://einestages
.spiegel.de/static/topicalbumbackground/3569/der_m_untergang.html. Accessed May 25,
2010.

Maase, Kaspar, and Wolfgang Kaschuba, eds. *Schund und Schönheit: Populäre Kultur um 1900.*
Cologne: Böhlau, 2001.

MacDonald, Callum A. "The United States, Appeasement and the Open Door." In *The Fascist
Challenge and the Policy of Appeasement*, edited by Hans Mommsen and Lothar Kettenacker. London: Allen & Unwin, 1983. 400–12.

Maltby, Richard, Melvyn Stokes, and Robert C. Allen, eds. *Going to the Movies: Hollywood and
the Social Experience of Cinema.* Exeter: University of Exeter Press, 2007.

Manos, Helene. *Sankt Pauli: Soziale Lagen und soziale Fragen im Stadtteil Sankt Pauli.* Hamburg:
Ergebnisse, 1989.

Marcuse, Harold. *The Legacies of Dachau: The Uses and Abuses of a Concentration Camp, 1933-
2001.* New York: Cambridge University Press, 2001.

Marczeweska, Hanna. "Controversies around the American Policy of Neutrality, 1935–1939."
American Studies 9 (1990).

Marshall, Barbara. "British Democratisation Policy in Germany." In *Reconstruction in Post-War
Germany: British Occupation Policy and the Western Zones, 1945-1955*, edited by Ian D.
Turner. Oxford: Berg, 1989. 189–214.

Martin, John Levi. "The *Authoritarian Personality* 50 Years Later: What Lessons Are There for
Political Psychology?" *Political Psychology* 22, no. 1 (2001): 1–27.

Mason, Timothy. *Nazism, Fascism, and the Working Class.* Edited by Jane Caplan. Cambridge,
UK: Cambridge University Press, 1995.

———. *Social Policy in the Third Reich. The Working Class and the "National Community."* New
York: Berg, 1993.

Massey, Doreen. *For Space.* London: SAGE, 2005.

Mayne, Judith. *Cinema and Spectatorship.* New York: Routledge, 1993.

Mazower, Mark. *Dark Continent: Europe's Twentieth Century.* New York: Alfred A. Knopf, 1999.

———. *Hitler's Empire: How the Nazis Ruled Europe.* New York: Penguin Press, 2008.

McElligott, Anthony. *Contested City: Municipal Politics and the Rise of Nazism in Altona, 1917–
1937.* Ann Arbor: University of Michigan Press, 1998.

McLaughlin, Robert L., and Sally E. Parry. *We'll Always Have the Movies: American Cinema
During World War II.* Lexington: University of Kentucky, 2006.

Medick, Hans. "'Missionaries in the Row Boat'? Ethnological Ways of Knowing as a Challenge to
Social History." *Comparative Studies in Society and History* 29, no. 1 (1987): 76–98.

Merritt, Anna J., and Richard L. Merritt, eds. *Public Opinion in Occupied Germany. The Omgus
Surveys, 1945-1949.* Urbana: University of Illinois Press, 1970.

Micheler, Stefan. "Homophobic Propaganda and the Denunciation of Same-Sex-Desiring Men
under National Socialism." *Journal of the History of Sexuality* 11, no. 1/2 (January/April
2002): 95–130.

Michelson, Annette. "The Estates General of the Documentary Film." *October* 91 (Winter 2000):
140–48.

Milgram, Stanley. *Obedience to Authority: An Experimental View.* London: Printer & Martin,
1974.

Moeller, Felix. *The Film Minister: Goebbels and the Cinema in the "Third Reich."* Stuttgart and
London: Axel Menges, 2000.

Moeller, Robert G. Review of *Stalingrad Erinnern: Stalingrad Im Deutschen Und Russischen Gedächtnis*, by Peter Jahn, ed. *Central European History* 38, no. 4 (2005): 697–99.

———. *War Stories: The Search for a Usable Past in the Federal Republic of Germany*. 2001. Berkeley: University of California Press, 2003.

———, ed. *West Germany Under Construction: Politics, Society, and Culture in the Adenauer Era*. 1997. Ann Arbor: University of Michigan Press, 2000.

Moiser, John. *The Blitzkrieg Myth: How Hitler and the Allies Misread the Strategic Realities of World War II*. New York: Harper Collins, 2003.

Mommsen, Hans. *Aufstieg und Untergang der Republik von Weimar*. Munich: Ullstein, 2001.

———. *Beamtentum im Dritten Reich. Mit ausgewählten Quellen zur nationalsozialistischen Beamtenpolitik*. Stuttgart: Deutsche Verlags-Anstalt, 1966.

Mommsen, Hans, and Lothar Kettenacker, eds. *The Fascist Challenge and the Policy of Appeasement*. London: Allen & Unwin, 1983.

Monteath, Peter. "Swastikas by the Seaside." *History Today* 50, no. 5 (May 2000): 31–35

Moore, Michaela Hoenicke. *Know Your Enemy: The American Debate on Nazism, 1933–1945*. Cambridge, UK: Cambridge University Press, 2010.

Müller, Corinna. "Variationen des Kinoprogramms. Filmform und Filmgeschichte." In *Die Modellierung des Kinofilms. Zur Geschichte des Kinoprogramms zwischen Kurzfilm und Langfilm 1905/6–1918*, edited by Corinna Müller and Harro Segeberg. Munich: Wilhelm Fink Verlag, 1998. 43–76.

Müller, Corinna, and Harro Segeberg, eds. *Kinoöffentlichkeit (1895–1920): Entstehung Etablierung Differenzierung / Cinema's Public Sphere (1895–1920): Emergence Settlement Differntiation*. Marburg: Schüren, 2008.

Muscio, Giuliana. *Hollywood's New Deal*. Philadelphia: Temple University Press, 1997.

Nazario, Luiz. "Nazi Film Politics in Brazil, 1933-42." In *Cinema and the Swastika: The International Expansion of Third Reich Cinema*, edited by Roel Vande Winkel and David Welch. New York: Palgrave Macmillan, 2007.

Neale, Steve. "Melodrama and Tears." *Screen* 27, no. 6 (November/December 1986): 6–23.

Necker, Sylvia. *Konstanty Gutschow, 1902–1978: Modernes Denken und volksgemeinschaftliche Utopie eines Architekten*. Hamburg: Dölling und Galitz Verlag, 2012.

Neil, Gregor. *Haunted City: Nuremberg and the Nazi Past*. New Haven: Yale University Press, 2008.

Neumann, Franz. *Behemoth: The Structure and Practice of National Socialism*. London: V. Gollanez, 1942.

Neumann, Klaus. *Shifting Memories: The Nazi Past in the New Germany*. Ann Arbor: University of Michigan Press, 2000.

Nichols, Bill. "Documentary Film and the Modernist Avant-Garde." *Critical Inquiry* 27, no. 4 (Summer 2001): 580–610.

Nikles, Bruno W. "Immer komplexer: Die Entwicklugn der techtlichen Regelungen zum Jugendschutz." *KJuG* 4 (2002): 119.

Noaks, Jeremy, ed. *Nazism*. Vol. IV. Exeter: University of Exeter Press, 1998.

Nolzen, Armin. "Die Gaue als Verwaltungseinheiten der NSDAP." In *Die NS-Gaue: Regionale Mittelinstanzen im zentralistischen Führerstaat*, edited by Jürgen John and Horst Möller. Munich: Oldenbourg Verlag, 2007.

O'Brien, Mary-Elizabeth. *Nazi Cinema as Enchantment*. Rochester: Camden House, 2004.

Offner, Arnold A. "The United States and National Socialist Germany." In *The Fascist Challenge and the Policy of Appeasement*, edited by Hans Mommsen and Lothar Kettenacker. London: Allen & Unwin, 1983. 413–27.

Oosterhuis, Harry. "Medicine, Male Bonding and Homosexuality." *Journal of Contemporary History* 32, no. 2 (April 1997): 187–205.

Otto, Gerhard, and Johannes Houwink ten Cate, eds. *Das organisierte Chaos: "Ämterdarwinismus" und "Gesinnungsethik." Determinanten nationalsozialistischer Besatzungsherrschaft.* Berlin: Metropol, 1999.

Pages, Neil Christian, Mary Rhiel, and Ingeborg Majer-O'Sickey, eds. *Riefenstahl Screened: An Anthology of New Criticism.* New York: Continuum, 2008.

Palmier, Jean-Michel. *Weimar in Exile: The Antifascist Emigration in Europe and America.* Translated by David Fernbach. London: Verso, 2006.

Palmowski, Jan. *Inventing a Socialist Nation: Heimat and the Politics of Everyday Life in the Gdr, 1945–1990.* New York: Cambridge University Press, 2009.

Parker, Simon. *Cities, Politics and Power: Critical Introductions to Urbanism and the City.* London: Routledge, 2011.

Parsons, Kermit C., and David Schuyler, eds. *From Garden City to Green City: The Legacy of Ebenezer Howard.* Baltimore: Johns Hopkins University Press, 2002.

Paschen, Joachim. *Hamburg vor dem Krieg. Bilder vom Alltag 1933–1940.* Bremen: Edition Temmen, 2003.

———. *Hamburg vor hundert Jahren.* Hamburg: Zeise Verlag, 1999.

———. *Hurra, Wir Leben noch! Hamburg nach 1945.* Gudensberg-Gleichen: Wartberg Verlag, 2003.

Paul, Gerhard, and Klaus-Michael Mallmann. *Die Gestapo—Mythos und Realität.* Darmstadt: Primus, 1996.

Paul, Heike, and Katja Kanzler, eds. *Amerikanische Populärkultur in Deutschland: Case Studies in Cultural Transfer Past and Present.* Leipzig: Leipziger Universitätsverlag, 2002.

Pendas, Devin O., Mark Roseman, and Richard F. Wetzell, eds. *Beyond the Racial State: Rethinking Nazi Germany.* Cambridge, UK: Cambridge University Press, 2017.

Peter, Karen, ed. *Ns-Presseanweisungen der Vorkriegszeit. Edition und Dokumentation.* Munich: Saur, 2001.

Petersen, Klaus. *Zensur in der Weimarer Republik.* Stuttgart: Metzler, 1995.

Petley, Julian. *Capital and Culture: German Cinema 1933–1945.* London: British Film Institute, 1979.

Petro, Patrice. *Joyless Streets: Women and Melodramatic Representation in Weimar, Germany.* Princeton: Princeton University Press, 1989.

Petropolous, Jonathan. *Art as Politics in the Third Reich.* Chapel Hill: University of North Carolina Press, 1996.

Petsch, Joachim. *Baukunst und Stadtplanung im Dritten Reich.* Munich: Carl Hanser Verlag, 1976.

Peukert, Detlev. *Die Edelweißpiraten: Protestbewegungen jugendlicher Arbeiter im Dritten Reich. Eine Dokumentation.* Cologne: Bund-Verlag, 1980.

———. *Grenzen der Sozialdisiziplinierung: Aufstieg und Krise der deutschen Jugendfürsorge von 1878–1932.* Cologne: Bund-Verlag, 1986.

———. *Inside Nazi Germany.* New Haven: Yale University Press, 1986.

———. *The Weimar Republic: The Crisis of Classical Modernity.* London: Allen Lane, 1991.

———. "Zur Erforschung der Sozialpolitik im Dritten Reich." In *Soziale Arbeit und Faschismus: Volkspflege und Pädagogik im Nationalsozialismus,* edited by Hans-Uwe Otto and Heinz Sünker. Bielefeld: K-T Verlag, 1986.

Phillips, Gene D. *Exiles in Hollywood: Major European Film Directors in America.* Bethlehem: Lehigh University Press, 1998.

Pike, David. *The Politics of Culture in Soviet-Occupied Germany, 1945–1949.* Stanford: Stanford University Press, 1992.

Pike, Frederick B. *FDR's Good Neighbor Policy: Sixty Years of Generally Gentle Chaos.* Austin: University of Texas Press, 1995.

Pine, Lisa. *Hitler's "National Community": Society and Culture in Nazi Germany.* London: Bloomsbury Academic, 2017.

———. *Nazi Family Policy, 1933–1945.* New York: Berg, 1997.

Pini, Udo. *Leibeskult und Liebeskitsch: Erotik im Dritten Reich.* Munich: Klinkhardt & Biermann, 1992.

Piper, Ernst. *Alfred Rosenberg: Hiters Chefideologe.* Munich: Karl Blessing Verlag, 2005.

Plagemann, Volker, ed. *Industriekultur in Hamburg: Des Deutschen Reiches Tor zur Welt.* Munich: Beck, 1984.

Polster, Bernd. *Swing Heil: Jazz im Nationalsozialismus.* Berlin: Transit, 1989.

Prakash, Gyan, and Kevin Michael Kruse. *The Spaces of the Modern City: Imaginaries, Politics, and Everyday Life.* Princeton: Princeton University Press, 2008.

Proctor, Robert. *The Nazi War on Cancer.* Princeton: Princeton University Press, 1999.

———. *Racial Hygiene: Medicine Under the Nazis.* Cambridge, MA: Harvard University Press, 1988.

Prümm, Karl. "Die Stadt ist der Film … Film und Metropole in den Zwanziger Jahren am Exempel Berlin." In *Im Banne der Metropolen,* edited by Peter Alter, 111–30. Göttingen: Vandenhoeck & Rupprecht, 1993.

Quayson, Ato. *Oxford Street Accra: City Life and the Itineraries of Transnationalism.* Durham: Duke University Press, 2014.

Raberg, Frank. "Wirtschaftspolitiker zwischen Selbstüberschätzung und Resignation: Oswald Lehnich, Württembergischer Wirtschaftsminister." In *Die Führer der Provinz. NS-Biographien aus Baden und Württemberg,* edited by Michael Kißenerand Joachim Scholtyseck. Konstanz: UVK, 1997. 333–59.

Rabinowitz, Paula. "Wreckage upon Wreckage: History, Documentary and the Ruins of Memory." *History and Theory* 32, no. 2 (May 1993): 119–37.

Rasp, Hans-Peter. *Eine Stadt Für Tausend Jahre: München, Bauten Und Projekte Für Die Hauptstadt Der Bewegung.* Munich: Süddeutscher Verlag, 1981.

Rau, Susanne. "Holsteinische Landestadt oder Reichstadt? Hamburgs Erfindung seiner Geschichte als Freie Reichstadt." In *Nordlichter. Geschichtsbewusstsein und Geschichtsmythen nördlich der Elbe,* edited by Bea Lundt. Cologne: Bohlau Verlag, 2004.

Reagin, Nancy. "Comparing Apples and Oranges: Housewives and the Politics of Consumption in Interwar Germany." In *Getting and Spending: European and American Consumer Societies in the Twentieth Century,* edited by Susan Strasser Charles McGovern, and Matthias Judt. Cambridge, UK: Cambridge University Press, 1998. 241–62.

———. *Sweeping the German Nation: Domesticity and National Identity in Germany, 1870–1945.* Cambridge, UK: Cambridge University Press, 2007

Rebentisch, Dieter. *Führerstaat und Verwaltung im Zweiten Welkrieg*. Stuttgart: Franz Steiner, 1989.

Reich, Jacqueline, and Piero Garofalo, eds. *Re-Viewing Fascism: Italian Cinema, 1922–1943*. Bloomington: Indiana University Press, 2002.

Reichel, Peter. *Der schöne Schein des Dritten Reichs: Faszination und Gewalt des Faschismus*. Munich: Carl Hauser, 1991.

Reimer, Robert C., ed. *Cultural History Through a National Socialist Lens: Essays on the Cinema of the Third Reich*. Rochester: Camden House, 2000.

Renneberg, Monika. *Science, Technology, and National Socialism*. Cambridge: Cambridge University Press, 1994

Rentschler, Eric. *The Ministry of Illusion: Nazi Cinema and Its Afterlife*. Cambridge, MA: Harvard University Press, 1996.

———. "Remembering Not to Forget: A Retrospective Reading of Alexander Kluge's 'Brutality in Stone.'" In "Alexander Kluge." Special issue, *New German Critique* 49, no. 1 (Winter 1990): 23–41.

Reuth, Ralf Georg. *Goebbels*. Translated by Krishna Winston. New York: Harcourt Brace, 1993.

Riccardo, Bavaj. *Von links gegen Weimar. Linkes antiparlamentarisches Denken in der Weimarer Republik*. Bonn: Dietz, 2005.

Ritzheimer, Kara. "Protecting Youth from 'Trash': Anti-*Schund* Campaigns in Baden, 1900–1933." PhD diss., Binghamton University, 2007.

———. *"Trash," Censorship, and National Identity in Early Twentieth-Century Germany*. Cambridge, UK: Cambridge University Press, 2016.

Robinson, Jennifer. *Ordinary Cities: Between Modernity and Development*. London: Routledge, 2006.

Roos, Julia. "Backlash against Prostitutes' Rights: Origins and Dynamics of Nazi Prostitution Policies." *Journal of the History of Sexuality* 11, no. 1/2 (January/April 2002): 67–94.

Roschlau, Johannes. "Ein Mädchen geht an Land." In *Fredy Bockbein trifft Mr. Dynamit: Filme auf den zweiten Blick*, edited by Christoph Fuchs and Michael Töteberg. Munich: Edition Text + Kritik, 2007. 109–14.

Roseman, Mark. "National Socialism and the End of Modernity." *American Historical Review* 116, no. 3 (June 2011): 688–701.

———. *The Past in Hiding: Memory and Survival in Nazi Germany*. New York: Metropolitan Books, 2001.

———. "The Uncontrollable Economy: Ruhr Coal Production, 1945–8." In *Reconstruction in Post-War Germany: British Occupation Policy and the Western Zones, 1945–1955*, edited by Ian D. Turner. Oxford: Berg, 1989. 93–124.

Rosenfeld, Gavriel D. "A Looming Crash or a Soft Landing? Forecasting the Future of the Memory 'Industry.'" *Journal of Modern History* 81, no. 1 (2009): 122–58.

———. *The World Hitler Never Made: Alternate History and the Memory of Nazism*. Cambridge, UK: Cambridge University Press, 2005.

Rosenkranz, Bernhard, Ulf Bollmann, and Gottfried Lorenz. *Homosexuellen Verfolgung in Hamburg, 1919–1969*. Hamburg: Lambda, 2009.

Ross, Corey. "Mass Culture and Divided Audiences: Cinema and Social Change in Inter-War Germany." *Past & Present* 193 (2006): 157–95.

Rossino, Alexander B. *Hitler Strikes Poland: Blitzkrieg, Ideology and Atrocity*. Lawrence: University of Kansas Press, 2003.

Roth, Karl-Heinz. "Ökonomie und politische Macht: Die 'Firma Hamburg' 1930–1945." In *Kein abgeschlossenes Kapitel: Hamburg im "Dritten Reich,"* edited by Angelika Ebbinghaus and Karsten Linne. Hamburg: Europäische Verlagsanstalt, 1997.

Rothenberger, Karl-Heinz. *Die Hungerjahre nach dem Zweiten Weltkrieg: Ernährungs- und Landwirtschaft in Rheinland-Pfalz, 1945–1950.* Boppard: Harald Boldt Verlag, 1980.

Rother, Rainer. "Leni Riefenstahl und der 'Absolute' Film." In *Mediale Mobilmachung I: Das Dritten Reich und der Film,* edited by Harro Segeberg. Munich: Wilhelm Fink Verlag, 2004.

Rothman, William. *Documentary Film Classics.* Cambridge, UK: Cambridge University Press, 1997.

Rouette, Susanne, and Pamela Selwyn. "Mothers and Citizens: Gender and Social Policy in Germany After the First World War." *Central European History* 30, no. 1 (1997): 48–66.

Rubin, Eli. *Synthetic Socialism: Plastics and Dictatorship in the German Democratic Republic.* Chapel Hill: University of North Carolina Press, 2008.

Said, Edward W. *Orientalism.* New York: Pantheon Books, 1978.

Sander, Ulrich. *Jugendwiderstand im Krieg: Die Helmuth-Hübener Gruppe, 1941/1942.* Bonn: Pahl-Rugenstein, 2002.

Sassen, Saskia. *The Global City: New York, London, Tokyo.* 2nd ed. Princeton: Princeton University Press, 2001.

Saunders, Thomas J. *Hollywood in Berlin: American Cinema and Weimar Germany.* Berkeley: University of California Press, 1994.

Schildt, Axel. "Auf Expansionskurs: Aus der Inflation in die Krise." In *Das Ufa-Buch. Kunst und Krisen. Stars und Regisseure. Wirtschaft und Politik,* edited by Hans-Michael Bock and Michael Töteberg. Frankfurt a.M.: Zweitausendeins, 1992.

———. "Einleitung." In *Hamburg im "Dritten Reich,"* edited by FZH. Göttingen: Wallstein, 2005.

———. "Jenseits Von Politik? Aspekte Des Alltags." In *Hamburg im "Dritten Reich, "* edited by FZH. Göttingen: Wallstein, 2005.

Schissler, Hanna. *The Miracle Years: A Cultural History of West Germany, 1949–1968.* Princeton: Princeton University Press, 2001.

Schivelbusch, Wolfgang. *The Culture of Defeat: On National Trauma, Mourning, and Recovery.* New York: Metropolitan Books, 2003.

———. *Three New Deals: Reflections on Roosevelt's America, Mussolini's Italy, and Hitler's Germany, 1933–1939.* 2006. New York: Picador, 2007.

Schmitz, Helmut, ed. *A Nation of Victims? Representations of German Wartime Suffering from 1945 to the Present.* Amsterdam: Rodopi, 2007.

Schneer, Jonathan. *London 1900: The Imperial Metropolis.* New Haven: Yale University Press, 1999.

Schnell, Ralf. *Literarische innere Emigration: 1933–1945.* Stuttgart: Metzler, 1976.

Schoonover, Thomas David. *Hitler's Man in Havana: Heinz Lüning and Nazi Espionage in Latin America.* Lexington: University of Kentucky Press, 2008.

Schreckenberg, Heinz. *Ideologie und Alltag im Dritten Reich.* Frankfurt a.M.: Peter Lang, 2003.

Schröder, Hans-Jürgen. "The Ambiguities of Appeasement: Great Britain, the United States and Germany, 1937-9." In *The Fascist Challenge and the Policy of Appeasement,* edited by Hans Mommsen and Lothar Kettenacker. London: Allen & Unwin, 1983. 390–99.

———. *Marshallplan und westdeutscher Wiederaufstieg: Positionen, Kontroversen.* Stuttgart: Steiner, 1990.

Schubert, Dirk. "Stadtplanung als Ideologie: Eine theoretische, ideologiekritische Untersuchung der Stadt, des Städtebaus und Wohnungsbaus in Deutschland Von Ca. 1850 bis heute." PhD diss., Freie Universität Berlin, 1981.

Schulte-Sasse, Linda. *Entertaining the Third Reich: Illusions of Wholeness in Nazi Cinema*. London: Duke University Press, 1996.

———. "The Jew as Other under National Socialism: Veit Harlan's Jud Süss." *German Quarterly* 61, no. 1 (Winter 1988): 22–49.

Schulz, Andreas. *Lebenswelt und Kultur des Bürgertums im 19. Und 20. Jahrhundert*. Munich: Oldenbourg, 2005.

Schwartz, Vanessa R. *Spectacular Realities: Early Mass Culture in Fin-De-Siecle Paris*. 1998. Berkeley: University of California Press, 1999.

Scobie, Alexander. *Hitler's State Architecture: The Impact of Classical Antiquity*. University Park: Pennsylvania State University Press, 1990.

Scott, James C. *Seeing Like A State: How Certain Schemes to Improve the Human Condition Have Failed*. New Haven: Yale University Press, 1998.

Sebald, W. G. *On the Natural History of Destruction: With Essays on Alfred Andersch, Jean Améry and Peter Weiss*. London: Hamish Hamilton, 2003.

Segeberg, Harro. "Erlebnisraum Kino: Das Dritte Reich als Kultur-und Mediengesellschaft." In *Mediale Mobilmachung I: Das Dritte Reich und der Film*, edited by Harro Segeberg, 11–42. Munich: Wilhelm Fink, 2004.

———, ed. *Mediale Mobilmachung I: Das Dritte Reich und der Film*. Vol. Mediengeschichte des Films Band 4. Munich: Wilhelm Fink Verlag, 2004.

Segeberg, Harro, and Corinna Müller, eds. *Die Modellierung des Kinofilms: Zur Geschichte des Kinoprogramms zwischen Kurzfilm und Langfilm 1905/06–1918*. Munich: Wilhelm Fink, 1998.

Semmens, Kristin. *Seeing Hitler's Germany: Tourism in the Third Reich*. New York: Palgrave Macmillan, 2005.

Sennett, Alan. "Film Propaganda: Triumph of the Will as a Case Study." *Journal of Cinema and Media* 55, no. 1 (Spring 2014), 45–65.

Sennett, Richard. *The Fall of Public Man*. New York: Knopf, 1977.

———. "The Public Realm." In *The Blackwell City Reader*, edited by Gary Bridge and Sophie Watson. Malden: Wiley-Blackwell, 2010.

Shandley, Robert. "Dismantling the Dream Factory: The Film Industry in Berubbled Germany." In "German Studies Today." Special issue, *South Central Review* 16, no. 2/3 (Summer-Autumn 1999): 104–17.

———. "Rubble Canyons: *Die Mörder sind unter uns* and the Western." *German Quarterly* 74, no. 2 (Spring 2001): 132–47.

Shepherd, Ben. "The Clean Wehrmacht, the War of Extermination and Beyond." *Historical Journal* 52, no. 2 (2009): 455–73.

———. *War in the Wild East: The German Army and Soviet Partisans*. Cambridge, MA: Harvard University Press, 2004.

Shull, Michael S., and David E. Wilt. *Doing Their Bits: Wartime American Animated Short Films, 1939–1945*. 2nd ed. Jefferson: McFarland, 2004.

Sigel, Lisa Z. "Filth in the Wrong People's Hands: Postcards and the Expansion of Pornography in Britain and the Atlantic World, 1880–1914." *Journal of Social History* 33, no. 4 (Summer 2000): 859–85.

Singer, Ben. "Modernity, Hyperstimulus, and the Rise of Popular Sensationalism." In *Cinema and the Invention of Modern Life*, edited by Leo Charney and Vanessa Schwartz. Berkeley: University of California Press, 1995. 72–99.

Skelton, Carl. *Soft City Culture and Technology: The Betaville Project*. New York: Springer, 2014.

Smaill, Belinda. *The Documentary: Politics, Emotion, Culture*. New York: Palgrave Macmillan, 2010.

Smaldone, William. *Confronting Hitler: German Social Democrats in Defense of the Weimar Republic, 1929–1933*. Lanham: Lexington Books, 2009.

Smelser, Ronald. *Robert Ley: Hitler's Labor Front Leader*. New York: Berg, 1988.

Sneeringer, Julia. *A Social History of Early Rock 'n' Roll in Germany: Hamburg from Burlesque to the Beatles, 1956-69*. London: Bloomsbury, 2018.

———. *Winning Women's Votes: Propaganda and Politics in Weimar Germany*. Hill: University of North Carolina Press, 2003.

Spector, Scott. *Prague Territories: National Conflict and Cultural Innovation in Kafka's Fin de Siècle*. Berkeley: University of California Press, 2000.

———. "Was the Third Reich Movie-Made? Interdisciplinarity and the Reframing of 'Ideology.'" *American Historical Review* 106, no. 2 (April 2001): 460–84.

Spiker, Jürgen. *Film und Kapital: Der Weg der deutschen Filmwirtschaft zum nationalsozialitischen Einheitskonzern*. Berlin: Verlag Volker Spiess, 1975.

Spode, Hasso. "Arbeiterurlaub im Dritten Reich." In *Angst, Belohnung, Zucht und Ordnung*, edited by Carola Sachse et al. Opladen: Westdeutscher, 1982.

Srelczyk, Florentine. "Far Away, So Close: Carl Froelich's *Heimat*." In *Cultural History Through a National Socialist Lens*, edited by Robert C. Reimer, 109–32. Rochester: Camden House, 2000.

Stacey, Jackie. *Star Gazing: Hollywood Cinema and Female Spectatorship*. London: Routledge, 1994.

Stachura, Peter D., ed. *The Shaping of the Nazi State*. London: Croom Helm, 1978.

Stahr, Gerhard. *Volksgemeinschaft vor der Leinwand: Der nationalsozialistische Film und sein Publikum*. Berlin: Hans Theissen, 2001.

Staiger, Janet. *Interpreting Films: Studies in the Historical Reception of American Cinema*. Princeton: Princeton University Press, 1992.

Stargardt, Nicholas. *The German War. A Nation Under Arms, 1939–1945*. New York: Basic Books, 2015.

Stark, Gary D. *Banned in Berlin: Literary Censorship in Imperial Germany, 1871–1918*. New York: Berghahn Books, 2009.

———. "Cinema, Society, and the State: Policing the Film Industry in Imperial Germany." In *Essays on Culture and Society in Modern Germany*, edited by Gary D. Stark, and Bede Karl Lackner. Arlington: Texas A&M University Press, 1982.

———. *Entrepreneurs of Ideology: Neoconservative Publishers in Germany, 1890–1933*. Chapel Hill: University of North Carolina Press, 1981.

Steakley, James D. "Cinema and Censorship in the Weimar Republic: The Case of *Anders Als Die Andern*." *Film History* 11, no. 2 (1999).

Steege, Paul. *Black Market, Cold War: Everyday Life in Berlin, 1946–1949*. Cambridge, UK: Cambridge University Press, 2007.

Steege, Paul, et al. "The History of Everyday Life: A Second Chapter." *Journal of Modern History* 80 (2008): 358–78.

Steinbach, Peter. *Widerstand gegen den Nationalsozialismus*. Berlin: Akademie Verlag, 1994.

Steinweis, Alan E. "Weimar Culture and the Rise of National Socialism: The Kampfbund für Deutsche Kultur." *Central European History* 24, no. 4 (1991): 402–23.

Stephenson, Jill. *Hitler's Home Front: Württemberg Under the Nazis.* London: Hambledon Continuum, 2006.

Stewart, Jacqueline Najuma. *Migrating to the Movies: Cinema and Black Urban Modernity.* Berkeley: University of California Press, 2005.

Stibbe, Matthew. *Germany 1914–1933.* New York: Routledge, 2010.

Stieg, Margaret F. "The 1926 German Law to Protect Youth against Trash and Dirt: Moral Protectionism in a Democracy." *Central European History* 23, no. 1 (Mar 1990).

Storim, Mirijam. *Ästhetik im Umbruch: Zur Funktion der 'Rede über Kunst' um 1900 am Beispiel der Debatte um Schmutz und Schund.* Tübingen: Max Niemeyer, 2002.

Stubbs, Julie R. "Rescuing 'Endangered Girls': Bourgeois Feminism, Social Welfare, and the Debate over Prostitution in the Weimar Republic." PhD diss., University of Michigan, 2001.

Stüber, Gabriele. *Kampf gegen den Hunger 1945–1950: Die Ernährungslage in der britischen Zone Deutschlands, insbesondere in Schleswig-Holstein und Hamburg.* Neumünster: K. Wachholtz, 1984.

———, ed. *Zonenbeirat. Zonal Advisory Council, 1946–1948. Protokolle und Anlagen 1.–11. Sitzung 1946/47.* Düsseldorf: Droste Verlag, 1993.

Sugrue, Thomas J. *The Origins of the Urban Crisis: Race and Inequality in Postwar Detroit.* Princeton: Princeton University Press, 2005.

Süss, Dietmar. *"Ein Volk, Ein Reich, Ein Führer": Die Deutsche Gesellschaft im Dritten Reich.* Munich : C. H. Beck, 2017.

Swett, Pamela. *Selling Under the Swastika: Advertising and Commercial Culture in Nazi Germany.* Stanford: Stanford University Press, 2014.

Szaloky, Melinda. "Sounding Images in Silent Film: Visual Acoustics in Murnau's 'Sunrise.'" *Cinema Journal* 41, no. 2 (Winter 2002): 109–31.

Szobar, Patricia. "Telling Sexual Stories in the Nazi Courts of Law: Race Defilement in Germany, 1933–1945." *Journal of the History of Sexuality* 11, no. 1/2 (January/April): 131–63.

Szodrzynski, Joachim. "Die 'Heimatfront' zwischen Stalingrad und Kriegsende." In *Hamburg im "Dritten Reich,"* edited by FZH. Göttingen: Wallstein, 2005. 633–85.

Szöllösi-Janze, Margit. *Science in the Third Reich.* Oxford: Berg, 2001.

Taylor, Philip M., ed. *Britain and the Cinema in the Second World War.* London: Macmillan, 1988.

Taylor, Richard. *Film Propaganda: Soviet Russia and Nazi Germany.* 1979. 2nd and revised ed. New York: St. Martin's Press, 1998.

Tegel, Susan. *Nazis and the Cinema.* London: Hambledon Continuum, 2007.

Templin, David. *Wasser für die Volksgemeinschaft: Wasserwerke und Stadtentwässerung in Hamburg im "Dritten Reich."* Munich : Dölling und Galitz Verlag, 2016.

Tent, James F. *Mission on the Rhine: Reeducation and Denazification in American Occupied Germany.* Chicago: University of Chicago Press, 1982.

Thomas, June Manning. *Redevelopment and Race: Planning a Finer City in Postwar Detroit.* Detroit: Wayne State University Press, 2013.

Thompson, Kristin. "The Concept of Cinematic Excess." In *Narrative, Apparatus, Ideology: A Film Theory Reader,* edited by Philip Rosen. New York: Columbia University Press, 1986.

———. *Herr Lubitsch Goes to Hollywood: German and American Film After World War I.* Amsterdam: Amsterdam University Press, 2005.

Timm, Annette. "Sex with a Purpose: Prostitution, Venereal Disease, and Militarized Masculinity in the Third Reich." *Journal of the History of Sexuality* 11, no. 1/2 (January/April 2002): 223–55.

Timpke, Henning, ed. *Dokumente zur Gleichschaltung des Landes Hamburg 1933.* Hamburg: Europäische Verlagsanstalt, 1964.

Toeplitz, Jerzy. *Die Geschichte des Films 1895–1928.* Munich: Rogner & Bernhard, 1979.

Tofahrn, Klaus W. *Chronologie der Besetzung Deutschlands 1945–1949: Daten, Dokumente, Kommentare.* Hamburg: Kovac, 2003.

Tonkiss, Fran. *Cities by Design: The Social Life of Urban Form.* Cambridge: Polity Press, 2013.

Tooze, Adam. *The Wages of Destruction: The Making and Breaking of the Nazi Economy.* 2006. New York: Penguin, 2008.

Töteberg, Michael. *Filmstadt Hamburg. Von Hans Albers bis Wim Wenders, vom Abaton zu den Zeise-Kinos: Kino-Geschichte(n) einer Großstadt.* Hamburg: VSA-Verlag, 1997.

Töteberg, Michael, and Volker Reissmann. *Mach dir ein paar schöne Stunden.* Bremen: Temmen, 2008.

Tratner, Michael. *Crowd Scenes: Movies and Mass Politics.* New York: Fordham University Press, 2008.

Trentmann, Frank. "Beyond Consumerism: New Historical Perspectives on Consumption." *Journal of Contemporary History* 39, no. 3 (July 2004): 373–401.

Trittel, Günter J. *Hunger Und Politik.* Frankfurt: Campus, 1990.

Tsing, Anna Lowenhaupt. *Friction: An Ethnography of Global Connection.* Princeton: Princeton University Press, 2005.

Tuan, Yi-Fu. *Space and Place: The Perspective of Experience* Minneapolis: University of Minnesota Press, 1977.

Turner, Ian D., ed. *Reconstruction in Post-War Germany: British Occupation Policy and the Western Zones, 1945–1955.* Oxford: Berg, 1989.

Vascik, George S. *The Stab-in-the-Back Myth and the Fall of the Weimar Republic: A History in Documents and Visual Sources.* London: Bloomsbury Academic, 2016.

Viano, Maurizio. "'Life Is Beautiful': Reception, Allegory, and Holocaust Laughter." *Film Quarterly* 53, no. 1 (Autumn 1999): 26–34.

Vogt, Timothy R. *Denazification in Soviet-Occupied Germany. Brandenburg, 1945–1948.* Cambridge, MA: Harvard University Press, 2000.

von Moltke, Johannes. "Home Again: Revisiting the New German Cinema in Edgar Reitz's 'Die Zweite Heimat' (1993)." *Cinema Journal* 42, no. 3 (Spring 2003): 114–43.

———. "Nazi Cinema Revisited." *Film Quarterly* 61, no. 1 (Fall 2007): 68–72.

———. *No Place Like Home: Locations of Heimat in German Cinema.* Berkeley: University of California Press, 2005.

———. "Trapped in America: The Americanization of the Trapp-Family or 'Papas Kino' Revisited." *German Studies Review* 19, no. 3 (October 1996): 455–78.

Wackerfuss, Andrew. *Stormtrooper Families: Homosexuality and Community in the Early Nazi Movement.* New York: Harrington Park Press, 2015.

Walker, Mark. *Nazi Science: Myth, Truth, and the German Atomic Bomb.* New York: Plenum Press, 1995.

Walkowitz, Judith. *City of Dreadful Delight: Narratives of Sexual Danger in Late-Victorian London.* Chicago: University of Chicago Press, 1992.

Wallace, David. *Exiles in Hollywood.* Pompton Plains: Limelight Editions, 2006.

Waller, Gregory A., ed. *Moviegoing in America: A Sourcebook in the History of Film Exhibition.* Oxford: Blackwell, 2002.

Wanmali, Sudhir, and Yassir Islam. "Rural Infrastructure and Agricultural Development in Southern Africa: A Center-Periphery Perspective." *Geographic Journal* 163, no. 3 (November 1997): 259–69.

Ward, Janet. *Weimar Surfaces: Urban Visual Culture in 1920s Germany.* Berkeley: University of California Press, 2001.

Watkins, T. H. *The Great Depression: America in the 1930s.* Boston: Little, Brown, 1993.

Weckel, Ulrike, and Edgar Wolfrum, eds. *"Bestien" und "Befehlsempfänger." Frauen und Männer in NS-Prozessen Nach 1945.* Göttingen: Vandehoeck & Rupprecht, 2003.

Weeks, Gregory. *U.S. and Latin American Relations.* New York: Longman, 2008.

Wehler, Hans-Ulrich. *Deutsche Gesellschaftsgeschichte.* 3rd ed. Band 4, 1914–1949. Munich: C. H. Beck, 1996.

Weihsmann, Helmut. *Bauen unterm Hakenkreuz. Architektur des Untergangs.* Vienna: Promedia, 1998.

Weinhauer, Klaus. "Handelskrise und Rüstungsboom. Die Wirtschaft." In *Hamburg im "Dritten Reich,"* edited by FZH. Göttingen: Wallstein Verlag, 2005.

Weinreb, Alice. "Matters of Taste: The Politics of Food and Hunger in Divided Germany, 1945–1971." PhD diss., University of Michigan, 2009.

———. *Modern Hungers: Food and Power in Twentieth-Century Germany.* New York: Oxford University Press, 2017.

Weisbrod, Bernd, ed. *Von der Währungsreform zum Wirtschaftswunder. Wiederaufbau in Niedersachsen.* Hannover: Hahn, 1998.

Weiss, Sheila Faith. *The Nazi Symbiosis: Human Genetics and Politics in the Third Reich.* Chicago: University of Chicago Press, 2010.

Weissman, Stephen. *Chaplin: A Life.* New York: Arcade, 2008.

Welch, David. "Cinema and Society in Imperial Germany 1905–1918." *German History* 8, no. 1 (February 1990): 28–46.

———. "Priming the Pump of German Democracy. British 'Re-Education' Policy in Germany after the Second World War." In *Reconstruction in Post-War Germany: British Occupation Policy and the Western Zones, 1945–1955,* edited by Ian D. Turner, 215–38. Oxford: Berg, 1989.

———. *Propaganda and the German Cinema 1933–1945.* Oxford: Clarendon, 1983.

———. *The Third Reich: Politics and Propaganda.* 1993. 2nd ed. London: Routledge, 2002.

Westermann, Edward B. *Hitler's Police Battalions: Enforcing Racial War in the East.* Lawrence: University Press of Kansas, 2005.

Wetzel, Kraft, and Peter Hagemann. *Zensur: Verbotene deutsche Filme 1933–1945.* Berlin: Volker Spiess, 1978.

Wetzell, Richard F. *Inventing the Criminal: A History of German Criminology, 1880–1945.* Chapel Hill: University of North Carolina Press, 2000.

Wiek, Peter. *Das Hamburger Etagenhaus 1870–1914: Geschichte, Struktur, Gestaltung.* Bremen: Edition Temmen, 2002

Wildt, Michael. *Am Beginn der "Konsumgesellschaft." Mangelerfahrung, Lebenshaltung, Wohstandshoffnung in Westdeutschland in den fünfziger Jahren.* Hamburg: Ergebnisse, 1994.

———. *Generation des Unbedingten.* Hamburg: Hamburger Edition, 2003.

———. *Hitler's Volksgemeinschaft and the Dynamics of Racial Exclusion: Violence against Jews in Provincial Germany, 1919–1939.* New York: Berghahn Books, 2012.

————. *Volksgemeinschaft als Selbstermächtigung. Gewalt gegen Juden in der deutschen Provinz 1919–1939*. Hamburg: Hamburger Edition, 2007.

Wilms, Wilfried, and William Rasch, eds. *German Postwar Films: Life and Love in the Ruins*. New York: Palgrave Macmillan, 2008.

Winkel, Roel Vande, and David Welch, eds. *Cinema and the Swastika: The International Expansion of Third Reich Cinema*. New York: Palgrave, 2007.

Winkler, Allan M. *Franklin D. Roosevelt and the Making of Modern America*. New York: Pearson, 2006.

Wischermann, Clemens. *Wohnen in Hamburg vor dem Ersten Weltkrieg*. Münster: Coppenrath, 1983.

Witte, Karsten. "Film im Nationalsozialismus: Blendung und Überblendung." In *Die Geschichte des deutschen Films*, edited by Wolfgang Jacobson, Anton Kaes, and Hans Helmut Prinzler. Stuttgart and Weimar: Verlag J. B. Metzler, 1993. 119–70.

————. "The Indivisible Legacy of Nazi Cinema." In "Nazi Cinema." Special issue, *New German Critique* 74 (Spring/Summer 1998): 23–30.

Wolf, Eric. *Europe and the People Without History*. Berkeley: University of California Press, 1997.

Woods, Rodger. *The Conservative Revolution in the Weimar Republic*. New York: St. Martin's Press, 1996.

Woods, Randall Bennett. *The Roosevelt Foreign-Policy Establishment and the Good Neighbor: The United States and Argentina, 1941–1945*. Lawrence: Regents Press of Kansas, 1979.

Wulff, Birgit. *Arbeitslosigkeit und Arbeitsbeschaffungsmaßnahmen in Hamburg 1933–1939*. Frankfurt a.M: Lang, 1987.

Yelton, David K. *Hitler's Volkssturm: The Nazi Militia and the Fall of Germany 1944–1945*. Lawrence: University of Kansas Press, 2002.

Zepp, Mariane. *Redefining Germany: Reeducation, Staatsbürgerschaft und Frauenpolitik im US-amerikanisch Nachkriegsdeutschland*. Göttingen: Vandehoeck & Rupprecht, 2007.

Ziegler, Reiner. *Kunst und Architektur im Kulturfilm 1919–1945*. Konstanz: UVK 2003.

Zimmermann, Peter. "Der Propaganda-, Kontroll- und Lenkungsapparat." In *Die Geschichte des dokumentarischen Films in Deutschland*, edited by Peter Zimmermann and Kay Hoffmann. Vol. III. Stuttgart: Philipp Reclam, 2005. 75–81.

————. "Der 'Kampf ums Dasein'. Eugenik, Rassismus und Antisemitismus." In *Die Geschichte des dokumentarischen Films in Deutschland*, edited by Peter Zimmermann and Kay Hoffmann. Vol. III. Stuttgart: Philipp Reclam, 2005.

————. "Sukzessive Verstaatlichung der Filmindustrie und Entwicklung der Kulturfilm-Produktion." In *Die Geschichte des dokumentarischen Films in Deutschland*, edited by Peter Zimmermann and Kay Hoffmann. Vol. III. Stuttgart: Philipp Reclam, 2005. 93–101.

Zukas, Alex. "Lazy, Apathetic, and Dangerous: The Social Construction of Unemployed Workers in Germany during the Late Weimar Republic." *Contemporary European History* 10, no. 1 (2001): 25–49.

INDEX

ACKNOWLEDGMENTS

This book has been in the making many more years than I care to admit. By now there are too many people to mention by name, people who have shaped my thinking, who have argued with me, shared their thoughts, and forwarded articles, who have inspired and encouraged me when I was ready to toss everything into the rubbish, and who have shared the many moments of joy. I would like to thank the expert staff who facilitated my work and answered my questions at the Hamburger Staatsarchiv, the Forschungsstelle für Zeitgeschichte in Hamburg, the Cinegraph Hamburg, Gallerie Morgenland in Eimsbüttel, the Geschichtswerkstatt Barmbek, Stadtteilarchiv St. Pauli, the Film- and Fernsehmuseum in Hamburg, the Hamburger Denkmalschutzamt, the Zeitzeugenbörse in Hamburg, the Bundesarchiv Berlin, the Bundesarchiv Filmarchiv, the Kinemathek Berlin, and the Tagebucharchiv in Emmendingen. In particular, I thank Volker Reißmann for his invaluable guidance through the Hamburger film thicket and his last-minute assistance with the illustrations for this book.

The Rackham School of Graduate Studies, the Department of History, the Eisenberg Institute for Historical Studies, and the Sweetland Writing Center, all at the University of Michigan, as well as the Quinn Foundation and my new home—the Department of History at the University of Pennsylvania—provided generous financial support. I wish to thank my editor, Robert Lockhart, for his enthusiasm, his patience, and his guidance. I am grateful to the anonymous reviewers for their most helpful suggestions and pointed criticisms. Special thanks are due to Jay Slagel, who read and edited the entire manuscript and who, from a distance, taught me more about writing than anyone before or since.

At Michigan, I was lucky to learn from and later teach alongside the most wonderful scholars. Kathleen Canning and Geoff Eley have been with this project from the outset. They have been my teachers, my mentors, my dissertation chairs, my colleagues, and my friends. Kathleen taught me how to govern my sources; her theoretical edge and her gentle insistence on defining one's terms continue to serve as my guide. Geoff's historiographical nuance and his genuine curiosity have pushed me to read more widely, to think more broadly, and to project my questions to different audiences. Many more colleagues at Michigan and elsewhere have offered advice, commentary, and encouragement along the way. I am particularly grateful to Kerstin Barndt, Andrew Bergerson, Hans Michael Bock, Erica Carter, Dario Gaggio, Moritz Föllmer, Peter Fritzsche, Karl Christian Führer, Joshua Hagen, Sabine Hake, Gabrielle Hecht, Alf Lüdtke, Dirk Moses, Douglas Northrop, Amy Offner, Greg Parker, Roberta Pergher, Johannes Roschlau, Mark Roseman, Axel Schildt, Julia Sneeringer, Scott Spector, Maiken Umbach, Johannes von Moltke, Ulrike Weckel, Dorothee Wierling, and Michael Wildt.

My friends held my feet to the fire and ensured that all the talk about work-life balance was more than mere talk. Amy and Brian, Tanya and Phil, Roberta and Mark, Dirk, Kathleen and Hubert, Sarge, Matthew, Gabrielle and Paul, Raz and Anat, Timo S., Bill, Carlo, Marcy, Daniel, Ben, Alejandro and Ismael have enriched my life with delicious meals, a constant supply of hugs, countless distractions, late-night messages, unexpected escapes, sounding boards and hard truths, love, encouragement, and much needed laughter. Though less critical to the final shape of the book, the many forms of support Cai provided throughout most of my life were central in more ways than I can express. Emi watched over my children when they were little; Lucas served as role model when they were older. Andrzej taught me how to find balance. Doug and Melle, independently and in their uniquely beautiful ways, have helped me to hold it all together. They will always be family to me.

My parents introduced me to the joy of reading and the magic of stories. Their unconditional love has enabled me to stand tall rather than hide under the covers. Karl encouraged me to think big. Christa modeled the strength and perseverance necessary to push through the hard stuff with a smile. Lisa alone understands why sometimes you have to go dancing. My favorite humans in the whole world—Lukas, Yannik, and Timo—grew up with this book, and this book grew around them. Their roaring laughter and probing questions, their volatile yet gentle love, the silly fights, the repeated visits to the ER, their spontaneous hugs and brimming smiles as much as their shit-talking contests and stunts of all imaginable kinds kept me anchored in the three-dimensional world. Their energy has proven as inexhaustible as their capacity for joy. Years ago, much younger versions of themselves asked the questions that capture the discontents of writing this book. "Who ever invented peace?" Lukas queried. "Why do you have to work *every* day?" Timo demanded to know, and Yannik wondered, "How do you erase something that's in print?" *On Screen and Off* doesn't answer their questions, but rather its very existence poses them anew.

CPSIA information can be obtained
at www.ICGtesting.com
Printed in the USA
JSHW050333231221
21501JS00001B/1